ALL ABOUT ST

OTHER TITLES IN THE "ALL ABOUT..." FINANCE SERIES

All About Options, 2nd Edition
by Thomas McCafferty (0-07-045543-0)

All About Bonds and Bond Mutual Funds, 2nd Edition
by Esmé Faerber (0-07-134507-8)

All About Futures
by Thomas McCafferty and Russell Wasendorf (1-55738-296-4)

ALL ABOUT STOCKS

Second Edition

ESMÉ FAERBER

McGraw-Hill

New York San Francisco Washington, D.C. Auckland Bogotá
Caracas Lisbon London Madrid Mexico City Milan
Montreal New Delhi San Juan Singapore
Sydney Tokyo Toronto

Library of Congress Cataloging-in-Publication Data

Faerber, Esmé.
   All about stocks : the easy way to get started / Esmé Faerber.
     p. cm.
   ISBN 0-07-134508-6
   1. Stocks.   2. Investments.   I. Title.
   HG4661.F34 2000
   332.63'22—dc21   99-39400
                                          CIP

McGraw-Hill

A Division of The McGraw·Hill Companies

2 3 4 5 6 7 8 9 0   DOC/DOC   0 9 8 7 6 5 4 3 2 1 0

ISBN 0-07-134508-6

The sponsoring editor for this book was Stephen Isaacs, the editing supervisor was John M. Morriss, and the production supervisor was Elizabeth J. Strange. It was set in Palatino per the IPROF design specs by Deirdre Sheean of the Hightstown McGraw-Hill Desktop Publishing Unit.

Printed and bound by R. R. Donnelley & Sons Company.

McGraw-Hill books are available at special discounts to use as premiums and sales promotions, or for use in corporate training programs. For more information, please write to the Director of Special Sales, McGraw-Hill, Professional Publishing, Two Penn Plaza, New York, NY 10121-2298. Or contact your local bookstore.

This publication is designed to provide accurate and authoritative information in regard to the subject matter covered. It is sold with the understanding that the publisher is not engaged in rendering legal, accounting or other professional service. If legal advice or other expert assistance is required, the services of a competent professional person should be sought.
From a Declaration of Principles Jointly Adopted by a Committee of the American Bar Association and a Committed of Publishers and Associations.

This book is printed on recycled, acid-free paper containing a minimum of 50% recycled de-inked paper.

CONTENTS

PREFACE

This new edition of *All About Stocks* is updated and introduces many changes and improvements over the first edition. The Internet and the growth of index mutual funds have had significant ramifications for the stock market, and they have changed the way individual investors invest in stocks. Not only do investors have more information, but through the Internet, they are able to buy and sell stocks without talking to anyone. Among the many changes to this book is the information necessary to use the Internet, for investors who are willing to take charge of their own portfolios. Stock prices and stock markets are constantly changing. There are stocks that have increased in value by several hundred percent in very short periods of time, and at the other extreme, stocks that have faded into oblivion. Moreover, the stock market has achieved new highs over the past four years (1995 to 1999) with annual returns of over 30 percent for many of the blue-chip stocks. This is an aberration, and in future years it will not be so easy for investors to earn these abnormally large returns. When the market becomes more broad-based to include small and mid-cap stocks, returns will revert to their normal average range of 7 to 10 percent, and investors will have to be more discriminating in their choices of investments, in order to earn positive returns.

Investing in the stock market can have a substantial effect on your financial well-being. This book is written to provide a practical guide for existing and potential stock investors. By understanding the basics of investing, the economic and financial conditions of companies, and the nature of stock markets, investors will be better able to assess investment opportunities. Investing your own money in stocks is difficult for most investors, particularly beginning investors, but by knowing what to expect, investors will be able to use strategies to manage their portfolios more effectively.

There are many myths concerning investing in the stock market, and this book does not fall into the category of offering methods to get rich quickly. In fact, many sophisticated investors in the stock market know just how difficult it is to outperform market averages consistently over long periods of time. Investors should also be aware that suggested methods or techniques of beating the stock market may not live up to their expectations.

The first chapter begins with a discussion of the fundamentals of investing, what stocks are, the different types of stocks, and the advantages of investing in them.

The second chapter compares the risks and returns of stocks with other financial investments. Within the context of the risk-return tradeoff, the selection of investments is introduced.

The third chapter includes an overview of the economic influences that have a bearing on the valuation of stocks. Understanding the relationships between the economy and the stock and bond markets is of great significance for stock investors. The latter part of the chapter includes tables on how to read the stock quotations listed in financial newspapers and the electronic media.

The fourth chapter discusses how and where securities are traded, including the Internet. The first part of the chapter has an overview of the types of brokerage firms and what to look for in the selection of a broker. This is followed by a discussion of both the costs and mechanics of trading stocks. An understanding of the types of orders and how the stock markets work can only benefit stock investors, and lead to reductions in the costs of trading.

Chapter 5 examines the use of fundamental analysis as a means of identifying stocks that are undervalued or that present buying opportunities. The next chapter provides an overview of technical analysis, as a method for selecting stocks.

Chapter 7 evaluates an array of different investment theories and introduces the efficient market hypothesis, the capital asset pricing theory, and later theories. An understanding of these theories will assist individual investors in the choice of their investment strategies and equity style preferences, and whether to be active or passive (buy-and-hold) investors. The chapter concludes with a discussion of formula buying plans, which can assist investors in their timing decisions of the market.

Chapter 8 is an all-new chapter which discusses the styles of equity investing, namely value and growth. Value and growth stocks differ in their financial characteristics and performance. An awareness and understanding of these styles can assist investors in the choice of the individual stocks that they are most comfortable holding.

Chapters 9 and 10 include information on mutual funds and closed-end funds. Investments in these funds are analyzed as to how they work, their risks, how to buy and sell them, their disadvantages, caveats, and whether these investments are suitable for you. These chapters include index mutual funds, and the new unit investment trust tracking stocks of the different stock market indexes, namely DIAMONDS, Spiders, and the Nasdaq 100 tracking stock.

Chapter 11 discusses portfolio management.

Investing money in the stock market is not easy, and the aim of this book is to make the task a little less difficult. The rapid dissemination of financial information through the Internet will have the effect of increasing the risk-return tradeoff. Understanding this tradeoff and how stock markets work should make investors more comfortable with their stock selections.

Esmé Faerber

ACKNOWLEDGMENTS

The preparation of this book was greatly facilitated by the people at the McGraw-Hill Publishing Company, most notably Stephen Isaacs and John Morriss, who were a pleasure to work with.

I would also like to thank the following people for their assistance with computer software and hardware: Jennifer Faerber, Michael Faerber, and Bill McKenna at Rosemont College. I am grateful for their efforts, which saved me many hours of trial and error on the computer.

Other people who very willingly provided me with information and investment materials were James H. Gately and Tisha Findeison of the Vanguard Group and my friend Marsha Bolden, Esq., who provided me with invaluable advice. I am especially appreciative of their help.

A special note of thanks goes to my husband, Eric, and our children, Jennifer and Michael, for their patience and continued support.

CHAPTER 1

Why Invest in Common Stocks? *

KEY CONCEPTS

- Stock market versus bond market
- Investment plan
- What are common stocks?
- Characteristics of common stocks
- Classes of common stock
- Types of common stock
- What is preferred stock?

There are many compelling reasons why investors should invest in common stocks. For one, people are living longer and are going to need more money for retirement, and for medical and other expenses. Consequently, they are going to have to save more and invest it in assets that earn satisfactory rates of return to fund these increasing expenses.

The key to success is to set aside more for savings and then invest it wisely. Investments are made to generate future purchasing power that will keep ahead of inflation and provide investors with a sense of financial security. If rates of return earned on these

---

*Some of the material in this chapter has been previously published by Esme Faerber in *All About Bonds and Bond Mutual Funds* (McGraw-Hill, New York, 2000).

investments are meager, this sense of security can quickly change to a sense of frustration. In order to generate future purchasing power, rates of return need to exceed the rate of inflation and cover the taxes paid on the earnings. Should rates of return not exceed those of inflation and the taxes paid, then the investments are earning negative rates of return and are losing purchasing power.

Table 1-1 shows the savings rates that investors are currently able to earn on their money market investments.

Why are investors attracted to these low-yielding alternatives? The answer lies in the fact that bank-savings-account and certificate-of-deposit investors tend to be conservative in their outlook, and they are reassured by the federal deposit insurance on bank accounts that they will not lose any of their principal. However, this risk-less, pay-less less type of investment strategy does not help these investors keep up with rising costs and growing anxieties about retirement.

This is a puzzling time for all investors, not just for conservative ones. With interest rates currently at a 20-year low, the bond and stock markets are at their record high levels. Consequently, many investors are reluctant to plunge into the stock and bond markets at this stage only to see a potential erosion of their savings in the event of a stock or bond market crash. The 10-percent decline in the U.S. stock markets in the six weeks from August 1998 sent many investors out of stocks. Yet when this decline is put into perspective, it is quite a healthy correction. The U.S. stock markets had

TABLE 1-1

Savings and Money Market Rates

Bank interest checking accounts	1.14%
Money market deposits	2.43%
Six-month certificates of deposit	4.28%
One-year certificates of deposit	4.39%
Five-year certificates of deposit	4.55%
U.S. Savings EE Bonds	5.06%
U.S. Savings I-Bonds	4.66%

Source: *The Wall Street Journal*, October 22, 1998.

increased roughly 25 to 30 percent each year for the three years just prior to August of 1998. As much as we would like it, stock markets cannot defy gravity and keep going up. They too have to correct and go down periodically.

The statistics on the stock markets for long periods of time are much more compelling, showing how stocks have outperformed bonds and other fixed-income investments. The bottom line is that over long periods of time, common stocks have outperformed all other investments. The Ibbotson and Sinquefield study summarized in Table 1-2 shows the average yearly returns earned for the investments in different portfolios of securities for the 67-year period from 1926 to 1993.

Common stocks of large companies had nominal average yearly returns of 12.3 percent over the 67-year period of the study and were only surpassed by the returns earned by the common stocks of small firms, which averaged 17.6 percent per year. Long-term corporate bonds and long-term government bonds lagged behind, with 5.9 percent and 5.4 percent respectively, while Treasury bills returned only 3.7 percent. Nominal returns are those which are not adjusted for inflation. The *real* average yearly rate of return, the nominal rate minus the rate of inflation, is 9.1 percent for common stocks of large companies and 14.4 percent for the common stocks of small companies. This surpasses by far the

TABLE 1-2

A Comparison of Investment Portfolios, 1926–1993

	Nominal Average Returns	Standard Deviation of Returns	Real Average Returns
Common stocks of large companies	12.3%	20.5%	9.1%
Common stocks of small firms	17.6%	34.8%	14.4%
Long-term corporate bonds	5.9%	8.4%	2.7%
Long-term government bonds	5.4%	8.7%	2.2%
U.S. Treasury bills	3.7%	3.3%	0.5%

Source: R. G. Ibbotson and R. A. Sinquefield, *Stocks, Bonds, Bills and Inflation: Historical Return,* Irwin, Chicago, 1994, p. 32.

returns earned on corporate bonds (2.7 percent), government bonds (2.2 percent), and Treasury bills (0.5 percent). Figure 1-1 depicts the comparison graphically. Put another way, the significance of these returns becomes quite apparent. Table 1-3 shows the power of compound interest if $1000 had been invested in each of these types of securities in 1926 at these corresponding annual real rates of return for the same 67-year period. The clear winner is small stocks, in which a $1000 investment for 67 years would have grown to $8.2 million, compared with $342,182 for large stocks. Bonds and Treasury bills did not fare very well. The astute reader will obviously ask, "So why bother with other investments when

FIGURE 1-1

Real Annual Rates of Return, 1926–1993

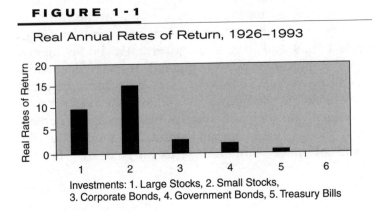

Investments: 1. Large Stocks, 2. Small Stocks, 3. Corporate Bonds, 4. Government Bonds, 5. Treasury Bills

TABLE 1-3

Value of $1,000 Invested at Different Rates of Return for 67 Years

	Amount 1926	Rate	Amount 1993
Common stocks of large companies	$1000	9.1%	$ 342,182.89
Common stocks of small companies	$1000	14.4%	$8,213,790.82
Long-term corporate bonds	$1000	2.7%	$ 5,959.64
Long-term government bonds	$1000	2.2%	$ 4,297.44
U.S. Treasury bills	$1000	0.5%	$ 1,396.77

you can get higher rates of return from investing in common stocks, which also provide the greatest hedge against inflation?"

There are a number of reasons, one of which concerns the variability of the returns. The standard deviation of the returns measures the riskiness of the portfolios. As expected, Treasury bills have the least risk due to their relatively short maturities and the fact that there is almost no chance of the U.S. government defaulting on them. Risk increases for long-term government bonds, which surprisingly have a slightly greater risk than long-term corporate bonds. Corporate bonds generally pose greater risk of default than government bonds. This anomaly is primarily due to the sharp increases in interest rates in the late 1970s and early 1980s, which had a negative effect on bond prices. Finally, the greatest risks are those experienced by portfolios of large common stocks (20.5 percent) and small common stocks (34.8 percent).

What this means is that common stock prices are historically more volatile than the other types of investments. Investing in common stocks will produce higher real rates of return (after adjusting for inflation) than most other investments, but investing in common stocks requires a longer time horizon so that the variability of the returns can be averaged out. This is confirmed by the Ibbotson study in which common stocks produced negative returns in 18 of the 65 years from 1926 to 1990, compared with only one negative year in the 65 for Treasury bills (Petty, p. 118).

Ken Gregory, a money manager in San Francisco, estimates that the risk of losing money on an investment in a basket of common stocks resembling the Standard & Poor's (S&P) Index diminishes over time: 30 percent for a one-year period versus 15 percent for a three-year period and between 3 and 4 percent for a ten-year period (Gottschalk and Donnelly).

The historical data from Ibbotson and Sinquefield clearly shows that with longer holding periods, stocks are less risky and outperform bonds and money market investments. If an investor has a long time horizon, it does not matter if there is a 10 percent decline in the stock market in any one year, because over a longer period of time, stock markets, historically, have always consistently outperformed other types of investments.

In a September 1998 *Wall Street Journal* article Professor Jeremy Siegel of the Wharton Business School wrote that even though stocks could be considered overvalued at that time, they would continue to provide superior returns over longer periods of time. The two major reasons he cited were information technology, which would spur corporate growth and profits, and globalization (Siegel, p. A22). Professor Siegel predicted annual real rates of return from stocks to be around 7 percent in future years. This is lower than the stellar returns of the past few years, but this would still be higher than the returns of bonds and "sitting on the sidelines" in money market securities.

STOCK MARKET VERSUS BOND MARKET

Despite the fact that stocks are volatile, historically, they have outperformed bonds over long periods of time. The following section compares stocks to alternative investments in the bond markets to give the investor a clearer picture of the differences in the rates of return and the risks.

Bond investments offer less variability in returns than common stocks: 8.4 percent for long-term corporate bonds versus 20.5 percent for common stocks in Ibbotson and Sinquefield. However, if there is a long investment period, the higher variability risks for common stocks can be averaged, resulting in higher returns for stocks.

Common stocks represent ownership in a corporation, whereas bonds are IOUs and bondholders are debt-holders, or creditors. Investors in common stocks are the owners of a corporation and are entitled to voting rights and a claim on income and assets. As to the latter, common stockholders stand last in line in their right to share in the income and assets. Shareholders are entitled to receive dividends only after the bondholders and preferred stockholders have been paid. Similarly, in bankruptcy, the claims of bondholders are settled first, while common stockholders are last in line for the collection of any remaining proceeds from the liquidation of assets.

Investors in common stocks are not guaranteed dividends. Dividends on common stocks are declared at the discretion of the company's board of directors. If the board decides to use the money for alternative purposes or if earnings go down, dividends may be reduced or may not be declared. By contrast, investors in bonds can count on a steady stream of interest income. Thus, investors who cannot tolerate the reduced or terminated flows of current income should not buy common stock.

Investors are strongly attracted to common stocks for their ability to provide for capital growth over long periods of time, as the Ibbotson study confirms. Bonds also offer the potential for capital appreciation (an increase in the selling price over the purchase price), but investors invest in bonds primarily for current income.

This comparison of some of the characteristics of stocks and bonds highlights the following reasons why investors should also consider investing some of their portfolios in bonds:

- Due to the higher volatility of stocks over bonds, investors might not want to be 100-percent invested in stocks. According to an earlier Ibbotson study, stocks were three times more volatile than bonds in the 64 years after 1926. The worst year for U.S. intermediate-term bonds was 1994, in which they fell 5.1 percent in value. The worst year for stocks was 1991, when stock prices fell by 43.3 percent (Zuckerman, p. C1). By diversifying and investing some of their portfolios in bonds, investors may lower their risk of loss due to a stock market downturn.
- In the current economic climate, bonds offer positive real rates of return. Bonds offer a steady stream of income, whereas stockholders are not guaranteed the receipt of dividends. If inflation remains low, around the current 1.5-percent annual rate and bonds continue to yield nominal returns between 5 and 6 percent, then bonds can still provide positive real rates of return of around 4 percent, which exceed those of bank accounts and Treasury bills. The S & P dividend yield for stocks is currently around 1.5 percent, which means that bond returns exceed those of common stocks with regard to income. Stocks of small companies generally pay no dividends.
- Investors who are risk-averse or have shorter investment horizons might shun stocks in favor of bonds to protect against possible downturns in the stock market, which could cause losses in principal in the short term.
- With the recent, excessively high valuations in the stock market, it may be a good time to take some profits in some of these stocks and put the money into bonds, if there is a short-term need for some of this money.

■ Investors in high tax brackets can reduce their federal, state, and/or local taxes by investing in municipal bonds and government bonds.

For long periods, however, investing in common stocks offers the following advantages over bonds:

■ The potential for greater average rates of return.
■ The ability to reduce federal, state, and local income taxes. Capital gains on common stocks are only taxed when the stocks are sold (at lower marginal rates than ordinary income such as interest and dividends), whereas interest income from bonds (and dividends from common stocks) are taxed when they are earned.
■ The potential for keeping ahead of the rate of inflation.

Table 1-4 summarizes some of the conditions conducive in choosing stocks and bonds. Investing in the stock market provides for the long-term growth of a portfolio. Investors who have a long time horizon (more than 5 to 10 years) and who do not need the income from the investments should stick with stocks. Investing in the bond markets provides for current income. These investments

TABLE 1-4

Stocks Versus Bonds

STOCKS	BONDS
1. Provide long-term growth.	1. Provide current income.
2. Need a long time horizon.	2. Have a shorter time horizon.
3. Require investors who do not need the principal from the stock investments to live on.	3. Require low current and future inflation rates.
4. Require investors who can withstand the volatility of the stock markets.	4. Favor risk-averse investors.
5. Provide potential for capital gains, which are taxed at lower tax rates than current income.	5. Municipal bonds and government bonds can lower federal, state, and local taxes.
6. Provide a store of value.	

are more suitable for investors who are risk-averse and who have shorter time horizons for the money.

There are other factors to consider. If you have a long time horizon but you have difficulty sleeping at night when the stock market goes down, then stocks may not be right for you.

INVESTMENT PLANNING

Before making investment decisions, each investor should assess his or her financial situation and then devise an investment plan. Unless you are fortunate in your planning to have chosen extremely wealthy parents, you will need to think about your future financial planning.

Before embarking on an investment plan, you need to determine your financial net worth (what you own minus what you owe), because then you will know how much you can afford to invest. A portion of your funds should be kept in liquid investments—such as bank money market accounts, money market mutual funds, Treasury bills, and other money market securities—for living expenses and for any emergencies. The amount to keep in these liquid investments for your emergency/living expense fund will vary according to individual circumstances. An examination of your personal assets will determine how much to keep. A conservative rule of thumb is to keep three to six months' worth of expenses in liquid investments. Keeping too much in liquid investments is not a good idea, since it may result in a loss of current and future purchasing power (see Table 1-1 for money market returns).

Once an emergency fund has been created, an investment program should be started for the medium- and long-term future. Even on a modest starting salary, consistently setting aside a small amount for savings can make a difference over time. The secret is to *pay yourself first*. Rather than waiting until the end of the month to see what is left for savings, at the beginning of the month, write a check to your investment account. Certain mutual funds allow investors to deposit amounts as small as $25 per month on a regular monthly basis.

Now take a look at Figure 1-2; it shows the steps in the investment planning process.

FIGURE 1-2

Investment Plan

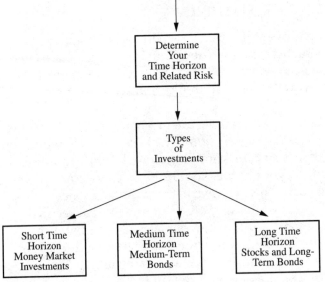

List Your Objectives

List your goals and objectives for your medium- and long-term investment plan. This will determine how much you need to invest to reach your goals and the appropriate types of investments to make. For example, the following objectives have a time horizon:

- Buy a car in two years
- Save for a down payment on a house in five years
- Fund a college education in 10 years
- Accumulate a retirement fund in 25 years

Determine Your Time Horizon and the Related Risks

The types of investments you choose can then be geared to the time horizons of your objectives. The first two objectives have short- to medium-term time horizons, which means that the investments chosen should focus on generating income and preserving principal. Investing the money set aside for the purchase of a car in 2 years in the stock market would be risky, since over a short period of time, the chances of losing money in the stock market can be quite high.

Types of Investments

Investments for your emergency fund should be *liquid*, which is the ability to convert them into cash without losing very much of your principal in the conversion. Examples of these are U.S. Treasury bills, commercial paper, bankers' acceptances, money market mutual funds, short-term (6-month) certificates of deposit, money market bank deposits, and savings and checking accounts.

Investments for short- and medium-term horizons should produce higher yields than money market investments, and the maturities should match the time period for which you will need the money invested. Investments in two-year and five-year U.S. Treasury notes, for example, will provide current income with virtually no risk of default on the interest and principal amount invested. Other options for these shorter maturities are U.S. government agency notes, short-term U.S. Treasury bonds, and short-term bond mutual funds.

Investing options to fund a college education in 10 years are greater and could include a mixture of common stock and bonds. With a 25-year time horizon, the mix of investments should be weighted more heavily toward stocks than bonds. This is because over long periods of time, stocks have outperformed bonds and most other investments, which means that if the past is a reflection of the future, you can expect average yearly returns of 7 percent for stocks versus 4 to 5 percent for bonds. Investors who are nervous about stock market corrections or crashes might consider investing

TABLE 1-5

Guidelines for Building an Investment Portfolio

1. Pay off all high-interest credit card debts first and then make extra payments to your mortgage account.
2. Cut all frivolous spending to increase amounts saved.
3. Pay yourself first, at the beginning of the month.
4. Open up an automatic investment plan to encourage regular savings.
5. Contribute to retirement plans.
6. Map out your investment plan, listing all your objectives.
7. Determine the level of risk that you are comfortable with for your investments.
8. Increase the rates of return on your investments within comfortable levels of risk.
9. Review your investment strategy with regard to taxes. High-tax-bracket investors should increase their municipal bond holdings.
10. Review your investment plan once or twice a year.

some of their retirement savings in 30-year U.S. Treasury bonds. Bonds are not riskless securities. They too suffer from changes in interest rates, economic changes, and the risks that affect the markets, the types of bonds, and their quality. Before investing in bonds, stocks, or mutual funds, you should be aware of the risks and nuances affecting them.

Ultimately, the key to building a large portfolio is to get your finances in order. Table 1-5 provides some guidelines.

WHAT ARE COMMON STOCKS?

Common stocks represent ownership in a corporation. For example, if a company has 100,000 shares of common stock outstanding and you buy 10,000 shares, you are a 10-percent owner of that company. A corporation can have one shareholder or numerous shareholders, as in the case of IBM Corporation. However, owning the common stock of a large corporation does not carry the same ownership rights as owning a house, for example. Shareholders of IBM cannot tell IBM management how to run the company or what types of computers they should be producing. This is because shareholders' rights are limited.

FIGURE 1-3

Responsibilities of Shareholders

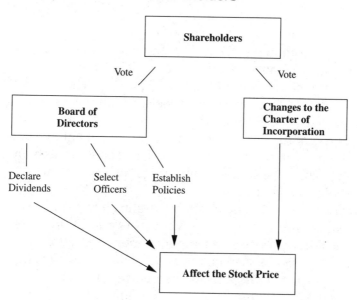

The relationship of shareholders to management and the board of directors is illustrated in Figure 1-3.

Common shareholders are the true owners of a corporation in that they are the only group with a claim to the company's profits.

When a new company is formed, common stock is sold to shareholders to raise money for the company. Companies also sell bonds to raise funds. Shareholders invest in the common stock of companies to earn a return on their money.

CHARACTERISTICS OF COMMON STOCKS

Ownership of common stock is evidenced by a stock certificate. On the front is the name of the issuing company, the name of the owner of the shares, the number of shares represented by the certificate, the identifying serial number, the name of the register, and the par value of the stock. The back of the stock certificate normally includes an assignment statement which must be signed by the holder of the stock when the holder decides to transfer ownership of the shares.

Voting Rights

A characteristic of common stock is that the shareholders can vote on important issues facing a corporation as well as for membership to the board of directors, as illustrated in Figure 1-3. The board of directors, in turn, selects officers to run the corporation.

Common shareholders must also approve any changes to the charter of incorporation. For example, if the management of a corporation wanted to take over another corporation through the issuance of new common shares, the management would have to get the shareholders' approval.

Instead of attending the shareholders' meeting to vote in person, many shareholders use a *proxy* vote. A proxy is a legal document which gives a designated person temporary power of attorney to vote for an absentee signee shareholder at the shareholder meeting.

With this setup, it would appear, theoretically, that shareholders choose the board of directors and determine the important issues facing management. In reality, however, the system often works with the opposite bent. Most often, management chooses the slate of candidates to stand for the board of directors as well as the important issues to be voted on by the shareholders. These choices are then sent out on proxy cards to be voted on by shareholders.

Occasionally, proxy battles occur which provide shareholders with a real choice. This happens when there are two opposing groups (an outside group versus the board of directors and management) who solicit the shareholders' proxy votes. Dissident shareholders have at times used their strength to bring about changes in top management. In late 1993, when Borden Inc.'s shareholders saw their dividends cut and the stock price fall to new lows, they brought pressure on the board of directors to remove the chief executive.

Corporations use either the *majority voting procedure* (also known as the *statutory* method) or the *cumulative voting procedure.* Under the majority voting procedure, the number of votes a shareholder has equals the number of shares he or she holds. The majority of votes cast determines the issue or the director elected. With cumulative voting, shareholders are entitled to a total number of votes equal to the total number of shares owned multiplied by the number of directors being elected. Shareholders can cast all of their votes for a single candidate or split them up as they see fit. Cumulative voting gives increased weight to minority shareholders, enabling them to elect at least one director.

A simple example will illustrate the difference between majority voting and cumulative voting. Assume that a company has 1000 shares outstanding and that there are two candidates to be elected to the board of directors. Under majority voting, the minority shareholder with 300 shares will be able to cast 300 votes for each of the two candidates. However, under cumulative voting, a minority shareholder with 300 shares in an election for two candidates could vote all 600 votes for one candidate. This method is advantageous for minority shareholders if they get together and place all their votes for one candidate who may be more sympathetic to their interests.

Claim on Income

As owners of the corporation, common shareholders have a right to share in the net income, after bondholders and preferred stockholders have been paid. This net income may either be retained by the corporation (and reinvested by the corporation) or paid out in dividends to shareholders. The corporation that retains income increases the value of the firm, which leads to an increase in the value of the stock. This benefit to the shareholders takes the form of capital gains (when shareholders sell their common stock at prices that are higher than the purchase price). Of course, shareholders benefit directly when the corporation pays out its earnings in dividends.

Dividends

When the board of directors of a corporation decides to pay out its earnings or part of its earnings in dividends, all the common shareholders have a right to receive them. If the board of directors decides not to declare a dividend, the shareholders will receive nothing. Companies are not legally required to pay dividends, even if they are profitable and they have paid them in the past.

However, companies are legally required to pay interest to their bondholders on their debt. This is an important distinction for investors who rely on regular inflows from their investments.

Declaration of Dividends Four dates are important in the declaration of dividends:

The first is the *date of announcement*, which is when the board of directors announces the dividends.

The second is the *date of record*, which determines which shareholders are entitled to receive the dividends. Only those shareholders who own the shares of that company on the date of record are entitled to receive the dividends. If shares are purchased after the record date, the owners will not be entitled to receive the dividends.

The third date, known as the *ex-dividend date*, is important because stock traded on the ex-dividend date does not include the dividend. The ex-dividend date is two business days prior to the date of record. When common stock is bought, it takes three business days for the settlement to go through. Thus, if the record date for a company's dividend is Friday, November 20, 1998, the ex-dividend date is Wednesday, November 18, 1998. Investors who buy these shares on Tuesday, November 17, 1998 (the day before the ex-dividend date), will receive the dividends because the transaction will be recorded in the ownership books for that company in three working days, which is November 20, 1998.

The fourth date is the *payment date*, which is the date the company pays the dividends.

Dividend payments are important to shareholders, and so companies often make their dividend policies known to investors. Rightly or wrongly, investors use dividend payments as a yardstick or mirror of the company's expected earnings, so any changes to dividend payments may have a greater effect on the stock price than a change in earnings. This explains the reluctance of management to cut dividends when earnings decline. Similarly, there may be a lag in increasing dividends when earnings increase. Management wants to be sure they can maintain the increased dividends from increased earnings.

Shareholders who rely on income from their investments will purchase the stock of companies that have a history of paying regular dividends out of their earnings. These companies tend to be older and well-established; their stocks are referred to as *income stocks*, or *blue-chip stocks*.

Young companies that are expanding generally retain their earnings; their stocks are referred to as *growth stocks*. Growth stocks appeal to investors who are more interested in capital appreciation.

Types of Dividends

Dividends can be paid in various forms or a combination of these forms:

- Cash
- Stock: dividends and splits
- Property
- Special distributions

Cash Dividends In order to pay cash dividends, companies need to have not only the earnings but also enough cash. Even if a company shows a large amount in its retained earnings on the balance sheet, it is not enough to ensure cash dividends. The amount of cash that a company has is independent of retained earnings. A company can be cash poor and still be very profitable.

Most American companies pay their regular cash dividends on a quarterly basis, while some companies pay their dividends semiannually or annually.

Stock Dividends Some companies choose to conserve their cash, and they declare stock dividends. By paying stock dividends, companies recapitalize their earnings and issue new shares. This does not affect the companies' assets and liabilities. See Table 1-6 for an example of a company's balance sheet before and after a 10-percent stock dividend.

Amounts from retained earnings are transferred to the common stock and additional paid in capital accounts. This does not affect the amount in the total equity section of the balance sheet. The amount transferred depends on the market value of the common stock and the number of new shares issued through the stock dividend. In this example, there are 10,000 additional shares at a market price of $5 per share. The retained earnings account is debited for $50,000 ($5 × 10,000 shares), and $10,000 (10,000 shares ×

TABLE 1-6

The Effects of a Stock Dividend on a Balance Sheet

XYZ Company Balance Sheet Before a Stock Dividend			
Current Assets	$100,000	Current Liabilities	$50,000
Fixed Assets	200,000	Long-Term Liabilities	50,000
		Equity: Common Stock 100,000	
		$1 Par 100,000 Shares Outstanding Additional	
		Paid in Capital 30,000	
		Retained Earnings 70,000	
		Total Equity	200,000
Total Assets	$300,000	Total Liabilities & Equity	$300,000
After 10 Percent Stock Dividend (Market Price $5 per Share)			
Current Assets	$100,000	Current Liabilities	$50,000
Fixed Assets	200,000	Long-Term Liabilities	50,000
		Equity: Common Stock 110,000	
		$1 Par 110,000 Shares Outstanding Additional	
		Paid in Capital 70,000	
		Retained Earnings 20,000	
		Total Equity	200,000
Total Assets	$300,000	Total Liabilities & Equity	$300,000

$1 par value) is added to the equity account. The other $40,000 ($4 premium over par value × 10,000 shares) is added to the additional paid-in capital account.

The astute investor will realize that a stock dividend does not increase the shareholder's wealth. With a stock dividend, shareholders will receive more shares of that company's stock, but because the company's assets and liabilities remain the same, the price of the stock will decline to account for the dilution. For the shareholder, this can be likened to a slice of cake. The slice can be divided into two, three, or four pieces. No matter how many ways you slice the piece of cake, the overall size of the cake remains the same. After a stock dividend, the shareholders receive more shares, but their proportionate ownership interest in the company remains the same.

Stock dividends are usually expressed as a percentage of the number of shares outstanding. For example, if a company announces a 10-percent stock dividend and it has 100,000 shares outstanding, the total shares outstanding will be increased to 110,000 shares after the stock dividend.

Stock Split A stock split is like a stock dividend in that there is an increase in the number of shares issued on a pro rata basis while the assets, liabilities, equity, and earnings remain the same. The only difference between a stock split and a stock dividend is technical in nature.

From an accounting point of view, a stock dividend of greater than 20 to 25 percent is recorded as a stock split. A 100-percent stock dividend is the same as a 2-for-1 stock split. A small medical imaging company, Adac Labs, split its shares 2 for 1 because the company felt that the price of the stock was too high and that with a lower price the shares would become more marketable. The stock was trading in the $50 range, so an investor owning 100 shares before the split (with a value of $5000) would own 200 shares after the split with a value of approximately $25 per share $(50 \div 2)$.

With the stock market boom of the last few years, many companies have split their stock as their prices have risen to historic highs. Some examples of recent stock splits include Intel (2-for-1), Cisco Systems (3-for-2), Walt Disney Company (4-for-1), Johnson & Johnson (2-for-1), and Texas Instruments (2-for-1).

Occasionally, companies announce *reverse splits,* which reduce the number of shares and increase the share price. When a company's stock has fallen in price, a reverse split will raise the price of the stock to a respectable level. Another reason for raising the share price is to assist the company in staying on the Nasdaq Stock Market, which has minimum price requirements, or to get a listing on the Nasdaq. For example, a stock that is trading in the cats-and-dogs range of $1 would trade at $10 with a 1-for-10 reverse split. Of course, the number of shares outstanding would be reduced by 10 times after the split.

Are there advantages to stock dividends and stock splits? If shareholder wealth is not increased by stock dividends and stock splits, why do companies go to the trouble and expense?

The first advantage from the company's point of view is a conservation of cash. By substituting a stock dividend for a cash dividend, a company can conserve its cash or use it for other attractive investment opportunities. It is for this latter reason that the company's earnings power might be increased and the stock price may be bid up, thus benefiting the shareholders. If this is the case, however, shareholders would be better off without stock dividends because the costs associated with them are borne by the shareholders. The costs of issuing new shares, transfer fees, and revising the company's record of shareholders is paid by shareholders (from the company's earnings).

When the price of the stock is reduced due to the split, it may become more attractive to many potential small investors because of the lower price. The increased marketability of the stock may push up the price. If the company continues to do well financially, stockholders will benefit in the long run by having more shares of a company whose stock price has continued to go up in price.

Stock dividends and stock splits do not increase the wealth of the stockholder from the balance sheet point of view, whereas cash dividends directly increase the shareholder's monetary wealth and reduce the company's cash and reinvestment dollars.

Property Dividends Property dividends are occasionally declared by corporations, whereby shareholders receive securities or assets of the corporation. For example, when a corporation spins off a subsidiary, shareholders could receive assets or shares of that subsidiary.

Special Distributions Companies sometimes make special distributions in various forms, like extra dividends, spin-offs, and split-offs:

- *Extra Dividends:* Companies may wish to distribute an extra dividend to their shareholders on a one-time or infrequent basis. The company may have had a particularly good quarter financially, or there may be some other reason for this type of distribution. The company's decision to use a special distribution rather than increase regular dividends is because this is a one-time occurrence. Companies would not want to increase their dividend rates if they could not continue paying those increased rates into the future.

- *Spin-Offs* Some companies will spin off some or all of their shares of a subsidiary company and distribute them proportionally to their shareholders.

The Pepsi Cola Company (stock ticker symbol PEP) wanted to focus its attention on its soft drink and snack food businesses, so it spun off its restaurant businesses to shareholders. The restaurant businesses that were spun off to Pepsi shareholders were the Pizza Hut, Kentucky Fried Chicken, and Taco Bell chains. These food businesses now trade under the name Tricon Global (stock ticker symbol YUM). Pepsi shareholders received one share of YUM for every 10 shares owned of Pepsi as of the record date. The market value of the Pepsi stock would have fallen by the value of the YUM shares distributed.

In spin-offs, shareholders have the option of keeping the additional shares that they receive or selling them. In many cases the shares of the spin-off companies have outperformed their parent companies. When they become stand-alone companies, they can grow and expand in directions in which they are no longer hindered by their parent companies. AT&T (ticker symbol T) spun off their equipment supplier, Lucent Technologies (ticker symbol LU), to their shareholders, and as a stand-alone company, the stock of Lucent Technologies has outperformed the stock of AT&T by a large margin.

This is not always the case. Tele-Communications Inc. (TCOMA) spun off its Satellite Company (TSATA) to its shareholders. The share price of TSATA has steadily gone down, while the price of TCOMA has gone up. A short time later, AT&T took over TCOMA in a stock deal. For every TCOMA share, holders received 0.77 AT&T shares.

- *Split-Offs* Split-offs do not occur that frequently and differ from spin-offs. In a split-off, shareholders are offered a choice of keeping the shares that they own in the existing company or exchanging them for shares of the split-off company.

Tele-Communications Inc. (TCOMA) split-off some of their subsidiary companies to form the TCI Ventures Group and offered shareholders the choice of either keeping their existing shares in Tele-Communications Inc. or exchanging them for an equal number of shares in the TCI Ventures Group.

In a split-off, there is an exchange of shares, whereas with a spin-off, shareholders receive additional shares in another company.

While it is obvious that the shareholders benefit from receiving cash and property dividends, they also benefit when earnings are not paid out but are reinvested in the company. This increases the value of the company and hence the value of its stock. Thus, the claim on income is an important characteristic for common stock-holders.

Claim on Assets

In the event of the liquidation of a company, the common share-holders have a residual claim on the assets of the company. However, this is only after the claims of the debt-holders have been satisfied. In other words, common shareholders' claims on assets are third in line behind those of the debt-holders and the preferred stockholders. If there are insufficient assets to fulfill the claims of the debt-holders and preferred stockholders, the common shareholders will come away receiving nothing, as is often the case during bankruptcy.

Limited Liability

The limited liability feature of a corporation limits the amount of the loss of common shareholders in the event of bankruptcy. The most that common shareholders can lose is the amount of their investment in the common stock.

Preemptive Rights

For those corporations that include preemptive rights in their charters, stockholders are allowed to maintain their proportionate share of ownership. This means that when the company issues new shares, they must first be offered to the existing shareholders. For example, if a shareholder owns 10 percent of the company's stock, that shareholder is entitled to purchase 10 percent of the new shares. Thus, existing shareholders have the first right of refusal on purchasing the new shares.

Certificates called *rights* are issued to shareholders, giving them the option to purchase a stated number of new shares at a specific price during a specific period. These rights may be exercised (which allows the purchase of new common stock at a lower price than the market price), sold, or allowed to expire.

Classes of Common Stock

Some corporations issue different classes of common stock which may have different characteristics. For example, Ford Motor Company has two classes of common stock, Class A and Class B. Class B shares are owned by the Ford family and some board members. The key characteristic of this class of shares is that it controls 40 percent of the total voting rights to Ford Motor Company. Class A Ford shares have limited voting rights (Hall, p. 42). There are fewer Class B shares than Class A shares.

In other companies with more than one class of common stock, there may be different dividend rates. For example, Food Lion Inc. pays its Class A stockholders a larger dividend than it pays its Class B stockholders. However, its Class A stock has no voting rights.

Some companies have issued a *tracking stock*, which is a class of shares that is tied to the performance of a part of the business of the company. General Motors was the first to issue these shares in 1984 and 1985 for their subsidiaries Electronic Data Systems and Hughes Electronics. In 1999, Donalson, Lufkin & Jenrette (DLJ) issued a tracking stock for their Internet brokerage business (trading symbol DIR). The Internet brokerage company DIR competes with DLJ for business, which creates a potential conflict for the board of directors of DLJ, which serves both sets of shareholders. In fact, both

Electronic Data Systems and Hughes Electronics shareholders sued
General Motors on the grounds that they were treated unfairly. The
court ruled against the Electronic Data Systems and Hughes
Electronics shareholders. This decision is currently being appealed.

Despite this and other potential conflicts of the same board of
directors serving two sets of shareholders with different interests,
several companies are considering the issuance of tracking stocks,
such as General Electric Co., Walt Disney Co., and Du Pont Co.

TYPES OF COMMON STOCKS

There are many types of common stocks, and they behave differently, even though all common stocks represent ownership interests in companies. As mentioned earlier in this chapter, there are
blue chip stocks, which pay dividends, and there are *growth stocks*,
which generally do not pay dividends. Being able to classify stocks
into categories is useful for investors because these different types
of stocks vary with regard to their returns, quality and stability of
their earnings and dividends, and their relationship to the various
risks affecting the companies and the market.

Blue-Chip Stocks

Blue-chip stocks may be defined as those of companies that have
had a long history of paying dividends. These are the quality,
established companies that have developed leadership positions in
their respective industries. Due to their importance and large size,
these companies have built stable earnings and dividend records.
Most, if not all, of the companies in the Dow Jones Industrial
Average are considered to be blue-chip companies.

Not all blue-chip companies are the same. Wal-Mart is the
leader among the discount retailers, and it does not pay as high a
dividend as Ford Motor Company or Exxon Corporation. Wal-
Mart pays an annual dividend of $0.20 per share, whereas Ford's
annual dividend is $1.84 per share and Exxon's is $1.64 per share.
Wal-Mart's sales and earnings have been growing rapidly, and the
company has retained their earnings to fuel future growth. Wal-
Mart does not fit the profile of a typical blue-chip company
because it does not pay much of a dividend and it has not had

such a long history of paying out dividends. Ford and Exxon have also been growing their sales and earnings, but they have elected to pay out a higher percentage of their earnings in dividends and both have long histories of paying dividends. Table 1-7 shows some other blue-chip stocks that have a very long history of paying dividends. Blue-chip companies appeal to investors who seek quality companies which have a history of growing profits and paying out regular dividends. They tend to be less risky in periods of economic uncertainty because of their dependable earnings. Currently, blue-chip stocks have run up considerably in price because of the flight to quality by investors and the fact that these stocks are traded actively. In other words, they are both liquid and marketable. While investors hold these stocks as a store of wealth in anticipation of future capital appreciation, they can also count on receiving regular dividend income.

Income Stocks

Companies that have a record of paying higher than average dividends may be defined as income stocks. Income stocks tend not to appreciate in price as much as blue-chip stocks, since the companies are more mature and are not growing as quickly. This does not mean that these companies are not profitable or are about to go out of business. On the contrary, these companies choose to pay out much higher ratios of their earnings in dividends than other companies. Some examples of income stocks are utility companies such as Texas Industries (ticker symbol TXU), with a current dividend yield of 4.9 percent; Houston Industries (ticker symbol HOU), with a current

TABLE 1-7

Blue-Chip Stocks

Name of Company	Dividends Paid Since	Ticker Symbol
Eli Lilly	1885	LLY
Coca-Cola Company	1893	KO
General Mills	1898	GIS

dividend yield of 4.7 percent; and Western Resources (ticker symbol WR), with a current dividend yield of 6.1 percent.

Investors invest in income stocks for the higher dividend yields, and also because the industries these companies operate in are not exposed to great deals of risk.

Growth Stocks

Companies that have exhibited sustained growth in sales and earnings at a high rate over a period of time are called growth stocks. Growth stocks like Wal-Mart (WMT) and Intel (INTC) have been growing their earnings in the high double digits. Both pay out very small amounts of their earnings in dividends, and, because of their leadership positions in their respective industries, they can also be classified as blue-chip companies. Some growth companies pay no dividends, such as Cisco Systems (CSCO), which has been growing its sales in the 30-percent annual range for the past few years. Instead of paying their earnings out in dividends, these companies retain them and reinvest them to finance their rapid growth.

For the quality growth companies—Cisco Systems, Microsoft (MSFT), Intel, Dell Computer (DELL)—investors are willing to pay higher P/E ratios (price/earnings). (See the chapter on Fundamental Analysis for an explanation of P/E ratios.) Table 1-8 is a comparison of the current P/E ratios of some of the more actively traded growth stocks and value stocks. Since investors do not receive returns in the form of dividends, they are buying these stocks for their capital appreciation. For investors in the high marginal tax brackets there are tax advantages to buying growth stocks owing to their low yields and high appreciation. Dividends are currently taxed as ordinary income, which in the highest tax bracket is 39.6 percent, whereas the capital appreciation of the stock is taxed at the lower capital gains rate of 20 percent if the holding period is at least a year.

Value Stocks

Value stocks may be defined as the stocks of companies that are currently out of favor with investors for some reason, such as disappointing earnings for the quarter, and are therefore trading at lower-

than-average earnings multiples. For example, at the end of a period of economic expansion, auto companies may trade at lower P/E
ratios than the stocks of other companies because the expectations
from investors for the auto companies are low. Investors have relatively low expectations for their immediate future growth, so these
stocks trade at lower prices relative to their earnings and dividends.
Patient investors with longer time horizons are willing to purchase
these stocks and wait for their prospective earnings increases.

Table 1-8 compares some of the characteristics of growth
stocks with those of value stocks. Investors are willing to pay 350
times 1999 earnings for Yahoo, the Internet search engine, because
of its potential future sales and earnings, whereas the potential
strengths of value stocks are not as evident or visible. Unisys
Corporation has been in the process of restructuring its operations
for a few years and seems about to turn the corner. It posted profitable earnings in the most recent quarter, but the stock is only trading at five times its earnings. Value investors look for stocks whose
prices do not reflect their intrinsic worth and are willing to buy
stocks when they have temporary setbacks in the hope that they
will overcome their earning and asset valuation setbacks in the
future. For example, the price of oil has fallen to $12 per barrel,

TABLE 1 - 8

Growth Stocks versus Value Stocks

Company	Symbol	Stock Price	P/E Ratio	Earnings per Share	Dividends per Share
Growth Stocks					
Intel	INTC	$110	33.77	$3.25	$0.16
Cisco Systems	CSCO	$ 80	81.98	$0.94	——
Yahoo	YHOO	$216^{15}/$_{16}$	Negative	-$0.18	——
America Online	AOL	$ 94^{7}/$_{8}$	307.5	$0.30	——
Value Stocks					
Unisys Corp.	UIS	$ 29^{5}/$_{16}$	5.93	$4.82	——
Bear Stearns	BSC	$ 44	10.86	$3.89	$0.60
Schlumberger Ltd.	SLB	$ 48	18.40	$2.69	$0.75

which has depressed the price of the oil service and oil drilling companies. At the time of this writing, the stock of Schlumberger is trading near its 52-week low of $48 per share. This may be a temporary situation, because once the Asian economies recover from their economic woes, there will be a greater demand for oil, which will push the price up from the historic low price.

Table 1-8 compares the P/E ratios of a sampling of growth stocks and value stocks. The growth stock P/Es are extremely high. For 1999, analysts expect Yahoo to turn in a small profit per share of $0.60, which would have it trading around 366 times earnings. In other words, investors are willing to pay $366 to buy Yahoo stock for each expected $1 in earnings for 1999. The P/E ratios of the value stocks are comparatively low and are lower than the average P/E for the Dow Jones Industrial Average, which is around 24.7, and for the Standard & Poor's 500 Index of stocks, which is about 29.58.

Cyclical Stocks

These are the stocks of companies that move with the state of the economy. When the economy is in recession, these stocks perform poorly. During periods of expansion, these stocks do very well. Examples of cyclical stocks are the capital equipment companies, the home builders, the auto companies, and all the other sectors that are tied to the fortunes of the economy. With an expected downturn in economic activity for 1999, analysts downgraded stocks such as Deere (DE), the farm equipment maker, and Cummins Engine (CUM), the diesel engine manufacturer. The downgrade resulted in a reduction in their stock prices, as new investors avoided buying and existing shareholders sold them. These stocks can also be considered as value stocks for the patient investor who is willing to buy them and hold them until there is an economic turnaround.

Defensive Stocks

These are the stocks of companies whose prices are expected to remain stable or do well when the economy is declining. These stocks are virtually immune to changes in the economy and are not so affected by downturns in the business cycle. Examples of these types of stocks are the drug companies, food and beverage companies, public utility companies, consumer goods companies, and even the auto parts manufacturers. In a recession, people generally wait to replace their cars and are more likely to spend more to repair them. The drug companies have predictable earnings, which puts them into the defensive category. And with their pipelines of biotechnology drugs, they also fall into the growth stock category. If the economy continues in a deflationary environment, some of the supermarket chains, which are viewed as defensive type stocks, may fall out of this category. Supermarket chains generally have low profit margins. If they are not able to pass on higher prices, they may not do as well as they have in the past.

More-aggressive investors buy these defensive stocks ahead of an economic downturn and hold them until better economic times in the future.

Speculative Stocks

Speculative stocks may be defined as the stocks of companies with the potential for large increases in price. These companies do not have earnings records and are considered to have a high degree of risk. There is a good probability that these companies could incur losses in the future and a small probability of very large future profits. Either way, with these types of stocks, there is a higher possibility of larger price gains or losses than with other types of shares.

Speculative stocks include relatively new companies with promising ideas in the development stages. Recently, this group is represented by the Internet companies, technology, and biotech companies. Many of the Internet companies have no earnings, but their stock prices have shot up into the stratosphere in expectation of potential future profits. The book seller Books-A-Million launched a Website and within the week saw its stock price rise from $3 $\frac{1}{16}$ to $38 $\frac{15}{16}$ per share. This is more than a twelvefold increase for a company that has not incurred profits.

Due to their high risk, investing in speculative stocks requires a strong stomach and the ability to sleep well at night under any circumstances. These stocks will deliver either high capital gains or high capital losses.

Penny Stocks

Penny stocks are the stocks of companies that have low prices—in the $1 or less range—and there is some doubt as to the future ongoing operations of these companies. These companies are extremely speculative. Many of the penny stocks have been promoted by boiler room (illegal) sales operators by cold-calling unsophisticated investors and stressing the merits of buying these low-priced stocks. But as the saying goes, *there are no free lunches on Wall Street*. If a share is trading at $0.25, it is probably trading at its fair value, and there are very good reasons for the low price. If it goes up to $0.50, an investor will have made a 100-percent return, but if the company goes out of business, the investor will have lost his or her entire investment.

Foreign Stocks

The U.S. stock markets still account for the largest market capitalization of all the stock markets in the world, but foreign stock markets are growing in market share. Foreign stocks provide investors with the opportunities to earn greater returns and diversify their portfolios. Many of the larger foreign companies, such as the stocks in Table 1-9, trade as American Depositary Receipts (ADRs) on the U.S. markets (New York Stock Exchange, Over-the-Counter, and NASDAQ).

Large-, Medium-, and Small-Cap Stocks

These categories are based on the market capitalization of the companies, which is measured by the company's stock price multiplied by the number of shares outstanding for the company. These are currently defined as follows, but there are many variations in these amounts, depending on the source:

> Small-cap: less than $1 billion
>
> Medium-cap: $1 billion to $5 billion
>
> Large-cap: greater than $5 billion

The large-cap companies are the larger companies in the Dow Jones Industrial Average and Standard & Poor's Index. These large-cap companies account for over half the total value of the U.S. equity markets. They generally are the established blue-chip

TABLE 1-9

Foreign ADR Stocks

Company	Symbol	Price*	Country	Exchange
Siemens	SMAWY	$65.822	Germany	OTC
Royal Dutch Petroleum	RD	49\frac{3}{8}$	Holland	NYSE
Glaxo	GLX	67\frac{7}{8}$	Britain	NYSE
Volvo	VOLVY	25\frac{7}{16}$	Sweden	NASDAQ

* Prices are as of December 24, 1998.

companies, and they include such companies as Intel, Microsoft, IBM, Ford, Exxon, and many of the other large companies that lead their industries. With the explosive rise in the stock prices of Internet companies, this definition would now include the stock of Yahoo, the Internet search engine, which has a market capitalization of close to $25 billion. This goes to show that large-caps do not necessarily have to be established companies with earnings. The Internet market mania has catapulted many Internet stocks into the large-cap category, even though many may not have turned the corner into posting positive earnings.

The medium-cap stocks are companies that have the safety of significant assets in terms of their capitalization and include many not-so-well-known companies. Examples are Tyson Foods, Cooper Tire and Rubber, and Starbucks as well as less-known companies such as Marine Drilling and Global Marine.

The small-cap stocks are small in size and are generally not household names. This is the group of stocks that, according to the studies, will outperform the large-cap stocks over long periods of time. Over the past few years (1995–1998) this has not been the case; large-cap stocks have outperformed the small-cap stocks. Small-cap stock prices tend to be more volatile than the large- and mid-caps due to their higher exposure to risk. These companies hold the potential to be the Intels and Microsofts of tomorrow. However, in the process, many small companies will go out of business. Small-cap stocks have the additional risk of not having very many shares outstanding as well as not being actively traded.

Small-cap stocks are riskier investments, and investors should diversify their holdings of them to reduce their overall risk of loss.

What becomes apparent from these classifications of the types of common stocks is that companies can be classified in several different categories. Merck, the pharmaceutical company, can be classified as a blue-chip stock, a growth stock, a large-cap stock, and a defensive stock. This classification system is useful in the planning stages of the portfolio to determine the types of stocks that investors would want to own and their respective percentages of the portfolio. These concepts are discussed in Chapter 2.

WHAT IS PREFERRED STOCK?

Another type of stock is preferred stock, which also represents an equity ownership in a company. *Equity* is defined as capital invested in a company by its owners; *debt* is capital lent to the corporation, which must be repaid. Preferred stock is a hybrid type of security in that it has features resembling both debt and equity.

Fixed Dividend

Unlike common stock, the dividend rate on preferred stock is usually fixed. It may be stated as a percentage of the par value of the preferred stock or as a fixed dollar amount. The *par value* is a stated value; hence, a preferred stock issue with $100 par value and a dividend of 8 percent would pay $8 per share (8 percent of $100).

The fixed dividends of preferred stocks appeal to investors who rely on regular returns for income. In this regard, preferred stock resembles the regular returns of interest on bonds. However, the downside to a fixed dividend rate is that the price of the preferred stock is sensitive to changes in market rates of interest. For example, if an investor bought preferred stock for $100 a share that pays a dividend of $6 and market rates of interest subsequently go up to 8 percent, there will be downside pressure on the price of the preferred stock. New investors will not want to buy this preferred stock for $100 when the dividend is only $6, or 6 percent, because a current investment will return 8 percent. Thus, price fluctuations of preferred stocks tend to be greater than those of long-term bonds (Mayo, p. 233).

To counter these swings in preferred stock prices, many financial institutions and utility companies introduced *adjustable-rate preferred stock* in the early 1980s, when market rates were high. Dividend payments fluctuate with changes in market rates of interest as measured by the changes in a combination of U.S. Treasury securities. Dividends would move up and down within a stipulated minimum and maximum limit. For example, Bank of America Corporation's 9.25 percent (at offering) adjustable-rate preferred stock had a 6-percent minimum dividend rate and a 12-percent maximum rate. The rate was adjusted to changes in interest rates on a quarterly basis.

The advantage of adjustable-rate preferred stock is that the price of the preferred stock does not fluctuate as much with changes in market rates of interest.

Multiple Classes

Most companies have one class of common stock, but it is quite common to see companies with more than one series of preferred stock. Table 1-10 illustrates the different preferred stock issues of the Long Island Lighting Co., which is listed on the New York Stock Exchange.

Each class of preferred stock may have different features, such as a different dividend rate. One might be a *cumulative preferred* issue, which gives the holder the right to receive all missed dividend payments before common shareholders are paid. Another in the series might be a convertible preferred issue with a call provision. *Convertible preferred* stock can be converted by the holders into a fixed number of shares of the common stock of the underlying company. These issues can also be differentiated in their priority status with regard to claims on assets in the event of bankruptcy.

Claim on Income and Assets

As the name implies, preferred stock has a preference over common stock with regard to claims on both income and assets. Companies must pay the dividends on preferred stock before they can pay dividends to common stockholders. In the event of bankruptcy, preferred stockholders' claims are settled before those of

TABLE 1-10

Different Issues of Long Island Lighting Co.'s Preferred Stock

| 52 Weeks Net | | Stock | Sym | Div | % | PE | Vol | Hi | Lo | Close | Chg |
Hi	Lo										
$29^5/_8$	$22^5/_8$	LIL Co	LIL	1.78	7.7	11	1379	$23^3/_8$	$23^1/_8$	$23^1/_4$	...
$28^1/_4$	$22^5/_8$	LIL Co	pfA	1.99	7.5		7	$26^5/_8$	$26^5/_8$	$26^5/_8$	$-^1/_8$
110	102	LIL Co	pfC	7.66	7.2		1	106	106	106	...
70	53	LIL Co	pfE	4.35	7.6		41	57	56	57	+1
$26^3/_4$	$24^5/_8$	LIL Co	pfa	1.76	6.8		3	$25^7/_8$	$25^7/_8$	$25^7/_8$	$+^1/_4$

common shareholders. This makes preferred stock less risky than common stock, but it is more risky in comparison to debt.

In the case of multiple classes of preferred stock, the different issues may be prioritized in their claims to income and assets.

Cumulative Dividend

Most preferred stock issues carry a *cumulative feature,* which means that if the company fails to pay the dividend, it will have to make it up before it can pay any dividends to its common shareholders. This cumulative feature protects the rights of the preferred stock-holders. A preferred issue that does not have a cumulative feature is called a *noncumulative* preferred stock.

Convertible Feature

Some preferred stock issues have a convertible feature that allows the owners to exchange their preferred stock for common shares. The conditions and terms of the conversion are set when the pre-ferred stock is first issued. This would include the conversion ratio, which is the number of common shares the preferred stockholder will get for each preferred share, and the conversion price of the common stock.

Let's say, for example, that Company XYZ issues a new con-vertible preferred stock, which is sold at $100 per share and is con-vertible into five common shares of Company XYZ. The conversion ratio is 5:1, and the conversion price is $20 per share for the com-mon stock ($100 ÷ 5 shares). If the market price of the common stock were $15, it would not be advantageous for the preferred stockholder to convert, because the value after conversion would be $75 (5 shares at $15). However, if the price of the common stock rose to $20, there would be parity. The preferred stockholder still would not convert because the preferred stock pays a dividend. If the common stock rose above $20 per share, however, the preferred stockholder could share in the capital appreciation of the common stock by converting to common stock.

The decision to exercise the conversion option depends on three factors:

1. The market price of the common stock. It would have to be greater than the conversion price for the holder to share in capital gains.
2. The amount of the preferred dividend.
3. The amount of the common dividend.

The conversion feature provides the investor with the possibility of sharing in the capital gains through the appreciation of the common stock as well as the relative safety of receiving the preferred dividends before conversion.

Participation Feature

Some corporations include a participation feature to make the preferred stock issue more attractive to investors. This feature allows preferred stockholders to share in earnings beyond the stated dividend. After the preferred stockholders and common stockholders have received their stated dividends, the additional amounts of the company's earnings are available for distribution to the preferred and common stockholders.

Call Provision

A preferred stock issue with a call provision entitles the issuing company to repurchase the stock at its option from outstanding preferred stockholders. The call price is generally more than the preferred stock's par value.

The call provision is advantageous to the issuing company, but not to the holder of the preferred stock. This is because when market rates of interest fall significantly below the dividend rate of the preferred issue, companies are likely to exercise the call provision by retiring the issue and replacing it with a new preferred stock issue with a lower dividend rate.

The savings to the issuing company represents a loss of income to the preferred stockholders. When interest rates went down in 1989, Long Island Lighting Company retired several of its callable preferred stock issues.

Thus, not only do preferred stockholders suffer a loss of income when their high-dividend-rate preferred stock issues are called in, but the call provision also acts as a ceiling limit on the price appreciation of the preferred stock. When interest rates decline, there is an upward push on the price of high-dividend preferred stock issues. However, the price of the preferred stock will not rise above the call price.

The Securities and Exchange Commission (SEC) encourages companies issuing preferred stock to include a call provision. The reason for this position is to prevent companies from being stuck with high-dividend-rate preferred stock issues that they can't retire when market interest rates decline. As a result, most preferred stock issues have call provisions.

To entice investors to buy preferred stock issues during periods of high interest rates, companies include a *call protection* feature. This prevents the company from calling the issue for a period of time, generally for five years, but this may vary. After the call protection period, the issue is callable at the stated call price per share.

Investors should examine the terms of the call feature before investing, because the terms vary greatly from issue to issue.

REFERENCES

Faerber, Esmé: *All About Bonds and Bond Mutual Funds,* McGraw-Hill, New York, 2000.

Gottschalk, Earl C., Jr., and Barbara Donnelly: "Despite Market Swings, Stocks Make Sense," *The Wall Street Journal,* October 1989.

Hall, Alvin D.: *Getting Started in Stocks,* Wiley, New York, 1992.

Ibbotson, Roger G., and Rex A. Sinquefield: *Stocks, Bonds, Bills and Inflation: Historical Return (1926–1993),* Irwin, Chicago, 1994.

Ip, Greg: "The Days of Robust Stock Market Gains May Turn Into Just Single-Digit Returns," *The Wall Street Journal,* October 26, 1998.

Mayo, Herbert B.: *Investments,* 2d ed., Dryden Press, Chicago, 1988.

Petty, J. William, et al.: *Basic Financial Management,* 6th ed., Prentice Hall, Englewood Cliffs, NJ, 1993.

Siegel, Jeremy: "Why Stocks Are Still the Investment of Choice," *The Wall Street Journal,* September 16, 1998.

CHAPTER 2

Should I Invest in Common Stocks?

KEY CONCEPTS

- Types of risk
- Rate of return
- Inflation and taxes
- Selection of investments

The main advantage of investing in common stock, as pointed out in Chapter 1, is that historically, investors have received greater returns than those received from most other investments. These returns come in the form of dividends and capital gains. In addition, common stocks act as a store of value for the future.

The U.S. stock markets (and bond markets) have performed admirably through the 1990s due to low market rates of interest. Many traditional certificate of deposit (CD) investors have found the low returns of CDs (around 3 percent) to be unpalatable and have moved into the stock market to participate in the higher returns. The Dow Jones Industrial Average has more than tripled in the nine years of this decade (1990–1999), from about 3000 to about 11,000, as of this writing. The major part of this increase came between 1995 and May of 1999. Put another way, investors who bought most of the stocks in the Dow Jones Industrial Average would have seen their value increase by an average of 30 percent per year from 1995–1998. Of course, there are some stocks in the Dow Jones Industrial Average that have not appreciated in value.

It is this factor that makes some investors more nervous than others about investing in common stocks. You can lose some of your investment capital if the price of the stock falls below the purchase price. By contrast, if you invest $10,000 in U.S. Treasury notes and hold them through maturity, you will receive your $10,000 back plus interest. In other words, there is no erosion of capital.

To get the most from your investments, not only do you have to understand the investments, their risks, and their returns, but you also need to have an investment plan with specific objectives. The investment plan provides the direction you need to take in order to achieve your stated objectives. The first step is to review your financial position. This includes a budget review, in which you would list the following:

- All of your sources of income: salary, bonus, interest, dividends, and so on
- Your monthly living expenses, including taxes
- Your expenses for insurance: life, disability, health, home, auto

The excess of income over expenses will be used to fund your objectives. List the objectives, their time frames, and the total amount of money needed to fund them. This process is illustrated in Table 2-1.

TABLE 2-1

Personal Objectives*

Objective	Time Needed	Total Cost	Priority	Amount Needed to Fund Objectives
Emergency fund				
Buy a car				
Save for a house				
Education fund				
Savings and investment fund				
Retirement fund				

* All of your objectives should be listed, along with the time frame and total costs. The latter should be realistic. The priority is the degree of urgency.

The next step is to choose the investments that are most likely to help you achieve those objectives. The shorter-term objectives will need investments that are high in liquidity, while with the medium- and long-term objectives, there is more flexibility as to the types of investments. Your objectives will govern your investment decisions not only from the time perspective (short-term, medium-term, or long term) but also as to whether the emphasis is on current income, capital growth, or both. The most common investment objectives for most people fall into the following three categories:

- To provide current income
- To fund expenditures
- To save funds for retirement

These objectives will determine the limits of the risks you can take with the different types of investments. For example, if you rely on current income to meet your living expenses, you do not have much latitude in the levels of risk that your investments can be exposed to. Similarly, if you are investing money to fund a college education which begins three years hence, you do not want to experience an erosion of your capital due to the nonperformance of a particular investment. Funds set aside for long periods of time can better withstand the volatility of the stock market. That's why they are able to receive greater returns.

WHAT ARE THE TYPES OF RISKS AND HOW MUCH CAN I TOLERATE?

Understanding the risks associated with the different types of investments is an important step in investing. *Risk* is the uncertainty related to the outcome of the investment, and all investments are subject to risk of one type or another. This is probably what deters many investors from investing in stocks and prompts them to keep their money in CDs, bank accounts, and bonds. These passive investments (keeping money in an FDIC-insured checking account at a bank and earning whatever meager interest rate is currently being offered) will not keep up with the rate of inflation.

Business Risk

Business risk is the uncertainty related to a company's sales and earnings. Some companies are riskier by their nature than companies in other sectors and will see greater fluctuations in their sales and earnings. If sales and earnings decline significantly, there will not only be downward pressure on the stock price but also the risk that the company may not be able to cover its interest, principal, and dividend payments. The company could experience losses and, at worst, go out of business, which would make their securities (stocks and bonds) worthless.

Investors' expectations of a company's earnings will affect the price of the stock. When there is an anticipated decline in earnings, shareholders may sell their shares, which puts downward pressure on the stock's price. Similarly, if there is an anticipated increase in earnings, investors will be willing to pay higher prices for the stock.

The stock prices of cyclical companies tend to fluctuate up and down along with the business cycles of the economy. Therefore, they are more susceptible to business risk.

For more conservative investors, business risk can be reduced by investing in the common stocks of companies with stable earnings, as opposed to those of the cyclical companies.

Financial Risk

Financial risk refers to the amount of debt a company has in relation to its equity. The greater the amount of debt to the amount of equity, the higher the financial risk, because the company will need to earn at least enough to pay back its fixed-interest and principal payments. Failure of a company to meet these commitments can lead to bankruptcy.

Companies with very little or no debt have very little or no financial risk. Looking at a company's balance sheet reveals the amount of debt relative to its total assets and equity. Financial risk can be reduced by investing in companies with low debt-to-equity ratios (or debt-to-total-asset ratios).

What Can I Do about Business and Financial Risks?

Total risk can be broken down into two parts: unsystematic risk and systematic risk. *Unsystematic risk* pertains to the risks of the company, such as business and financial risk. It is also called *diversifiable*

risk, because it can be diversified away. This type of risk is associated with investing in only one company—putting all your eggs into
one basket. For example, had you taken your life savings of
$100,000 and invested it all, at $55 per share, in the common stock
of Boeing Corporation at the beginning of 1998, you would have
lost around 43 percent of your investment a year later. Boeing stock
fell to lows of around $31 per share. This dismal performance of
Boeing stock is compounded by having occurred in an overall market that is up around 20 percent for the same period. See Table 2-2.

   Suppose that instead of investing all your money in Boeing at
the beginning of the year, you decided to divide it up into three
stocks, as shown in Table 2-3. At the end of the year, the portfolio
would have grown by 17 percent, as opposed to the loss of 43 percent
from investing all your money in Boeing. The stock prices of Boeing
and Cisco declined and rose, respectively, due to company-related
events. Boeing Corporation experienced production problems during
the year and was not able to fill all their orders for aircraft. This result-

TABLE 2-2

Portfolio of Stocks

Date	Security	# Shares	Share Price	Symbol	Cost	Market Price (12/98)
1/98	Bought Boeing	1818	$55	BA	$100,000	$56,358

TABLE 2-3

Portfolio of Stocks

Date	Security	# Shares	Share Price	Symbol	Cost	Market Price (12/98)
1/98	Bought Boeing	606	$55	BA	$33,333	$18,786
1/98	Bought Cisco	833	$40	CSCO	$33,333	$63,308
1/98	Bought Pepsi	901	$37	PEP	$33,334	$35,139
					$100,000	$117,233

ed in Boeing posting losses for several quarters, which explains the nosedive in the stock to $31. By contrast, Cisco Systems is the leader in the production of routers (computer equipment needed to hook up to the Internet), and it consistently posted double-digit increases in sales. This explains the move in the stock price from $40 per share to $76 per share. The stock of Pepsi did not do very much, starting out at $37 per share and ending up at $39 per share.

Of course, you might think you should have invested the entire amount in Cisco Systems and not bothered with the other stocks. Hindsight always produces 20/20 vision. However, at the beginning of the year, you did not know that Cisco Systems would be the outperformer, so you invested in three stocks to reduce the variability in returns (risk).

By investing all your funds in the securities of several companies, you can reduce company-related risks, such as business and financial risk. Studies have shown that a portfolio composed of 20 different stocks can virtually eliminate all the company-related risks (Klemkosky and Martin, pp. 147–154). Thus, of the total risk, the unsystematic risk is reduced through diversification, and you are now left with the systematic risk, which cannot be reduced through diversification. Systematic risk is also known as *market risk*.

Investing in the same types of stocks is not diversification. For example, if you had invested in Boeing and several other aerospace companies, you would not have been able to protect yourself against the effects of a downturn in government orders for planes and missiles. The stocks of these companies would all have behaved the same way. To get the most from diversification, you need to invest in different types of stocks in different sectors of the economy as well as other types of investments, such as government bonds, corporate bonds, and foreign stocks.

Market Risk

Although investors can diversify their investments to virtually eliminate business and financial risks, market risk cannot be diversified away. Market risk is more encompassing. It refers to the movement of security prices in general, which tend to move together in response to external events (unrelated to the fundamentals of specific companies).

When the stock market goes up, most stocks go up in price, including those with less-than-spectacular sales, growth, and earnings. Similarly, if there is a sell-off in the stock market, it will include those stocks with better-than-average sales, growth, and earnings.

The external events that move security prices are unpredictable. They could range from news of a war in a remote part of the globe, an uprising in the Middle East, or a coup d'etat in a developing nation to the death of a prominent leader of a foreign nation, changes in the inflation rate, labor strikes, or floods in the Midwest. Any such event could trigger a sell-off in the stock market. Since these external events cannot be predicted, investors in the stock markets cannot do very much to avoid the short-term fluctuations in stock prices that accompany them.

Investors should bear in mind that over long periods of time, stock prices tend to appreciate in relation to their intrinsic value (their growth and earnings). In other words, it is more likely the investment fundamentals of a company that will determine the long-term returns for its stock.

Market risk highlights, in particular, the danger of investing short-term money in the stock market. If the money is needed when the market has declined, investors will need to sell out at a loss. Thus, investors in stocks should have a time horizon long enough so that they will not have to sell out in a down market.

What Can I Do about Market Risk?

If you have a short time horizon, your risk of loss increases with stocks. A study of S&P 500 stocks done by the Vanguard Group, the mutual fund company, compared the range of returns for stocks with different holding periods from 1950 to 1980. With a holding period of one year, annual returns averaged 11.4 percent from 1950 to 1980. The high during this period was 52.3 percent for a one-year period, and the low was a negative 26.3 percent. If you had invested funds in the one particular year that the market went down by 26.3 percent, you would probably never want to invest in common stocks again (Keown et al, 1996, p. 232). Table 2-4 shows the range and average returns for different holding periods during this same period.

From this table, you can see that the variability, or risk, is reduced as the holding period increases. Patient investors who can afford long holding periods can significantly reduce the market

TABLE 2-4

Range and Average Returns for S&P 500 Stocks for Different Holding Periods, 1950–1980.

	1 Year	5 Years	10 Years	15 Years	20 Years	25 Years
High	52.3%	20.1%	16.4%	13.9%	11.6%	10.2%
Average	11.4%	9.3%	8.5%	8.4%	8.4%	8.9%
Low	−26.3%	−2.4%	−1.2%	4.3%	6.5%	7.9%

Source: Vanguard Group as reported in Keown, et al., *Basic Financial Management*, 7th ed., Prentice Hall, N.J., 1996, p.232.

risk of investing in stocks. However, investors in stocks cannot escape from market risk completely. There will always be volatility in the stock markets. However, with the reinvestment of dividends and capital gains, the range of returns will be less variable over longer holding periods.

Using asset allocation to create a balanced portfolio of different types of investments can also reduce the effects of market risk. The bond and stock markets do not always rise and fall in tandem. During a stock market decline, the bond market could be rising, which provides some form of balance for shorter-term objectives.

Purchasing Power or Inflationary Risk

Putting money under the mattress may avoid market risk, but this may not alleviate *purchasing power risk*. If prices in the economy keep rising (inflation), the real purchasing power of the investor's dollars is reduced. In other words, future dollars will purchase less in goods and services than they would today. Purchasing power risk has the greatest effect on investments that have fixed returns (bonds, savings accounts, and certificates of deposit) and no returns (non-interest-bearing checking accounts and the hoard under the mattress).

Assets whose values move with general price levels, such as common stocks, do better during periods of slight to moderate inflation. To protect against purchasing power risk, investors should choose investments whose anticipated returns are higher than the anticipated rate of inflation.

Of all the financial assets, such as bonds, money market securities, and common stocks, common stocks have fared the best during periods of low to moderate inflation. During periods of high inflation, all financial assets do poorly, including common stocks. However, common stocks perform less poorly than bonds and money market securities in these circumstances.

Interest Rate Risk

Interest rate risk refers to the changes in market rates of interest affecting all investments.

Interest rates do affect common stocks, but less directly than fixed-income securities. High market rates of interest tend to depress stock prices, and low interest rates tend to go hand in hand with bull markets. High market rates of interest prompt many investors to sell their stocks and move into the bond markets to take advantage of the higher coupon rates of bonds. When interest rates come down, more investors move into the stock markets from the bond and money markets.

The trend is your friend and *don't fight the trend* are a couple of common sayings with regard to interest rates. Investors should be aware of market rates of interest. By analyzing trends and responding, you can protect against substantial losses due to adverse changes in market rates of interest.

Political Risk

Political risk refers to changes in the political environment that affect companies' stocks and bonds. For example, government intervention in the private sector, currency devaluations, changes in government, and taxes can all affect a company's profits. Pharmaceutical stocks were battered by fears of the price controls in the Clinton health plan proposal of the early 1990s.

Since political events often occur with very little warning, it may be difficult for investors to anticipate which foreign companies will be adversely affected. It is easier to avoid investing in companies in troubled countries than to anticipate the possible political events that could send stock prices plunging.

Liquidity Risk

Liquidity risk refers to the uncertainty about converting an investment into cash without losing a significant amount of the funds invested. Certain investments are more liquid than others; the greater the liquidity of the investment, the easier it is to buy and sell without sacrificing a price concession. When making a particular investment, investors should consider two factors:

- The length of time it will take to sell that investment
- The relative certainty of the selling price

Funds that are to be used in a short period of time should be invested in securities high in liquidity (savings accounts, Treasury bills, money market mutual funds, for example). A Treasury bill can be sold very quickly with only a slight concession in selling price, whereas a 20-year-to-maturity junk bond may not only take time to sell but may also sell at a significant price concession.

This is especially true for bonds that are thinly traded, that is, relatively few bonds are traded and the trades take place only with large spreads between the bid and asked prices. Thinly traded bonds basically are *not marketable,* which is to say they cannot be sold quickly.

Common stocks of actively traded companies on the stock exchanges can be sold quickly and hence are marketable and liquid (there is a small spread between the bid and asked prices). However, inactively traded common stocks listed on the stock exchanges and on the over-the-counter markets may be marketable but not liquid. The spreads between the bid and asked prices may be wide and the sale price may be less than the purchase price, resulting in losses. This could be a problem for an investor who needs to sell inactively traded common stocks unexpectedly. If there are few or no buyers for the stocks, the investor will have to sell them at a lower price to entice buyers. Investors should anticipate liquidity risks with inactively traded common stocks and medium- and long-term bonds.

Foreign Currency Risks

If you think you can escape from all these risks by investing in the stocks of foreign companies, keep in mind *foreign currency risks.*

A rise in the dollar against a foreign currency can decimate any returns and result in a loss of capital when the stocks are sold. For example, a 10 percent increase in the price of a British stock is negated by a 10 percent rise in the price of the dollar to the British pound.

THE RELATIONSHIP BETWEEN RISK AND RETURN

It is evident that risk cannot be avoided even with the most conservative investments (savings accounts and Treasury bills). By understanding and recognizing the different levels of risk for each type of investment, the total risk can be better managed in the construction of an investment portfolio.

There is a direct correlation between risk and return. The greater the risk in an investment, the greater the potential return to entice investors. In most cases, however, investing in securities with the greatest return and, therefore, the greatest risk can lead to financial ruin if everything does not go according to plan.

Being aware of the risks pertaining to the different types of investments is of little consequence unless you are aware of your own feelings toward risk. How much risk you can tolerate depends on many factors, such as the type of person you are, your investment objectives, the amount of your assets, the size of your portfolio, and your time horizon for the investments.

How nervous are you as an investor? Do you check your stock prices every morning in the financial newspapers? Can you sleep well at night if your stocks have declined below their acquisition prices? If you do watch the prices of your stocks every day, call your broker every time that your stocks fall by a point, and do not sleep well at night when your stocks are down, you do not tolerate risks well. In this case, your portfolio should be weighted toward conservative investments that generate income through capital preservation. The percentage of your portfolio allocated to stocks may be low to zero, depending on your comfort zone. Figure 2-1 illustrates the continuum of risk tolerance. If you are comfortable with accepting more risks, you would invest a greater percentage of your portfolio in stocks.

FIGURE 2-1

Continuum of Risk Tolerance

Percentage Allocation to Stocks

0%		100%
Nervous Investor	Moderate Risk Tolerance	Risk Seeker, Speculator

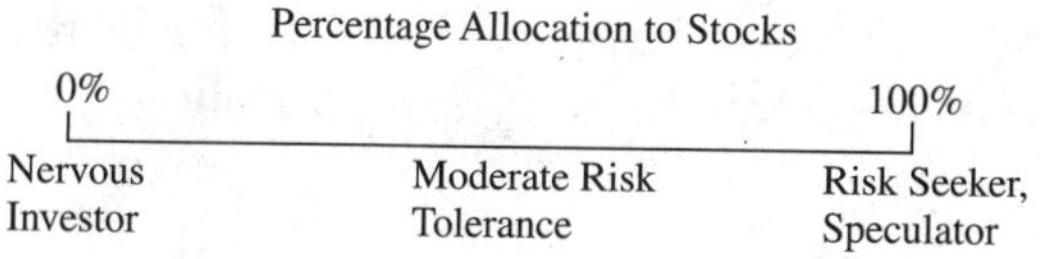

Moving along the continuum of greater risk-seeking, if you buy stocks and forget about them until you are reminded about them by someone else, your tolerance for risk is much greater and your portfolio can include a large percentage of stocks.

The risk-seeker or speculator will look for investments with the greatest rates of return, even though the investments may be extremely volatile and there may be a good chance that some of the principal will be lost.

Bear in mind that there are other factors you need to consider when allocating your investment funds to different types of investments. Understanding your tolerance for risk is an important step in determining how much of your portfolio should be allocated to common stocks.

There is a wide range of returns associated with each type of investment. As pointed out in Chapter 1, there are different classifications for stocks, such as growth stocks, income stocks, and speculative stocks. Income stocks generally are lower risk and offer returns mainly in the form of dividends, whereas growth stocks generally offer higher returns in the form of capital gains and are more risky. Investors should be aware of this broad range of risks and returns for these different types of investments so that an acceptable level of risk can be found. Figure 2-2 illustrates the risk-return tradeoff, in general, for the different types of investments. Bear in mind that you would likely be exposed to more risk with certain junk bonds, for example, than with certain blue-chip stocks. The Ibbotson studies (1994) show that over the period from 1926 to 1993, real returns on a portfolio of large common stocks averaged 9.1 percent a year with risks of 20.5 percent, while a portfolio of long-term government bonds averaged real rates of return of 2.2 percent with risks of 8.7 percent. For the same period, common stocks had negative returns in 20 of the 67 years, while Treasury bills had negative returns for only one of the years. The risk-return relationship shows that for accepting higher levels of risk in an investment, you should be rewarded with higher returns. Similarly, for lower levels of risk, you can expect lower returns.

Knowing your acceptable levels of risk will assist you in the determination of the types of investments for your portfolio.

FIGURE 2-2

General Risks and Returns for Different Types of Investments

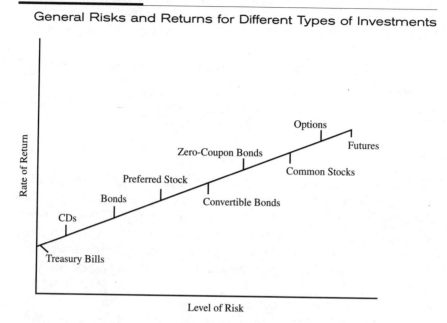

WHAT IS MY RATE OF RETURN?
===

Investors invest in order to earn a return, which may be in the form of income (interest and dividends) or capital appreciation (when the price of the investment rises between the time of purchase and sale). Some investments, such as savings accounts and certificates of deposit (CDs), offer only income with no capital appreciation. Others, such as common stocks, which may or may not pay dividends, also offer the potential for capital appreciation. If the price of the stocks goes down, there will be capital losses. The simple definition of total return includes both income and capital gains and losses.

Why is calculating a return so important? There are two reasons. First, it is a measure of the growth or decline of your investments. Second, it is a yardstick with which to evaluate the performance of your investments against your objectives. The total rate of return can be calculated as follows:

Rate of return = (ending value − beginning value)
+ income/gross purchase price

Spreads and commissions should be included in the calculations. For example, if a stock was purchased at the beginning of the year for $1000 (including the commission) and was sold for $1200 at the end of the year (net proceeds received after deducting the commission), and earned a dividend of $50, the rate of return is 25 percent:

$$\text{Rate of return} = \frac{(1200-1000)+50}{1000}$$

$$= 25\%$$

This rate of return is not very accurate, particularly if the investment is held for a long period of time, over a year. This is because the time value of money is not taken into account. The *time value of money* is a concept that recognizes that a dollar today is worth more in the future because of its earnings potential. A dollar invested at 3 percent for one year would be worth $1.03 at the end of one year. Similarly, a dollar to be received at the end of one year would be worth less than a dollar at the beginning of the year.

The simple average rate of return of 25 percent discussed above does not take into account the earnings capacity of the interest received. In other words, the $50 of dividends received would be reinvested, which would increase the rate of return above 25 percent.

Using the time value of money to calculate the rate of return will give a more accurate rate of return figure. However, it is more difficult for the average person to calculate. The rate of return on a stock will equate the discounted cash flows of the future dividends and the expected sale price of the stock to the current purchase price of the stock. This formula works better for bonds than for common stocks because the cash flows for bonds are much more certain than those for common stocks. The coupon rate for bonds is generally fixed, whereas dividend rates on common stocks may fluctuate. When companies are experiencing losses, they may cut their dividends, as Westinghouse Electric Company (now CBS Corporation) did in 1994. On the positive side, if earnings increase, companies may increase their dividend payout ratios. There is even less certainty over the sale price of a stock into the future. Bonds are retired at their par price ($1000 per bond) at maturity; but when selling a stock in the future, you would be guessing at the sale price.

Whichever formula you use to calculate the rate of return on stocks, you need to be aware that there could be wide fluctuations in return from year to year. This is due primarily to the fluctuations in the prices of stocks, since dividend income tends to be relatively stable. Thus, at any point in the future, the price of the stock could be up or down from the acquisition price.

However, between 1926 and 1992, there have been only 20 down years in the stock market. If investors had time on their side during these down years and stayed in the stock market, they would have recouped their losses (Clements, p. 13).

Clearly, many investors dream of trebling their investments overnight by buying stocks. This could happen, but it is not the order of the day. Currently, the stocks of many Internet companies have risen 200 to 300 percent in very short periods of time, but if they can go up this rapidly, they have the potential to go down by that much and more. However, the superior results obtained by stocks are compelling.

According to the Ibbotson and Sinquefield study (1994), common stocks of large companies had nominal (not adjusted for inflation) average yearly returns of 12.3 percent over the 67-year period from 1926 to 1993, while returns earned by common stocks of small companies averaged 17.6 percent per year during that same period. These average returns are useful yardsticks of performance. Investors should follow the various stock market indexes, such as the Dow Jones Industrial Average and the Standard & Poor's 500 Index, to help them gauge the performance of the stock markets.

Investors in the stock markets need to be aware that their money will always face the risk of price fluctuation despite the long-term profitability of the stock markets. Investors who have a low tolerance for risk and who need investments with capital preservation should not invest in common stocks. Similarly, if investors need their money in less than five years, they should avoid stocks.

If investors have a long time horizon, they can invest in a diversified portfolio of stocks, which, despite all the risks, will more than likely generate superior returns to other investments.

INFLATION AND TAXES

There are two important factors affecting the rate of return on investments—inflation and taxes. If an investor earns 5 percent per year and inflation is 3 percent for the same period, the *real rate of return* is only 2 percent. If inflation rises to 5 percent or higher, investors holding fixed-income securities yielding 5 percent will not be jumping for joy at the prospect of zero to negative rates of return. That is why market prices of fixed-income securities (bonds) decline so rapidly when the inflation rate rises: bondholders receive fixed amounts of interest. To entice additional investors, market prices of existing bonds on the secondary markets will go down in price in order to make their rates of return more competitive (to include the rate of inflation).

The Ibbotson and Associates studies (1994) report that the highest real rates of return (adjusted for inflation), for the 67-year period from 1926 to 1993 were for common stocks (over Treasury bills and bonds). Common stocks had their highest real rates of return in years when inflation was low. In years when inflation was high (above 6 percent), the real returns on common stocks were negative. To put this another way, in relation to other investments, the returns of stocks were less negative than those of bonds and Treasury bills.

Consequently, the stock market offers investors the most favorable real rates of return in a low-inflation economy, whereas a high-inflationary environment produces negative real rates of return on most investments, both bonds and stocks. If you anticipate inflation, choose investments that will yield rates of return that will protect against the inflationary erosion of purchasing power.

Taxes also diminish the investor's rate of return. Dividend and interest income are taxed at ordinary rates at the federal level. At the time of this writing, long-term capital gains (requiring a holding period of greater than one year) are taxed at a lower rate than the top marginal tax bracket rate. For 1998, the highest tax rate bracket was 39.6 percent; the long-term capital gains rate was 20 percent.

The reinstatement of the lower capital gains rate is advantageous for investors in higher tax brackets who have investments that generate long-term capital gains. For these investors, common stocks with capital appreciation potential become attractive investments.

Since taxes (federal, state, and possibly local) are levied on dividends (interest) and capital gains, it is advisable to compare different investments on the basis of their after-tax rate of return. The after-tax rate of return is calculated as follows:

After-tax rate of return = (1 − tax rate) (before-tax rate of return)

For example, an investor in the 39.6 percent marginal tax bracket who invests in securities yielding 10 percent would have an after-tax rate of return of 6.04 percent:

$$\text{After-tax rate of return} = (1 - .396)(.10)$$
$$= 6.04\%$$

This after-tax rate of return can be compared to the rate of return of a municipal bond, which is tax-free at the federal level. In many cases, taxes can affect your choice of investments. Effective tax planning may reduce the level of taxes paid.

Inflation, taxes, and commissions all reduce the rate of return. Investors should consider these factors to ensure that after they have been deducted, their investments still yield positive returns.

SELECTION OF INVESTMENTS

Understanding the risk-return trade-off is an important step in the investment process and, of course, involves the level of risk that you feel comfortable with. Returns on common stocks may be higher than those received on other investments, but the risks of holding common stocks are greater than those of bonds and Treasury bills.

There is no perfect investment, so investors should understand the different types of investment securities, their risk characteristics, and their expected returns. Keep in mind that these can change over time, and investors may need to anticipate these changes in order to be successful.

As mentioned earlier in this chapter, there are two factors that reduce some of the risk: diversification and time. Diversification reduces unsystematic risk, which consists of business and financial risk. By investing in different types of securities, among various companies in different industries, the risk of loss in the total portfolio is reduced. For example, when the stock of one company in the portfolio declines, there may be increases in the other stocks which will offset the loss. However, diversification does not reduce market risk. If the entire stock market declines, the stocks of even a diversified portfolio will generally also decline. Since the bond and stock markets often move together, diversification across markets does not provide immunity from market risk.

Time, however, can help combat market risk. With a long time horizon, investors can wait for stock prices to recover from a down market.

The decision about the types of securities to invest in will depend on the investor's objectives, the characteristics of the investor (marital status, age, family, education, income, net worth, and the size of the portfolio), the level of risk tolerance, the expected rate of return, and the economic environment. The flow chart in Figure 2-3 looks at some of the factors in the selection of different types of investments.

For example, if an investor's objectives are to seek capital growth and this investor is a young, single professional with an excellent salary, he or she may be able to tolerate greater risk in order to receive higher returns. With a long time horizon and less need for income generation from these assets, a greater portion of this investor's portfolio should be invested in common stocks. *Asset allocation* in this case could be as follows:

Stocks	80%
Bonds	10%
Money market equivalents	10%

A more conservative asset allocation model would be:

Stocks	60%
Bonds	30%
Money market equivalents	10%

At the other extreme, an older, retired couple with limited net worth, whose objectives are income generation and capital preservation, should choose an entirely different allocation of their assets. They would not be able to tolerate very much risk, and their time horizon would likely be shorter. In order to generate regular income, a greater proportion of their investment portfolio will go into fixed-income securities with varying maturities. Depending on their circumstances, there could be a small percentage allocated to common stocks to provide some capital appreciation. Their suggested asset allocation model might be set up as follows:

FIGURE 2-3

Selection of Investments

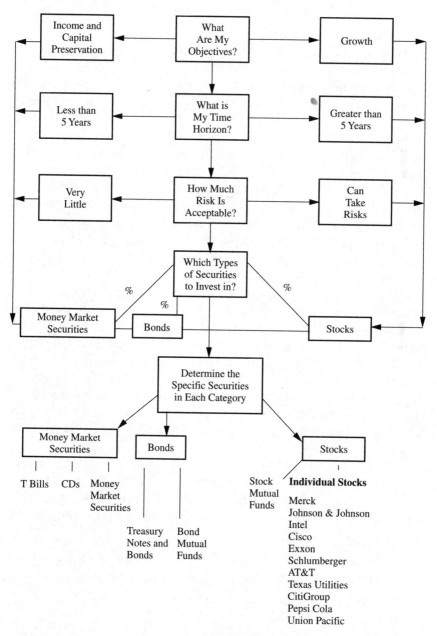

Stocks	15%
Bonds	65%
Money market equivalents	20%

The percentage amount allocated between bonds and money market equivalents will vary from couple to couple depending on their circumstances.

Asset allocation depends on the investment objectives, the financial characteristics, and the risk tolerance of each investor. What works for one family may not be appropriate for another. For example, the financial characteristics of two couples may be identical, but one couple may need to set aside greater amounts in money market securities to meet medical bills.

The important aspect of investing is having an asset allocation plan that signifies the broad mix of investments to strive for. This allocation plan is not cast in stone and should change to accommodate changes in personal and economic circumstances. See Table 2-5 for some guidelines on asset allocation.

After you have determined how you will allocate your portfolio to the broad categories of investments (stocks, bonds, and money market funds), the next step is the choice of individual securities. This requires a thorough investigation. For stocks, it may be useful to review the different categories of common stocks discussed in Chapter 1. For example, allocations of equal amounts of your total stock amount to value stocks, growth stocks, foreign stocks, blue-chip stocks, and small-cap stocks will also reduce the total risk of the portfolio. The portfolio of individual stocks listed at the bottom of Figure 2-3 can be classified as shown in Table 2-6.

Most of these companies are leaders in their respective industries, and there is a broad representation of different industry sectors. Noticeably absent from this portfolio are small-cap stocks, value stocks, and foreign stocks. This portfolio was chosen with the following considerations:

- Large-cap stocks instead of mid- or small-caps
- Growth stocks instead of value stocks
- U.S. stocks instead of foreign stocks

TABLE 2-5

Guidelines for Asset Allocation

1. Review your objectives and your personal financial circumstances. If you need to generate current income and preserve capital, your allocation should be weighted more towards bonds and money market securities. If you do not need current income and you are investing for capital growth in the future, your weighting should be more toward stocks.

2. Determine your tolerance for risk. If you can accept the volatility of the stock market, you can be comfortable investing in stocks. If not, your allocation should be weighted more toward bonds and money market securities.

3. Consider your time frame. If you are young and you have a long time horizon of, say, 25 years, allocate a larger percentage to stocks. If you have a short time frame, your allocation would be weighted more towards bonds with a lesser percentage in stocks.

4. Do not be too unrealistic in your expectations from your investments. The returns of the past two decades have been quite spectacular: long-term bonds in the 1980s returned on average around 13 percent annually, and stocks returned on average around 37 percent in 1995, 22 percent in 1996, and 33 percent in 1997, based on the S&P 500 Index. The past two decades have been abnormally good for both the bond markets and the stock markets due to the decline in interest rates from around 17 percent in 1980 to the current low of 4.7 percent. Lower your expectations to more realistic levels.

5. Consider the risk-return trade-off in your asset allocation model. How you allocate your assets can affect both your risks and returns. For example, according to Ibbotson and Associates (1994), a portfolio consisting of 100 percent long-term government bonds had an average annual return of 5.5% with risk of 11.3%. A diversified portfolio consisting of 63% Treasury bills, 12% long-term government bonds, and 25% in common stocks of large-companies had the same annual returns of 5.5%, but risk fell to 6.1%. A third portfolio during the same period consisting of 52% stocks of large companies, 14% long-term government bonds, and 34% Treasury bills returned 8% annually with 11.3% risk. This is the same risk as the first portfolio of bonds.

6. After determining your percentage allocation of the asset classes, you need to consider the individual assets within the classes. In a speech to the American Association of Individual Investors National Meeting, July 10, 1998, John J. Brennan used the example of a portfolio invested 100% in international stocks for the five-year period ending 1990. This portfolio, based on the Morgan Stanley EAFE Index, would have outperformed a portfolio of stocks based on the S&P 500 Index. However, in the five-year period from 1992–1997, a 100% portfolio of stocks based on the S&P 500 Index would have outperformed the portfolio of foreign stocks. To reduce the overall risk investors should divide their stocks into different types of classes and then choose the stocks for each class. The same should be done for bonds.

The selection of the types of stocks would depend on your individual preferences, the risks and returns, the fundamentals of the economy and of the stocks. The same process would apply to the division of the total amount allocated to bonds.

How you choose your stocks is discussed in later chapters. In many cases, investors invest in stocks suggested by friends and associates without even looking at the financial status of the companies. One of the easiest ways to lose money is to make a few uninformed investments in stocks and bonds. There are many ways to choose individual securities. Investors can rely on hot tips they hear at the hairdresser's, or preferably, they can be more scientific about their choices of investments.

The focus of this book is on common stocks, and so bonds and money market securities are not addressed, except in some cases for comparative purposes. There are many books written about bonds and money market securities to help you with the choice of these securities.*

The choice of individual stocks is guided by the investor's objectives and degree of risk tolerance, among other factors. *Blue-chip stocks* are the stocks of well-established companies that typically pay dividends. These stocks appeal to investors looking for both income and capital appreciation. In general, the dividend yield of these more conservative stocks tends to lessen the stock price volatility when the stock market declines. Nevertheless, during such declines, even good-quality stocks carry a moderate risk of capital loss. In addition to having stock prices that are more volatile, growth and emerging company stocks have higher business and financial risks. Moreover, these stocks usually do not pay dividends. Therefore, they would hold more appeal for investors looking for capital appreciation.

Most of the approaches used for selecting individual stocks fall into one of these two classifications: fundamental or technical analysis. Once you have identified which individual stocks to buy, the next step is to determine the amount to allocate to each stock. Timing, which involves forecasting price movements and diversification, will also play a part in the selection process. Through diversification of the investments in the portfolio, the risk of the entire portfolio can be minimized.

---

*Esmé Faerber, *All About Bonds and Bond Mutual Funds* (McGraw-Hill, New York, 2000).

TABLE 2-6

A Portfolio Weighted toward Large-Cap, Domestic Stocks

Company	Sector	Stock Classification
Merck	Drug company	Defensive stock
Johnson & Johnson	Drug company	Defensive stock
Intel	Semiconductor manufacturer	Technology/growth stock
Cisco Systems	Network communications	Technology/growth stock
Exxon	Oil company	Energy/blue-chip stock
Schlumberger	Oil service company	Energy stock
AT&T	Telecommunications company	Blue-chip utility company
Texas Utilities	Utility company	Income stock
CitiGroup	Financial services company	Blue-chip stock
Pepsi Cola	Beverage company	Defensive stock
Union Pacific	Transporatation stock	Cyclical stock

This is not a recommendation for you to buy any of these stocks. With the spectacular increases in the prices of many of these stocks, they are currently trading at very rich multiples to their earnings. Had these stocks been bought at lower prices, they would constitute good core holdings in a long-term portfolio.

Due to the inevitable changes in an investor's objectives, the portfolio should be revised about once a year and evaluated for overall performance.

REFERENCES

Brennan, John J.: "Strategic Asset Allocation in Today's Market," speech given to the American Association of Individual Investors National Meeting, Washington D.C., July 10, 1998.

Clements, Jonathan: "Why It's Risky Not to Invest More in Stocks," *The Wall Street Journal*, February 1, 1992, pp. C1,13.

Ibbotson, Roger G., and Rex A. Sinquefield: *Stocks, Bonds, Bills and Inflation: Historical Return (1926–1993)*, Dow Jones-Irwin, Chicago, 1994.

Klemkosky, Robert C., and John D. Martin: "The Effect of Market Risk on Portfolio Diversification," *Journal of Finance*, March 1975, pp. 147–154.

Keown, Arthur J., et al.: *Basic Financial Management*, Prentice Hall, Saddle River, NJ, 1996.

CHAPTER 3

How to Read the Financial Pages*

KEY CONCEPTS

- The relationship between the state of the economy and the financial markets
- Monetary policy and the markets
- Fiscal policy and the markets
- The dollar and the markets
- Stock markets and how to read stock quotations
- Ticker tape trades
- Mutual fund quotations

The easy years of earning 30 percent annual returns on stocks (1995 to May 1999) and double-digit returns on bonds (the 1980s and early 1990s) seem to be over. Instead, returns on these investments may be coming back to the normal annual levels of around 7 to 10 percent for stocks and 5 percent for bonds. This means that investors are going to have to be more careful in the selection of their investments. By understanding the relationships between the economy and the bond and stock markets, investors will be better able to make decisions regarding the types of investments to have

---

*Portions of this chapter have been previously published by Esmé Faerber in *Managing Your Investments, Savings, and Credit* (McGraw-Hill, New York, 1992); and in *All About Bonds and Bond Mutual Funds* (McGraw-Hill, New York, 2000).

in their portfolios. Companies operate within the economic environment. By being able to forecast future economic performance, investors are able to invest more profitably.

To better explain the relationship between stock prices and the overall economic environment, the first part of this chapter presents a brief overview of some of the key terms used to measure the economy and their effects on the stock markets. The latter part of the chapter focuses on stock indexes and the different stock price quotations in the newspapers.

The clearest picture of the economy and financial markets is gained through hindsight, but after-the-fact information is too late for investment decisions. By interpreting economic and financial market indicators, investors are looking for early signs of changes in the direction of the stock and bond markets. On the other hand, the astute reader will observe that if economists and financial analysts can't agree on the state of the economy, how is the lay individual to come up with any more definitive answers?

For individual investors, it is not important if the forecasted numbers are not in agreement because, after all, economists and analysts all base their forecasts on the same information. What is important, however, is to be able to use either their forecasts or the key statistical indicators to predict changes in the direction of the economy and the financial markets. An understanding of the economic indicators can help you make timely decisions in the stock and bond markets.

If earnings are related to interest rates and levels of risk, and are influenced by the state of the economy, it then becomes important to understand the relationship between the markets and the economy.

WHAT IS THE STATE OF THE ECONOMY?

The U.S. economy is currently growing at an average annual rate of about 4.2 percent (1998), but, economic weakness in Asia and Latin America could cause corporate profits in the U.S. to fall. This weakness affects not only the large multinational corporations but all companies that do business in Asia and Latin America.

Such changes in the economy often have an impact on interest rates and inflation, which both directly affect the stock and bond markets.

Investors are better equipped to plan their investment strategies if they are able to understand and forecast the state of the economy. This section explains the most common economic indicators that can be used to identify trends in the economy.

Gross domestic product (GDP) is a measure in dollar value of the economy's total production of goods and services. Comparing the current GDP with previous periods indicates the economy's rate of growth (or lack of it). An increasing GDP indicates that the economy is expanding and companies have greater opportunities to increase their sales and earnings. The current expectation is that GDP will slow somewhat in the near future. Slower economic growth also slows corporate profits, which impacts inventories. With slower sales, companies experience a buildup in inventories, which means they likely will slow down production to adjust for this buildup. However, the state of the economy is far more complex than the mere correlation of two variables. To better assess the state of the economy, many measures—the inflation rate, unemployment rate, national income, international trade, and manufacturing capacity, among others—need to be considered.

Inflation distorts the accuracy of the measurement of growth, so there is a measure of the *real* growth of an economy's output, referred to as real GDP. *Real GDP* is adjusted for price level changes and measures each period's goods and services using prices which prevailed in a selected base year. A comparison of real GDP figures with those of prior periods provides a more accurate measurement of the real rate of growth. Gross domestic product is therefore a measure of the economic health of a country. Inflation in the U.S. has been low recently and has not significantly detracted from real GDP.

A more narrowly focused measure of a nation's output is *industrial production,* which measures manufacturing output. The manufacturing sector generally leads the economy's short-term swings. Currently, the weakness in Asia has led to a downturn in factory production.

The *unemployment rate* is the percentage of the nation's labor force that is out of work, and it is another indicator of the economy's strength (or weakness). Currently, the United States has a tight labor market. In April 1998, the unemployment rate stood at 4.3 percent, the lowest in 28 years. A growing economy and a low unemployment rate in combination have traditionally fueled inflation. Concern arises when rates for labor rise faster than productivity gains. This is why the bond and stock markets pay so much attention to the utterances of the Federal Reserve chairman, especially his periodic speeches to Congress about interest rates. When there is even a shadow of inflation on the horizon, the Federal Reserve will raise short-term interest rates.

The other side of the coin is a high unemployment rate. Governments become concerned when the unemployment rate rises above a certain level (about 7 percent), and they will stimulate the economy (through fiscal and monetary policies) to reduce the unemployment rate. These actions may also stimulate inflation, however.

Inflation is defined as the rate at which the prices for goods and services rise in an economy. Inflation often characterizes a growing economy in which the demand for goods and services outstrips production, which in turn leads to rising prices. In other words, there is too much money chasing too few goods and services.

The *Consumer Price Index* (CPI) is one measure of inflation. It is calculated monthly by the Bureau of Labor Statistics. The Bureau monitors the changes in prices of items (such as food, clothing, housing, transportation, medical care, and entertainment) in the CPI. It is a gauge of the level of inflation and is more meaningful when it is compared to the CPIs of previous periods.

Some economists believe that the CPI fuels inflation, similar to a cat chasing its tail. For instance, social security payments and many cost-of-living increases in employment contracts are tied to increases in the CPI. So the CPI may indeed exacerbate the level of inflation.

When the level of inflation is high (relative to previous periods), governments will pursue restrictive economic policies to try and reduce the level of inflation.

The *Producer Price Index* (PPI) is announced monthly and monitors the costs of raw materials used to produce products. The PPI is a better predictor of inflation than the CPI because when prices of raw materials increase, there is a time lag before consumers experience these price increases.

Another key indicator is the Commodity Research Bureau's *Commodity Price Index*, which is a measure of raw material prices.

When this index rises significantly over a six-month period, it is a warning that inflation is on the horizon.

The *Leading Inflation Index*, developed by Columbia University's Center for Business Cycle Research, is an index that anticipates cyclical turns in consumer price inflation. When it moves up with commodity prices, it is a clear signal that inflation is ahead.

When an economy is in recovery, the *manufacturing capacity utilization rate* is a key indicator to watch. This indicator measures how much of the economy's factory potential is being used. Economists worry about inflation when the nation's factory capacity utilization rises above 82.5 percent. For example, when a recovery is robust and the economy is growing rapidly, but interest rates remain low, there will be a decline in unemployment, which will give rise to increased wage pressures and increased prices of goods.

Inflation has a detrimental effect on the bond and stock markets as well as on the economy. When the level of inflation increases, real GDP falls (recall 1980 in the U.S., for example). Similarly, when inflation declines, real GDP increases (1983 in the U.S.). This inverse relationship may not always hold up, though, as the economy of the mid-1990s proved. Despite lower levels of inflation, real GDP showed insignificant growth, which translated into the economy taking a long time to move out of recession.

Housing starts are released monthly and show the relative strength in housing production. An increase in housing starts relative to previous months indicates optimism about the economy; more people are buying homes. Thus, strength in housing starts is an indicator of consumer confidence in the economy.

Economists have designed an index of *leading indicators* to forecast economic activity. This index includes data series ranging from stock prices, new building permits, and the average work week to changes in business and consumer debt. By analyzing this monthly index, economists hope to be able to forecast economic turns and give advance warning of any turn in the stock market, which can impact the bond markets. In reality, however, by the time the leading indicators point to an economic turn, the stock market has already reacted to the change.

These, then, are some of the elements of the overall economic picture. By examining such indicators and statistics, investors may be better able to fine-tune their opinions and forecasts of the economy.

THE EFFECTS OF THE ECONOMY ON THE STOCK MARKET

Generally, there is a strong correlation between a company's performance and its stock price, which is also tied to the strength of the economy. When the economy is strong (real GDP is growing, unemployment is falling, raw material orders are increasing, investment spending is up), most firms see sales increase, followed by corresponding increases in earnings, which allow for increases in dividends and growth for the companies. This generally translates into higher stock prices.

The relationships between the components of the economy are exceptionally complex and should not be oversimplified. For example, an expanding economy can also result in rising prices (inflation), higher wages, increased competition, higher interest rates, and higher taxes, all of which could have a detrimental effect on companies' earnings. Thus, the relationship between the economy and the stock market is not a simple one. It is generally true, however, that during periods of prosperity, the stock prices of earnings-driven companies tend to go up.

The opposite is true during a recession, when there is a downturn in economic activity. Companies will eventually feel the effects of that poor economic activity. Sales will likely slow down, leading to reduced earnings and, consequently, lower stock prices.

An expanding economy is generally accompanied by a strong stock market due to strong earnings, and a declining economy by a weak stock market. However, we should be wary of blanket generalizations. Not all companies will suffer during periods of economic downturn. Similarly, not all companies will do well during periods of economic growth. Investors still need to analyze each individual company—its potential sales and earnings growth and its financial position—to ascertain whether or not to purchase that company's stock.

Investors are always concerned about inflation. Rising prices in an economy have a detrimental effect on the bond market, which may then affect the stock market. With rising prices, the fixed returns received on bonds buy less and less over time. This drives bond prices down, which may then cause jitters on the stock markets.

For the past three years, an economic period characterized by low inflation, falling interest rates, and an expanding economy, the stock and bond markets have moved up together. There are always shorter periods of time when the stock and bond markets decouple, but over longer periods, they tend to move together.

A persistently strong economy with strong corporate profits can overheat, cause prices to rise, and scare the bond markets, which are sensitive to even a suggestion of inflation. Higher interest rates will continue to depress both the bond and the stock markets. Thus, by forecasting the direction of the economy, investors can better anticipate the direction of the stock market.

Investors should, therefore, follow the actions of the Federal Reserve Bank, which impact interest rates and the bond and stock markets.

MONETARY POLICY AND THE FINANCIAL MARKETS

Monetary policy can have a substantial impact on the economy and, thus, the financial markets. The Federal Reserve Bank (the Fed) is the central bank of the United States and works with the government to maintain financial stability and to devise and implement monetary policy. In addition, the Federal Reserve regulates the nation's banks and provides financial services to the U.S. government. The stability of the monetary system depends upon the supply of money in the economy. By regulating the supply of credit and money in the economy, the Federal Reserve Bank can affect the country's economic growth, inflation, unemployment, production, and interest rates.

How the Federal Reserve Changes the Supply of Money

The Federal Reserve Bank can increase or decrease the nation's money supply to provide a stable currency value, a reasonable level for interest rates, and sufficient money to fund transactions in the economy. The principal tools used by the Federal Reserve to change the supply of money are:

- Open market operations
- Reserve requirements
- Discount rate

Open Market Operations

The Federal Reserve buys and sells securities (mostly U.S. Treasury bills and repurchase agreements) in the open market to change the money supply and the reserves of commercial banks. Figure 3-1 illustrates the process when the Federal Reserve expands the money supply by buying securities on the open market. The Federal Reserve purchases the securities on the open market, which then expands their inventory of securities. Payment is made within three days by check, which is deposited in the commercial banks, expanding their deposits. This increases the reserves of the commercial banks and the reserves of the commercial banks at the Federal Reserve. The banks are then able to lend more money, which expands the nation's credit and money supply.

When the Federal Reserve wants to contract the money supply, it will sell securities from its portfolio in the open market. This has the effect of siphoning off money from the nation's money supply. Commercial banks' reserves are reduced, therefore reducing banks' ability to lend money. Figure 3-2 illustrates the contraction of the money supply by the Fed.

These open market operations are conducted by the Federal Open Market Committee (FOMC), which is composed of the president of the Federal Reserve Bank of New York, the board of governors, and the presidents of the other Federal Reserve banks

FIGURE 3-1

Transactions When the Fed Buys Securities on the Open Market

Federal Reserve Bank		Commercial Bank	
Inventory of securities increases when the Fed buys securities.	Reserves of the commercial banks increase.	Reserves of the banks increase, which allows banks to issue more credit.	Demand deposits increase when the Fed pays the sellers of the securities.

FIGURE 3-2

Transactions When the Fed Sells Securities on the Open Market

Federal Reserve Bank		Commercial Bank	
Inventory of securities decreases when the Fed sells securities.	Reserves of the commercial banks decrease.	Reserves of the banks decrease, which reduces banks' ability to issue credit.	Demand deposits are decreased when the Fed is paid by the buyers of the securities.

on a rotating basis. This committee meets every two weeks, and the minutes of its meetings are released to the public six weeks after each meeting. However, Federal open market transactions are reported in the newspapers the day after they occur. Bond traders are acutely aware of the Fed's actions with regard to buying, selling, or refraining from open market transactions.

Reserve Requirements

The Federal Reserve Bank requires banks to maintain reserves with the Fed. The percentage of banks' deposits held as reserves is determined by the Fed and is called the *reserve requirement*. The Fed can increase the money supply by reducing the reserve requirement: banks will need to keep less in reserve and can therefore increase their lending. The reverse is true when the Fed increases the reserve requirements, which increases interest rates.

Not only does the money supply increase or decrease due to changes in the reserve requirements, but there is also a multiplier effect on the money supply. This can be illustrated with a simple example:

Suppose you deposit $100 in bank X and the reserve requirement is 10 percent. Bank X now has $100 on deposit, of which $10 is kept on reserve and $90 is lent to corporation A. Corporation A deposits this $90 check in its bank, bank A. Bank A keeps $9 on reserve and lends the remaining $81. This process is repeated, which shows how the original $100 is increased through the banking system to expand the money supply. Figure 3-3 illustrates the multiplier process graphically.

FIGURE 3-3

The Multiplier Process

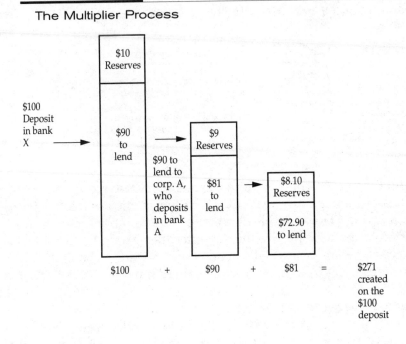

The Fed can stimulate the multiplier effect by lowering reserve requirements which correspondingly increases banks' capacities to lend.

The Fed does not pay interest on the reserves of the banks. Banks with excess reserves lend to banks that need to add to their reserves. These funds are called *federal funds* and are mostly provided on a short-term (one-day) unsecured basis, although there are occasions when these funds are provided on a longer-term basis. The rate that banks pay for these funds is called the *federal funds rate*, which is reported in the financial newspapers. The Fed can alter the money supply by changing the fed funds rate, and these changes to both the federal funds rate and reserve requirements are widely reported in the newspapers.

Discount Rate

The discount rate is the Fed's third tool. The discount rate is the rate of interest that the Fed charges banks when they borrow from the Fed. When the discount rate is too high, banks are discouraged from borrowing reserves from the Fed. When the discount rate is low or lowered, banks are encouraged to borrow. So by changing the discount rate, the Fed can expand or contract the money supply. Changes in the discount rate are reported in the newspapers.

Monitoring the changes in open market transactions, reserve requirements, and discount rates gives you a better feeling for the future direction of interest rates.

Defining the Money Supply

Before looking at the relationship between the money supply and the financial markets, we need to define the different measures of the money supply.

The narrowest measure of the nation's money supply is referred to as M-1, a broader definition as M-2, and the broadest category as M-3:

- M-1 consists of the nation's cash, coins, travelers' checks, checking accounts (NOW accounts, which are interest-bearing checking accounts, are included), and demand deposits.
- M-2 includes M-1 but also adds savings and time deposit accounts (e.g., CDs and money market deposit accounts of less than $100,000).
- M-3 includes M-1 and M-2 as well as time deposits and financial instruments of large financial institutions.

Which is the best measure of the economy's money supply? That is hard to answer because economists continue to debate this point. The Federal Reserves' preferred measure is M-2, which is America's broad money supply.

Interest rate changes explain this discrepancy. Short-term interest rates have fallen prompting investors to move their savings out of low-yielding bank deposits (included in M-2) into higher-yielding bonds, since long-term rates have remained relatively high. Economists argue that portfolio shifts make the definitions of the money supply unreliable as indicators of the state of the economy. For example, M-1 could increase without affecting M-2 when people transfer money from their savings accounts to checking accounts. There will be discrepancies between the classifications of the money supply from week to week, but investors should be more concerned with the overall changes over a period of time so that they can see a trend. By monitoring the Fed's open market transactions, changes in the reserve requirements and the discount rate, and the rate of growth or decline in the money supply, investors are better able to make their investment decisions.

In short, evidence suggests that changes in the money supply have an influence on nominal economic activity, but the influence on real economic growth is still hotly contested.

Impact on the Financial Markets

When the Fed pursues a restrictive monetary policy, it may sell securities on the open market to siphon money from the money supply; raise the reserve requirements, which reduces banks' capacity to lend money; raise the discount rate to discourage banks from borrowing money; or any combination of the three.

These changes in monetary conditions will have an effect on corporate earnings. When the money supply is decreased, interest rates go up, making it more costly for companies and individuals to borrow money. This causes them to delay purchases and leads to reduced sales. With lowered sales and higher credit costs, companies will have decreased earnings. This translates into lower stock prices and lower prices of existing bonds.

When interest rates are rising, investors earn more by investing in fixed-income securities and money market instruments. Therefore, many investors take their money out of the stock markets and invest in liquid short-term securities and longer-term debt securities, which puts more downward pressure on stock prices. Higher interest rates also translate into higher borrowing costs for margin investors. These investors will move their money to debt instruments to justify their higher interest costs.

Monetary policy has a direct effect on interest rates, and interest rates and the stock market are strongly correlated. Rising interest rates tend to depress stock market prices, and falling interest rates have the opposite effect. Stock market investors move into bonds when interest rates go up and out of bonds when interest rates go down.

This suggests that if investors anticipate changes in monetary policy, they can make the appropriate changes to their investment strategies.

FISCAL POLICY AND THE MARKETS

The goals of monetary and fiscal policy are the same: the pursuit of full employment, economic growth, and price stability. The government uses fiscal policy to stimulate or restrain the economy. The tools of fiscal policy are taxation, government expenditures, and the government's debt management. Changes in fiscal policy can affect the financial markets.

Taxation

The federal government uses taxation to raise revenue and also to reduce the amount of money in the economy. Taxation policies can stimulate or depress the economy and the stock markets. When taxes are increased, consumers have less money to invest and spend on goods and services, and corporations have reduced earnings, which leads to lower dividends.

Tax cuts, however, have the opposite effect. Individuals will have more money to spend and invest, and corporations will experience the benefits of greater consumer spending, along with lower corporate taxes, which generally leads to higher sales and earnings, and higher stock prices.

Government Spending

A tax cut has an effect similar to an increase in government spending. But whereas a tax cut has a favorable effect on savings and investments, government spending has a greater effect on the goods and services produced in the economy. Therefore, government spending also can be used as a tool to stimulate or restrain the economy.

Debt Management

When the government's revenues are less than its expenditures, it runs a deficit. Deficit spending can have a significant effect on the financial markets in general and the stock market in particular. The government can finance its deficit either by borrowing in the financial markets or by increasing the money supply.

Borrowing in the Financial Markets. By borrowing in the financial markets, the government drives up yields in the bond markets, which has a depressing effect on the stock market. By selling securities on the market, prices of government securities go down, which increases their yields. To counter the rate differential (between corporate and government securities), investors will invest in government securities rather than in corporate securities, which reduces the prices of corporate bonds, which leads to increased yields (on corporate bonds). Thus, borrowing in the market by the government has the effect of depressing bond prices and increasing interest rates. The opposite is true of the government buying securities in the market: bond prices are pushed up and interest rates are lowered.

When a government is faced with financing an increasing deficit, it will have to pay high rates of interest to attract buyers to invest in all its securities. This leads to higher interest rates in the economy. This has a depressing effect on stock prices and tends to drive up yields. The announced reduction in the U.S. budget deficit in 1998, for example, had the effect of a downward pressure on bond yields and increasing bond prices and stock prices.

Increasing the Money Supply. If the government increases the money supply, inflation may raise its ugly head, and inflation has a negative effect on the overall economy and particularly the bond and stock markets.

In summary, when a government is unable to reduce the growth of its deficit spending, there is an effect on the bond and stock markets. When a government is able to reduce its deficit spending, it is able to reduce its borrowing and pay down its debt, which lowers interest rates in the economy. Investors are constantly looking for policies or budgets that can effectively change the direction of growth of the deficit.

Increased government spending can be inflationary and can bring an immediate response from bondholders. Due to computerized global trading, bondholders can unload millions of dollars of U.S. Treasuries within hours and can send bond prices plummeting and long-term yields soaring. This is especially true for the U.S. Treasury bond market, which attracts a large amount of foreign investment due to the perception of the dollar as a safe-haven currency. This instant access to information also exhibits itself in the increased volatility of stock markets worldwide. Traders and large institutional stock investors can unload their positions very quickly, causing stock markets to reverse direction within minutes.

Fiscal policies affect the securities markets, and by anticipating changes in these policies, you can better formulate your investment strategy.

THE DOLLAR AND THE FINANCIAL MARKETS

Great attention is paid to the relative value of the dollar, the trade deficit, and whether the Japanese and the Europeans will continue to fund the budget deficit through the Treasury auctions. The financial markets react to these financial events. In fact, by now you have probably come to realize that the financial markets react on a daily basis to almost all economic, political, and financial announcements. In some cases, the markets anticipate the news. For example, the bond and stock markets may go up or down in anticipation of the announcement of the balance of trade figures for the quarter.

International Trade and the Dollar

There is a relationship between the markets, international trade, and the relative value of the currency. Readers of the financial press will come across an assortment of terms: *balance of payments, trade deficit* (not the same as a budget deficit), *current account surplus,* and *foreign portfolio investment,* for example, and wonder how these can guide (or misguide) economic policymakers. Great care should be used in interpreting balance of payments figures because of the complexities and ramifications involved.

Balance of payments is an accounting of all the transactions that take place between the residents of a country and the rest of the world. The balance of payments shows whether a country is a net importer or exporter of goods and services, whether foreigners are net investors in that country or the country is a net exporter of capital, and the changes in the country's reserves.

Balance of trade shows whether a country imports or exports more merchandise. The balance of trade is, therefore, the difference between a country's exports and its imports of merchandise. A balance of trade surplus indicates that the country exports more goods than it imports. A deficit indicates the opposite.

A balance of trade deficit is not necessarily a bad financial omen and should not be judged in isolation from the rest of the country's balance of payment figures. For example, Switzerland has had balance of trade deficits, but it also has surpluses in its balance of services account. As long as a country can finance its balance of trade deficit through its other current accounts and capital accounts, it is economically acceptable.

Current account is the first major section of the balance of payments, and it includes all the country's imports and exports of merchandise (balance of trade), services (balance of services), and transfers (which include foreign aid). A country with a current account surplus will be able to contribute to its capital and reserve accounts. A country with a current account deficit will have to finance it from capital inflows from abroad or run down its reserves.

Capital account indicates whether the country is a net importer or exporter of capital. In other words, has the rest of the world invested more in this country, or has this country invested more in the rest of the world? A country with a current account deficit needs to finance this deficit with imported capital or it will be forced to run down its reserves.

Reserve account includes liquid assets, such as gold, foreign currencies, special drawing rights (SDRs), and the country's reserve position at the International Monetary Fund. All of these can be converted into foreign currencies to settle the country's international claims.

International trade, investments, and the country's actual or relative reserves affect the value of its currency. When Americans buy goods from abroad, they pay in U.S. dollars, which are exchanged at the going rate into the foreign currency. Since 1973, most of the currencies of the industrialized nations have been allowed to float against each other. This means the value of one currency is measured against the value of other currencies through the forces of supply and demand. When there is great demand for a currency, it will appreciate in value relative to other currencies. When demand is low, the currency will lose value. Prices of currencies are determined on the foreign exchange markets, which are composed of international banks and foreign exchange traders.

Inflation and interest rates are important economic factors which influence a currency's value.

Inflation. High inflation in a country will cause the currency in that country to depreciate. For example, if inflation rises in the U.S. by 5 percent, the price of goods that originally cost $100 will increase in price to $105. As a result, American consumers may prefer to buy imported goods for the equivalent of $100. This will increase demand for foreign currencies and put downward pressure on the dollar. The theory of *purchasing power parity* addresses this issue by stating: If the prices of goods go up in one country relative to another, then in order to keep parity in prices of goods between the two countries, the currency must depreciate.

Inflation also has a detrimental effect on foreign investments, since foreigners will not invest in financial assets which will lose value. Therefore, higher inflation will put upward pressure on interest rates to attract foreign investors.

Rising interest rates exert downward pressure on the bond and stock markets, because investors sell their long-term bonds and stocks and invest in shorter-term securities whose yields increase as interest rates go up.

Interest Rates. When interest rates are higher in one country relative to another, foreigners will then invest in that country's T-bills, CDs, and other higher-yielding investments. This means a greater demand for that country's currency and, theoretically, an appreciation in value of that currency. The opposite holds true for low interest rates and lower rates of inflation.

The relationships between interest rates, inflation, and the value of a currency all add an important dimension to international investments.

This discussion points to the overall relationship between economic activity and the financial markets. Generally, if companies are experiencing greater earnings, an expanding economy may be accompanied by a booming stock market.

However, economic expansion can also spook the bond markets, which react to fears of inflation. Great care should be taken in not oversimplifying the relationships. A declining bond market can have a detrimental effect on the stock market during economic expansion because of fears of inflation and the anticipation of higher interest rates. Similarly, a declining economy can be associated with a rising bond market because of lower interest rates, which would have a positive effect on the stock markets. By forecasting the direction of the economy, investors can anticipate the direction of the bond and stock markets.

THE STOCK MARKETS AND HOW TO READ STOCK PRICES

The stock markets, where you buy and sell shares of stock, and the news and listings of the different stocks seem to take up a major portion of the financial pages. Stocks may be listed on the national exchanges, New York Stock Exchange (NYSE), American Stock Exchange (ASE), and/or regional exchanges. If stocks are not listed on these exchanges, they may be traded in the over-the-counter markets.

Exchanges

The New York Stock Exchange (NYSE) is the largest and the oldest exchange in the United States and has the most stringent listing requirements. See Table 3-1 for some of the listing requirements. Generally, the largest, best-known, and most financially secure companies that meet the listing requirements are listed on the NYSE. When a buy or sell order is placed for a company listed on the NYSE, the broker or registered representative transmits the order electronically to the floor of the exchange. The order is then taken to the trading post for that stock where the specialist will execute the order.

The ticker tape reports all the executed transactions. Investors can watch the trades on the ticker tape, which are shown during the day on financial news stations like CNBC. Investors who place orders to buy and sell shares receive confirmations of their executed trades from their brokerage firms.

The American Stock Exchange (AMEX) has less stringent listing requirements than the NYSE and generally has the listings of the younger, smaller companies.

TABLE 3-1

Listing Requirements for the NYSE, AMEX, and NASDAQ

	NYSE	AMEX	NASDAQ
Minimum number of shareholders	2000	800	400
Minimum pretax income	$2.5 million	$0.75 million	—

Source: www.friedlandassociates.com.

There are also regional exchanges (the Philadelphia and Pacific Exchanges, for example) that list the stocks of companies in their geographic areas. A company can be listed on the NYSE or AMEX and also be listed on a regional exchange.

For a variety of reasons, a number of companies that issue stocks to the public may not be listed on any of the above-mentioned exchanges. Instead, they are traded over-the-counter. The over-the-counter market (OTC) is linked by a network of computers and telephones. The most actively traded issues are listed on the NASDAQ (National Association of Securities Dealers Automated Quotations) national market system, and the less heavily traded issues are listed on the NASDAQ bid and ask quotations. The least actively traded issues are listed on the Additional Over-the-Counter Quotes. A stockbroker can, therefore, provide the bid and asked price for a particular stock by punching that company's code into the NASDAQ computer system. There are many large, reputable companies, such as Intel, Microsoft, Cisco, Dell, and MCI Worldcom, that have chosen to remain on the OTC market rather than move up to the AMEX or NYSE. The listing fees are lower on the over-the-counter market, which is another reason why a majority of the companies are small, capitalized companies.

In the OTC, orders are executed differently. A customer's order to buy is sent to the trading desk of the brokerage firm where the trader will contact *the market makers*, or *dealers*, in that stock for the lowest asked price. Market makers are the firms that buy and sell stocks out of their own inventories. A markup is added to the asked price. This amount can be ascertained from the listings of the stocks in the NASDAQ National Market Issues in the newspapers. Similarly, when selling a stock, an amount called a *markdown* is subtracted from the bid price. For OTC trades, a brokerage firm cannot charge a commission and act as the market maker in a trade. Thus, the brokerage firm would have to choose between charging a commission or the markup or markdown.

STOCK MARKET INDEXES

Stock investors are always anxious to know how the stock market is doing, whether the market is going up or down, and when to buy and sell stocks. There are a number of stock market indexes that give investors different measures of the stock market.

Stock market indexes can be very useful to individual investors in the following ways:

1. To determine how the stock markets are doing
2. As comparison benchmarks for the performance of individual portfolios and mutual funds
3. As forecasting tools for future trends

These aggregate measures give a glimpse into the movement of individual stock prices in the market. However, the relationships between the indexes and individual stocks need to be understood before any action is taken. For example, a panic attack is not necessary when the Dow Jones Industrial Average drops 150 points in any one day, nor should you order up champagne for the neighborhood when the NASDAQ Index goes up 40 points. This is because there are some basic differences between the indexes, and these need to be understood. In general, the different stock market indexes move up and down together, and by greater or lesser amounts. There are times when the different indexes diverge. These differences are because of the composition of the stocks in the index, the manner in which the index is calculated, and the weights assigned to each of the stocks.

The Dow Jones Industrial Average is composed of 30 blue-chip, large capitalized companies, whereas the New York Stock Exchange Composite Index includes all the stocks listed on the NYSE.

The manner in which the index is calculated can be as an average or as an index. An *average* is calculated by adding stock prices and then dividing by a number to give the average price. The Dow Jones averages are computed this way. An *index* is a more sophisticated weighting of stock prices, related to a base year's stock prices. Examples are the Standard & Poor's 500 Composite Index, the NYSE Composite Index, and the OTC Index.

The relative weighting of the individual stocks in each index differs. A *price-weighted* index is composed as follows: The share price of each stock in the index is added and then the total is divided by a divisor. The divisor is a number that is adjusted for stock splits. This is because when there is a 2-for-1 stock split, the price of the stock will be reduced by half. By making the changes to the divisor, the effects of the stock split will have no impact on the index. The Dow Jones averages are calculated on a price-weighted basis. With a price-weighted index, the higher-priced stocks are given more weight in the makeup of the index than lower-priced stocks.

A *market-value-weighted* index is composed using the market value of each company in the index. The weighting of each company is determined by the price of the stock and the number of shares outstanding, or the market capitalization of the company. Consequently, a company with a greater market capitalization will have a larger weighting in the index. Stock splits do not affect the index. The Standard & Poor's 500 Index is a market-value-weighted index.

An *equally weighted index* is composed by giving each stock the same weight, regardless of price or market capitalization. This method places an equal dollar value on each stock, as opposed to price-weighting, which uses an equal number of shares of each stock, and market-valuation-weighting, which views stocks in proportion to their market capitalization. An equally weighted index can be calculated using an arithmetic method or geometric method. The Value Line Index, which includes over 1650 smaller-company U.S. stocks, uses the geometric method.

These differences help explain the discrepancies between the rates of return of the different indexes. Following is a discussion of the most widely used stock indexes.

The Dow Jones Averages

The *Dow Jones Industrial Average* (DJIA) is the oldest and most widely quoted average. The DJIA is composed of the stock prices of 30 large blue-chip companies that are listed on the NYSE (see Table 3-2). The closing stock prices of each of the 30 stocks are added up each day and then divided by an adjusted divisor. This divisor is a very small number (.2119 in May 1999), which makes the DJIA a greater number than the average of the stock prices. When the Dow Jones Industrial Average was first introduced, it was calculated using a simple average, in other words, using the number of stocks in the calculation. However, because of stock splits and the addition of new stocks to replace

TABLE 3-2

Companies in the Dow Jones Averages

Dow Jones Industrial Average

AT&T	DuPont	McDonald's
Allied Signal	Eastman Kodak	Merck
Alcoa	Exxon	Minnesota Mining & Manufacturing
American Express	General Electric	Morgan, J.P.
Boeing	General Motors	Philip Morris
Caterpillar	Home Depot	Procter & Gamble
Intel	Hewlett Packard	Microsoft
Citigroup	IBM	SBC Communications
Coca-Cola	International Paper	United Technologies
Disney	Johnson & Johnson	Wal-Mart

Dow Jones Transportation Average

AMR Corp.	FDX Corp.	Southwest Air
Airborne Freight	GATX	UAL
Alex Baldwin	Hunt, J.B.	U.S. Airways
Burlington Northern	Norfolk Southern	U.S. Freightways
CNF Transportation	Northwest Air	Union Pacific
CSX Corp.	Roadway Express	Yellow Corp.
Delta Air	Ryder System	

Dow Jones Utility Average

American Electric Power	Edison International	Public Services Ent.
Columbia Gas System	Enron Corp.	Southern Company
Con Edison	Houston Industries	Texas Utilities
Consolidated Natural Gas	Pacific Gas & Electric	Unicom
Duke Energy	Peco Energy	Williams Company

stocks that were dropped, a divisor was employed to keep the average from changing for these events. This explains why the Dow Jones Industrial Average can be such a large number (currently near 11,000).

Due to the small number of companies in the Dow, care has been taken over the years to make sure that these companies are broadly representative of the market. Thus, in 1997, four companies—Bethlehem Steel, Texaco, Westinghouse (now CBS), and Woolworths (now Venator Group)—were dropped and were replaced by Hewlett-Packard, Johnson & Johnson, Travelers Group (now CitiGroup), and Wal-Mart.

There has been much criticism of the DJIA. First, the stocks are not equally weighted. Consequently, an increase of a higher-priced stock will have a greater impact on the DJIA than an increase of a lower-priced stock. Second, with a sampling of only 30 large, blue-chip stocks, the DJIA is hardly a representative measure of the market.

Yet the DJIA can be of use to investors. First, by looking at a chart of the DJIA over a period of time, investors can see the ups and downs of the market, which can help them decide when to buy and sell stocks. Second, the DJIA can be used as a yardstick, to compare how your blue-chip stocks and blue-chip mutual funds have performed in comparison to the DJIA for the same period of time. However, since the DJIA is composed of only 30 stocks (representing approximately 25 percent of the total market value of all the stocks traded on the New York Stock Exchange), investors can benefit as well from looking at more broad-based measures of the market. See Table 3-3 for a comparison of the DJIA, the S&P 500 Index, and the "Dogs of the Dow" for the past 10 years.

The *Dogs of the Dow* is an offshoot of the Dow Jones Industrial Average. This group is related to a strategy of investing in the 10 highest-dividend-yielding Dow stocks at the beginning of the year and then replacing them with the 10 highest-yielding stocks the next year.

Other Dow Jones averages are the *Dow Jones Transportation Average* (DJTA), which is composed of the stocks of the 20 major transportation companies; the *Dow Jones Utility Average* (DJUA,), which includes 15 major utility stocks; and the *Dow Jones Composite Average*, which combines the three Dow Jones indexes and consists

TABLE 3-3

Performance of the Indexes

Year	DJIA	S&P 500	Dogs of the Dow
1989	31.7%	31.5%	26.5%
1990	−0.4%	−3.2%	−7.6%
1991	23.9%	30.0%	34.3%
1992	7.4%	7.6%	7.9%
1993	16.8%	10.1%	27.3%
1994	4.9%	1.3%	4/1%
1995	36.4%	37.6%	36.5%
1996	28.6%	23.0%	27.9%
1997	24.9%	33.4%	21.9%
1998	18.4%	28.5%	11.5%[*]
10-Year Return	18.6%	19.00	18.1%[*]

[*]Through December 23, 1998

Source: Andrew Bary, *Barron's*, December 18, 1998. p. 16.

of all the stocks of the 65 companies. See Table 3-2 for a listing of the companies.

Standard & Poor's Index

The *Standard & Poor's 500 Index* (S&P 500) consists of 500 stocks listed on the New York Stock Exchange and on the NASDAQ. The 500 companies in the S&P 500 Index can also be broken down into the following indexes:

- The S&P Industrial Index, which consists of 400 industrial stocks
- The S&P Transportation Index (20 companies)
- The S&P Utilities Index (40 companies)
- The S&P Financial Index (40 companies)

The most often cited of the S&P indexes is the S&P 500 Index. The S&P 500 Index is a market-value-weighted index, which is computed by calculating the total market capitalization (value) of the 500 companies in the index and then dividing them by the total market capitalization of the 500 companies in the base year. This number is then multiplied by 10. The percentage increase or decrease in the total market value from one day to the next represents the change in the index.

With 500 stocks, the S&P 500 Index is more representative than the DJIA, with only 30 stocks. The S&P 500 Index occasionally adds and drops stocks to maintain a broad representation of the economy. In December 1998, Venator Group, formerly Woolworths, was dropped for the Internet stock AOL. This action caused some controversy in that AOL, due to the rapid rise in its stock price because of the speculation in Internet stocks, had a market capitalization of $70 billion, versus Venator's $830 million. By changing the index and replacing low-capitalization companies with high-capitalization ones, the index is sure to go up. The second point is that many mutual fund managers, whose funds are tied to the S&P Index, go out to buy the stocks that are added. This accounted for a 32-point rise in AOL's stock price during the week of the announced change, and it closed at around $136 per share. All this fuels speculation regarding future additions to the S&P 500 Index. Berkshire Hathaway, the largest company not in the S&P 500 Index, heads the list.

The S&P 500 Index is an important proxy for the performance of the larger stocks in the market, a case further confirmed by the growing popularity of S&P 500-indexed mutual funds. These indexed mutual funds outperformed most of the actively managed mutual funds in 1998. This was primarily due to the fact that many actively managed mutual funds were invested in value stocks and small-capitalization stocks, which had all underperformed the large growth stocks in the S&P 500 Index.

Since 1995, both the DJIA and the S&P 500 Index have more than doubled. The broader market for small-capitalization stocks has not participated in the four-year rally.

New York Stock Exchange Composite Index

The *New York Stock Exchange Composite Index* is a more broad-based measure than the S&P Index because it includes all the stocks traded on the NYSE. It is a market-value-weighted index, and like the S&P 500, relates to a base period, December 31, 1965. On that date, the NYSE Composite Index base was 50. In addition to the NYSE Composite Index, the NYSE also has indexes for industrial, utility, transportation, and financial stocks.

NASDAQ Composite Index

The *NASDAQ Composite Index* is a measure of all the stocks traded on the NASDAQ (National Association of Securities Dealers Automated Quotations) system. The NASDAQ Index shows more volatility than the DJIA and the S&P 500 Index because the companies traded on the over-the-counter market are smaller and more speculative. Thus, an increase in the NASDAQ Composite Index can be interpreted as investor enthusiasm for small stocks.

Which Is the Best Index to Use?

There is not an obvious answer to this question. Studies have shown that all the indexes are highly correlated with each other. In other words, they all move in the same direction together, but there are some differences. The NASDAQ and the AMEX indexes are not as highly correlated with the S&P 500 and the DJIA. This is not surprising since the NASDAQ and AMEX stock indexes are composed of companies that are younger, smaller, and riskier than the larger companies of the DJIA and S&P 500 Index. This is evidenced by the lack of participation of the mid- and smaller-capitalization stocks in the bull run of the large-cap stocks since 1995.

The best approach is to choose the index that most closely resembles the makeup of your stock portfolio.

Individual measures of the market are convenient indicators or gauges of the stock market. These indexes also indicate the direction of the markets over a period of time. By using these measures, it is possible to compare how well individual stocks and mutual funds have performed against comparable market indicators for the same period.

HOW TO READ COMMON STOCK QUOTATIONS

The format for reading stock price quotations is much the same for stocks listed on the NYSE, AMEX, and NASDAQ National Market

System. There are some variations in the amount of information listed about the companies. The listings of NYSE companies are the most comprehensive.

The market prices of listed stocks are quoted daily in the financial pages of newspapers. For example, a typical listing of a common stock from the financial pages would appear as follows:

							365 Days				
High	**Low**	**Stock**	**Sym**	**Div**	**Yld %**	**P/E**	**Vol 100s**	**High**	**Low**	**Last**	**Net Chg**
$72\frac{1}{4}$	$48\frac{3}{8}$	AT&T	T	1.32	1.8	21	66776	73	$71\frac{7}{16}$	73	$+1\frac{1}{16}$

Reading from left to right:

- The first two columns indicate the range of trading of the stock for the year. AT&T traded at its high of $72\frac{1}{4}$ per share and a low of $48\frac{3}{8}$ per share.

- The next columns show the name of the stock, AT&T, and the trading symbol, T.

- The column to the right of the stock symbol is the estimated amount of the dividend, which is $1.32 per share. Corporations may change the dividends that they pay from time to time. This number is based on the last quarterly or semiannual dividend payment.

- The dividend yield for AT&T is 1.8 percent. This can be calculated by dividing the expected dividend by the last, or closing, price of the stock ($1.32 \div 73$).

- The P/E (price/earnings) ratio indicates what price investors are willing to pay for a stock in relation to the stock's earnings. In other words, investors in AT&T stock are willing to buy the stock at 21 times its earnings. High P/E ratios indicate that buyers are willing to pay more for a dollar of earnings than low P/E ratio stocks.

- Volume in 100s indicates the number of shares traded for that day. In this case, 6,677,600 shares of AT&T were traded. By following the average daily volume, you can tell if there is any unusually heavy trading activity on a particular day.

- The next three columns indicate the high, low, and last price of the stock for that day. AT&T traded at a high of $73 and a low of $71^7/_{16}$ per share. It closed at $73 per share.

- The last column is the change in price from the previous day's closing price. In this case, AT&T closed up $1^1/_{16}$ from the previous day's close.

The reporting of the stocks on the over-the-counter markets is more or less the same as for the stocks on the exchanges. The only difference is that in some newspapers, the P/E ratios and dividend yields may be omitted.

HOW TO READ PREFERRED STOCK QUOTATIONS

Preferred stock is a hybrid of debt and common stock. It is listed with the common stocks on the stock exchange. Preferred stock is designated with a *pr* or *pf* after the name of the stock. Preferred stock pays dividends at a rate that is fixed at the time of its issue. Although the payments of preferred dividends are not legal obligations of companies, the companies cannot pay dividends to common stockholders until they have paid their preferred stockholders. Bearing in mind these differences, preferred stock is read the same way as common stock in the stock exchange quotations.

Following is a quotation of one of the preferred stock series of CitiGroup:

365 Day										
High	Low	Stock	Div	Yld %	P/E	Vol 100s	High	Low	Last	Net Chg
$56^5/_8$	$51^1/_2$	Citigroup pfF	3.18	5.9	—	3	54	54	54	$+^1/_2$

Reading from left to right:

- The first two columns indicate the range of trading of the stock for the year. CitiGroup's preferred F series traded at its high of $56^5/_8$ per share and a low of $51^1/_2$ per share.
- The next column is the name of the stock, CitiGroup preferred F.

- The column to the right of the stock is the amount of the dividend, $3.18 per share.
- The dividend yield is 5.9 percent. This can be calculated by dividing the dividend by the last, or closing, price of the stock (3.18 ÷ 54).
- There is no PE ratio for preferred stock issues because the earnings do not have a direct effect on the price of the issue.
- Volume in 100s indicates the number of shares traded for that day. In this case, 300 shares were traded. By following the average daily volume, you can tell if there is any unusually heavy trading activity in a day.
- The next three columns indicate the high, low, and last price of the stock for the day. For that day, CitiGroup's preferred F issue traded at a high of $54 and a low of $54 per share. It closed at $54 per share.
- The last column is the change in price from the previous day's close. In this case, it closed up $1/_2$ from the previous day's close.

HOW TO READ THE TICKER TAPE

On some of the financial television stations, such as CNBC, investors can watch the ticker tape broadcast during the day's trading hours of the New York Stock Exchange. There are two bands of trades. The upper band shows the trades of New York Stock Exchange transactions; the lower band shows the trades on the American Stock Exchange and NASDAQ. The example below illustrates the following trades on the ticker:

AOL $148^3/_8$ ↑ $2^5/_8$ DE $34^3/_4$ UIS 10,000s $34^5/_8$ ↑ $1^1/_8$

SUNW 10,000s $97^7/_8$↑ 1 CSCO 50,000s 99 ↑ $3^1/_8$

- The top row shows the trades of stocks on the NYSE. The stock symbol is listed first. The first one is AOL, followed by John Deere & Co. (symbol DE), and Unisys (symbol UIS).

- The bottom row shows the trades of stocks on the AMEX and the NASDAQ. AMEX stocks have three letters in their stock symbols, and NASDAQ stocks have four letters. The examples shown are both NASDAQ stocks: Sun Microsystems (SUNW) and Cisco Systems (CSCO).
- After the company symbol is the volume of the trade. If the trade consists of 100 shares, or one lot, the volume is omitted, as in the examples of AOL and DE. Volume of 200 shares would be shown as 2s, or two lots. Shares under 10,000 are shown with the hundreds omitted. Trades of over 10,000 shares show the numbers in full followed by an s. In the examples shown there were 10,000 shares of Unisys traded. Also 10,000 shares of Sun Microsystems and 50,000 shares of Cisco traded.
- To the right of the volume is the price of the stock traded. For AOL, there were 100 shares traded at $148^3/_8$ per share; 100 shares of Deere traded at $34^3/_4$ per share; 10,000 shares of Unisys at $34^5/_8$ per share; 10,000 shares of Sun Microsystems at $97^7/_8$ per share; and 50,000 shares of Cisco Systems at $99 per share.
- The arrow shows the direction from the opening price. AOL was up $2^5/_8$ from the opening price. Deere was unchanged; hence there is no arrow. A down arrow would show a decline from the opening price.

HOW TO READ EQUITY MUTUAL FUND QUOTATIONS

Equity Mutual Fund Quotations

Equity mutual fund quotations are found in the daily newspapers. Prices, or net asset values, of equity funds fluctuate on a daily basis, unlike money market funds, which have constant $1 per share prices. Following are two examples from the Vanguard Group of funds:

Name	N.A.V.	Net Chg	YTD % Ret
Vanguard Fds			
EqInc	24.11	−0.03	+14.4
WndsrII	29.16	+0.08	+13.7

- In the Vanguard Group of funds, the Equity Income Fund had a net asset value of $24.11 per share as of the close of that particular day. The Windsor II Fund, which is a growth and income equity fund, had a closing share price of $29.16 per share.
- The share prices for both funds changed overnight: the Equity Fund lost $0.03 from the previous day's close, and Windsor II increased by $0.08 from the previous day's close.
- The year-to-date percentage return for the Equity Fund was 14.4 percent and it was 13.7 percent for the Windsor II Fund.

Chapter 4 explains the basics of buying and selling stocks and how the markets work.

REFERENCES

Bary, Andrew: "Bound for the Pound?" *Barron's,* December 28, 1998, pp. 16–17.
Faerber, Esmé: *Managing your Investments, Savings, and Credit,* McGraw-Hill, New York, 1992.
Faerber, Esmé: *All About Bonds and Bond Mutual Funds,* McGraw-Hill, New York, 2000.

How to Buy and Sell Stocks

KEY CONCEPTS

- What kind of help do you need?
- How to select a stockbroker
- Types of accounts at brokerage firms
- Types of orders
- How short-selling works
- How the security markets work
- How orders are executed for stocks on the NYSE
- How orders are executed for stocks on the OTC

Most people work hard to earn their money, and they invest in stocks in the hopes of earning significant returns. They buy and sell stocks for investment or speculative purposes. Most investors buy stocks when they anticipate that the price of the stock will go up over time. This is known as establishing a *long position*, which is another way of saying that the investor owns the stock. The opposite of the long position is the *short sale*, in which investors speculate on the price of the stock going down. With a short sale, investors place a sell order, which means that they sell the security first and then buy the security back when, they hope, the price is lower. In other words, they are hoping to sell high and buy low. Short-selling is much more risky and complex than taking a long position, and it is discussed in more detail later in this chapter. Therefore, investors can profit not only by looking for undervalued stocks but also for overvalued stocks.

WHAT HELP DO YOU NEED?

The first question when investing in stocks is, Do you need financial help? If so, what kind of help? There are financial advisors who evaluate investors' financial situations and then formulate financial and investment plans. There are stockbrokers who provide investment advice as to which individual securities to invest in. Should you decide that you can evaluate your finances and choose securities without help, you may be a candidate for trading online. If you do not want to trade online, you can use a broker to place your trades.

Financial Planners

Virtually anyone who pays a fee of $150 and registers with the SEC can be a financial advisor. (There are some states that require registration as well.) Consequently, investors should do their homework before hiring a financial planner or advisor and evaluate their advice carefully.

Credentials
Ask the planner for his or her credentials. Some areas of expertise are:

- *Certified Financial Planner* (CFP), which means that this person has passed six three-hour examinations given by the Certified Financial Planning Board of Standards in Denver. You can call the Institute of Financial Planners at the toll-free number (800) 282-7526 or the National Association of Personal Financial Advisors at (888) 333-6659 to verify credentials. CFPs, in addition to passing the exams, must have three years of professional experience in finance and adhere to a code of ethics.
- *Chartered Financial Analysts* (CFA), have passed three exams given by the Association for Investment Management and Research and have had three years of professional

experience in the investment field. Again, there is a requirement to adhere to a code of ethical behavior.

- *Certified Public Accountants* (*CPAs*) have passed four three-hour exams given by the AICPA and have two years of public accounting experience. CPAs must also adhere to a strict code of ethical behavior. CPAs who work in the investment area generally specialize in providing tax advice.

- *Registered Investment Advisor* requires paying a registration fee of $150 to a federal government agency.

Lawyers and insurance people also become financial planners or advisors. Being aware of the orientation is helpful. None of the degrees and certifications, however, guarantee knowledge, skill, or integrity. They do, however, indicate that there is, or was, a seriousness of purpose in pursuing the credentials.

In addition to word of mouth recommendations, check up on any prospective financial advisor's license to operate. Accountants and lawyers who give financial advice as a major part of their business must be licensed as investment advisors with securities regulators. Financial planners, advisors, and money managers must be licensed by their states and if their businesses are large enough, with the SEC. Brokers must be licensed by their states and must register with the NASD (National Association of Securities Dealers) in Washington, D.C. Be aware that some states allow investment advisors and planners to operate without having to demonstrate any knowledge, skill, or experience. You should check up on your advisor's background, previous employment, and whether there are any past complaints or violations. There are many con artists just waiting for trusting clients to entrust them with their money. Advisors who oversee more than $25 million of investors' funds must register with the SEC, so check with the SEC. If they are not registered with the SEC, check with the state regulatory authorities. You can call the North American Securities Administrators Association (NASAA) in Washington, D.C. at (202) 737-0900 or reach them on the Internet at *www.nasaa.org.*

Even if the advisor works for a large firm, there is no guarantee of honesty. Evaluate the information given by your financial advisor and ask questions if you don't understand the advice. Never invest in something that you don't fully understand.

Compensation

Ask your financial advisor or planner how she or he is being compensated. Financial planners may be compensated on a *flat fee basis*, which could be an annual fee, an hourly fee, a percentage of the total assets, or a combination of these. Flat fees vary considerably. Currently, annual fees range from $1000 to $3000; hourly fees from $100 to $500 per hour; and percentage of assets from 0.5 percent to 1 percent. Some financial planners use a combination of a *fee plus commissions*, and others may charge on a *commission-only* basis. Investors can never be sure if they are getting objective advice, but knowing how their advisors are compensated can help them determine the relative objectivity of that advice. Keep a tally of how much is being spent on investment advice, and question whether you are getting your money's worth for it.

Stockbrokers

In order to trade securities, investors need access to the marketplace. This comes through brokerage firms. Should you decide that you need assistance in the selection of investments, you can use a stockbroker to act as your agent. Selecting a stockbroker is a personal decision. There are three basic types of brokers:

- Full-service
- Discount
- Online

The amount and level of services among these basic types of brokers differ, as do the ways they are compensated. The good news is that there are many brokers and brokerage firms to choose from. The following guidelines may be helpful.

HOW TO SELECT A STOCKBROKER
Services Required

Stockbrokers charge commissions for executing trades. These commission costs vary considerably and can impact the investor's profits and losses. The commission charged depends on both the number of shares traded and the share price.

Full-service national brokerage firms generally charge the highest fees and commissions, followed by regional full-service brokerage firms, which tend to be marginally cheaper. The discount brokerage firms discount their commissions and either charge no fees or reduced fees for miscellaneous services. Commissions are discounted even more at the deep-discount brokerage firms. For example, on a 100-share trade of a stock with a price of $30 per share, the typical commission charged at the different types of brokerage firms would fall close to the following range:

Type of Broker	Range
National full-service brokerage firms	$83–$91
Regional full-service brokerage firms	$78–$82
Discount brokerage firms	$40–$55
Deep-discount brokerage firms	$25–$35
Online brokerage firms	$ 7–$40

Paying $91 versus $7 for the same trade certainly would make a difference in the total return. In this example, paying 3 percent of the stock price (at a full-service broker) versus less than 1 percent (at the deep-discount broker) means that the stock would have to go up 6 percent to cover the transaction costs of the full-service commission broker, compared with 2 percent for the deep-discount broker. The more trades you make, the greater the significance of the commissions.

Individual brokers at full-service brokerage firms earn commissions on the volume of trades that they make. If pushed by their clients, brokers are sometimes willing to discount their commissions, particularly for clients with large accounts. Full-service brokers familiarize themselves with the financial circumstances of their clients, provide opinions about specific stocks and bonds, and provide research on request from clients. Investors are paying the higher commissions for the investment advice and research available from and through the brokerage firm. In essence, there is a personal relationship, which may be likened to hand-holding by the broker. The large national full-service brokerage firms offer a diversified range of financial service, in addition to information, research reports, and the execution of trades.

Compared with the full-service brokerage firms, the discount brokerage firms offer reduced commissions and in some, but not all, cases, reduced services. Brokers at discount brokerage firms execute trades for clients, but they may not provide the same personalized service as full-service brokers. In fact, investors may not have their own personal broker. Trades may be executed by a different broker—whoever answers the toll-free phone number—each time you call. Research may or may not be available for the asking. Some discount brokerage firms may provide research for free, but others may do so only for an additional charge. Due to the rapid growth of online brokerage firms, there is pressure to provide free research from the same sources used by the full-service brokerage firms. The trend is toward providing more free research and more service.

Electronic trading or online brokers allow investors to place their own trades using a computer linked to the Internet. Four million people currently use the Internet to make their trades and control their finances (Brooker, p. 89). This number is expected to grow to an estimated 21 million people by 2003, prompting many large full-service brokerage firms to set up online trading services for their clients. The costs of online trading can vary from $5 per trade to $40 per trade. Research is widely available through the various online trading services. Some charge nominal amounts for S&P reports or Zacks research reports, while others provide them for free. Investors online can tap into the government's EDGAR Website, *www.edgar-online.com*, where they can get the latest financial statements of all the publicly traded companies. See Table 4-1 for what to look for in online trading.

If you do not require information and research from a broker, you may not need the services of a full-service brokerage firm. In addition, if you do not need assistance in the selection of your stocks and you are comfortable using a computer, you could use an electronic brokerage firm. On the other hand, if you are new to investing and would require information and research about the market and the types of securities to buy, a full-service brokerage firm, or a discount firm that offers these services, would be worth the extra transaction costs.

TABLE 4-1

What to Look For in an Online Brokerage Firm

There are currently over 100 online trading firms to choose from. They will have different trading prices and they will offer a variety of services. In general you want an online brokerage firm that will give you **fast, reliable executions, immediate confirmations and free real time quotes**. If your orders take a long time to be executed, you may not have the right online broker. When you place a market order, it should be transacted instantaneously. You want your transactions transacted at **the best prices**. This can be determined by watching real time price quotes to see if your transaction was executed, with the best price passed on to you. You also want an online firm that provides you with **research**. In addition, to the above, your choice will depend on several factors such as:

> The kind of investor that you are
>
> The frequency with which you trade
>
> The services that you will require

If you are a long-term investor, requiring help with investment decisions and you want to trade online, look for an online brokerage firm that will give you personal service. You will probably find that the trading costs of such a firm will be on the higher end of the range, but you will be getting investment advice.

If you are a long-term investor who does not need any hand-holding, you want to look for lower-end trading commissions from an online broker that provides research, free real time quotes, a Web site that is easy to use, fast executions at the best prices.

If you are an active trader who is in and out of stocks within minutes or hours, you want a low-cost broker, who provides you with information that you need for trading. Active traders or *day traders* require the tick-by-tick trading activity of the individual stocks. They will need to know the highest bid prices and the lowest ask prices, in essence, the best available price for any stock in real time in order to be able to make quick nimble trades in and out of a stock. Some online traders will sell this information ranging up to $90 per month. However, E*Trade, the online broker, is providing Nasdaq Level II service to their active traders for free. This service provides the real time, buy-and-sell quotes of all the market makers conducting trades on all Nasdaq stocks. By being able to monitor the actual buy-and-sell quotes of the market makers, day traders can get a better insight into the possible direction of the movement of stock prices. Similarly with this information, day traders are able to profit by looking for price discrepancies between the quotes of the market makers by buying the shares of a stock from a lower quoted market maker and selling it to a higher priced market maker. Taking large positions in a stock and attempting to profit from fractional point moves is not for the fainthearted. Online trading has fostered the growth of day traders who seem to be involved in the unprecedented run-ups in the Internet IPO stocks. Before you jump onto the day trading bandwagon, you need to understand how the market works; you need the trading tools; and above all you need to be aware that the risk of loss is much greater than if you were a buy-and-hold investor.

Another consideration is the number of trades you will make in a year. If you are likely to have only a few trades a year, the difference in the commissions between a full-service and a discount broker may not be significant. However, if you expect to buy and sell securities on a frequent basis, the additional commissions charged by a full-service broker over an online broker will be significant. With the increased competition among brokerage firms, many full-service brokers will discount their commissions if asked.

Reputation

Selecting a broker or brokerage firm is a difficult decision that can be likened to choosing a physician. The choice can be approached in two ways: (1) you can choose a broker, or (2) you can choose a brokerage firm and then find a broker in that firm. There have been many complaints by investors of wrongdoing by brokers and brokerage firms.

Both a firm's size and membership on the stock exchange affect its reputation. Large national firms are known throughout the world. However, a small local firm may be renowned within a local community. If a stock brokerage firm is a member of the New York Stock Exchange, its brokers have most likely passed the exam given by the New York Stock Exchange and the National Association of Securities Dealers. In addition, member firms have a stricter set of rules of conduct. Investors can review their brokers' employment history, where they are licensed, and whether they have been disciplined or had any customer complaints or violations of NASD regulations by calling (800) 289-9999 or going to the Website *www.nasdr.com.*

Another consideration is the level and area of expertise of the broker. If the broker's expertise is in bonds or commodities and you are interested in stocks, you ought to continue your search for a broker with specialized knowledge in that area.

Above all, you ought to feel comfortable both when talking to your broker and with your broker's investment philosophy. Before making your final decision, find out whether any complaints have been lodged against your broker by calling the National Association of Securities Dealers' toll-free number. You should also ask about the fee structure for custodial services, account management, and transaction fees before making your final choice.

Caveats

The following are caveats regarding what to expect and what not to expect from your broker:

- Most stockbrokers make their living from commissions on trading securities. If the broker's salary is purely from commissions, as opposed to a straight salary, the broker may be biased toward encouraging you to make frequent changes to your portfolio. Brokers who encourage excessive trading, known as *churning*, in order to earn more commissions may be exposed to lawsuits and should be avoided, especially if your investment philosophy is a buy-and-hold strategy. Keep in mind that if brokers are paid a salary, they may have sales quotas to fill in order to cover some of the fixed costs of the brokerage firm.

- Most brokers are not financial analysts, and you should not assume they are experts in all aspects of investing. They may have an excellent feeling and working knowledge of many companies and their relative prices. However, if investors need information about stocks not followed by their broker, the broker should be able to obtain the relevant research information from the in-house research department or from sources available to the brokerage firm.

- Brokers are required professionally not to offer unsuitable investments to their clients. For example, if a broker suggests a risky, speculative security when the investor's objectives are income generation and safety of principal, the broker may be held accountable for the losses. To protect yourself, state your objectives in writing and give a copy to your broker (Clareman, p. 167). Don't rush into investments suggested by your broker if you are not sure about them. Ask for more information and weigh the advice or recommendations carefully before making your decision.

- Check your monthly statements for accuracy. If you see excessive buying and selling of securities in your portfolio, or any unauthorized trading, put your complaint in writing immediately. Do not acquiesce to any unauthorized trades, even if profitable; it could be disadvantageous for future unauthorized trades which lose money. In the case of excessive trading, you may be asked to sign an activity letter from the brokerage firm. Signing such a letter means that you approve of the excessive trading or unauthorized trades. If you don't approve, don't sign (Clareman, p. 168).

TYPES OF ACCOUNTS AT BROKERAGE FIRMS

Opening an account at a brokerage firm is as easy as opening a bank account. You will be asked basic information, such as your occupation and social security number, as well as more specific information about your financial circumstances. Brokers are required to get to know their customers, in order to be able to use their judgement with regard to sizable transactions and to whether credit can be used by their customers to finance trades.

You will be asked how you want your securities registered. If you decide on leaving the stock certificates in the custody of the brokerage firm, they will be registered in *street name* (in the name of the brokerage firm). Dividends on the securities are mailed to the brokerage firm, where they are then credited to the customer's account. The main disadvantage of registering stocks in street name is that the brokerage firm may not forward all the mailings of reports and news from the company to you. The advantage of holding securities in street name is that when you sell securities, you do not need to be concerned with delivering the signed stock certificates within the three days before the settlement of the transaction.

If you decide to have the securities registered in your own name, you can either have the certificates stored in the broker's vaults or have them mailed to you. In the latter case, you must store the certificates in a safe place. Since they are negotiable securities, it is a good idea to store your stock certificates in a bank safe deposit box. If they are stolen, you could face losses.

Three types of accounts can be used for buying and selling securities:

- Cash accounts
- Margin accounts
- Discretionary accounts

Cash Account

With a cash account, the investor is required to pay in full for the purchase of the securities on or before the *settlement date*. The settlement date is currently three business days after the order has been executed. If a stock is bought on a Monday, the payment is due on or before the Wednesday of that week, assuming that there are no public holidays within those three days. The Monday is referred to as the *trade date*. Should you not pay for your stocks by the settlement date, the brokerage firm will liquidate the securities. In the event of a loss, the brokerage firm can come back to you for the additional amounts. In general, for online trading accounts, the money should be in the account before the trade is made.

When stocks are sold, the certificates must be delivered within three days to avoid any charges (if securities are not held in street name). After the settlement date, the proceeds of the sale less commissions will either be mailed to you or deposited into a cash account with the brokerage firm. This depends on the arrangements made with the firm. It is a good idea to ask whether there are any fees charged for the management of the cash and money market account. If fees are applied, have the checks with your proceeds mailed to you. Interest rates on money market funds are currently so low (around 2 to 3 percent) that a 2 percent management fee could send your returns after taxes into negative territory.

Margin Account

A margin account allows the client of the brokerage firm to buy securities without having to pay the full cash price. The balance is borrowed from the brokerage firm. The maximum amount that the client can borrow depends on the margin requirement set by the Federal Reserve Board. For example, with a margin requirement of 50 percent, an investor buying stock worth $12,000 would have to put up at least $6000 in cash and could borrow the other $6000 from the brokerage firm. The brokerage firm would use the stock as collateral on the loan. These securities held in street name may also be loaned to other clients of the brokerage firm who are selling short. Short-selling is discussed later in this chapter.

The brokerage firm charges interest on the amount borrowed by the margin investor. Risks are greater in margin trading because using borrowed funds to buy stocks could lead to greater losses, if the stocks decline in price in addition to the interest costs. However, if the price of the stock goes up significantly, the rate of return is greater for the margin investor than for the cash investor because the margin investor has invested less money.

If stock prices decline in a margin account, the brokerage firm will send the client a *margin call.* This is a notice requesting that the investor pay additional money to maintain the minimum margin requirement. If the investor does not deposit additional funds, the firm can liquidate the securities. The investor would be liable for any losses incurred by the brokerage firm.

Certain transactions can only be performed with a margin account, selling stocks short and writing uncovered stock options, for example.

Discretionary Account

With this type of account, the investor agrees to allow the brokerage firm to decide which securities to buy and sell as well as the amount and price to be paid for buying and selling securities. For the unethical broker, a discretionary account is the answer to all prayers!

An investor should monitor the activity in a discretionary account on a monthly basis to determine if there is any excessive trading by the broker for the sole purpose of earning more commissions. This is called *churning,* that is, when stocks are turned over frequently, even though they have only moved up or down a few points. Unless you know and trust your broker implicitly, be careful with a discretionary account.

TYPES OF ORDERS

The size of an order will determine whether it is considered to be a round lot or an odd lot. A *round lot* usually means that the number of shares traded is 100 or in multiples of 100. For the very cheap stocks (penny stocks), a round lot may be 500 or 1000 shares, and for very high-priced shares, a round lot could be as low as 10 shares. These 10-share round lots are referred to as *cabinet stocks.*

Berkshire Hathaway A stock is a good example of a cabinet stock. It is currently trading at around $63,800 per share. This is the most expensive stock on the New York Stock Exchange.

An *odd lot* for most cabinet stocks consists of a trade of between one and nine shares. On regular-priced shares, an odd lot is from one to 99 shares, and for very cheap stocks, it is less than 500 shares.

Investors trading in odd lots will pay more to trade than investors trading in round lots. In addition to the fact that the price of the shares quoted may include a hidden fee, the commissions to execute the odd lot trades are generally higher.

Orders for stocks in excess of 10,000 shares are called *block trades.* These are typically placed by institutional customers and are handled in a variety of ways. Commissions are much lower and orders are executed very quickly. By knowing the types of orders to use and how they are executed, investors may be able to lower their transaction costs and avoid any misunderstandings with their brokers.

Market Order

The most common of all orders placed is the *market order.* The market order is an instruction to buy or sell a stock at the best available price at the time the order is executed. If you obtain a price quote from your broker on CitiGroup stock, for example, and you place an order to buy 100 shares without specifying the price, you are placing a market order. Market orders are given priority in the communications system of the brokerage firm so that the order can quickly reach the exchange floor or the over-the-counter desk. Usually, market orders are executed within a few minutes (or even a few seconds) of being placed. There are a few situations where a market order may not be executed: when there are curbs on the exchange floor, for example, or if trading on that particular stock has been halted.

Typically, the order is executed at or close to the quoted price, due to the prompt execution of the market order. However, if the stock is actively traded at the time the order is placed, there may be a greater price deviation from the quoted price. For example, a market order placed to buy a newly issued stock that begins trading for the first time on the secondary market could be executed at a very much higher price than the offering price. The issuance of new stocks is discussed more fully later in the chapter. When there is a fast-moving market for a particular stock or stocks, a market order may be transacted at a significant price discrepancy from the price quoted. Recent examples of the fast moving markets for stocks are the Internet-related stocks, such as Amazon.com, Yahoo, and E-bay.

These fast markets have a bearing on online trading. Even if investors receive real-time quotes, in a fast market, the quotes may not indicate what is actually happening in the market. By the time the order is placed online, the market may have moved considerably, making the quote that you received only an indication of what has happened. Market orders are executed on a first-come, first-served basis, which means that if there are many orders ahead of yours, the execution price may be significantly different from the quoted price. In such markets, it may be better to use limit orders to protect against the risks of large price deviations.

Market orders are usually *day orders,* which means they expire at the end of the day. In other words, if the order is not executed on the day it is placed, it expires.

Limit Order

A *limit order* is an instruction to buy or sell a stock at a specified price. The specified price can be different from the market price. In other words, when you place a limit order, you are specifying the maximum price at which you are willing to buy a stock or the minimum price that you will accept to sell a stock. For example, if you think the price of a stock is going to fall from its current price, you could place a limit order to buy that stock at a specified lower price. If you want to buy 100 shares of CitiGroup, which over the past months has fluctuated between $49 and $73 per share, you could place a limit order to buy CitiGroup at $60 or lower, even though the market price is currently $63 per share. The length of time that the order stands before being executed or expiring depends on the instructions given to the broker:

- Good for the week (GTW)
- Good for the month (GTM)
- Good until cancelled (GTC)

If you do not specify a time limit, it is assumed to be a day order; and if the price of CitiGroup does not go down from $63, the order will be cancelled at the end of the day.

Similarly, a limit order to sell stock is placed above the current market price. For example, when Unisys Corporation's stock was trading at $34 per share, an investor who thought the stock would continue on an upward trend could put in a limit order to sell at $38 per share or better.

The advantage of a limit order is that investors have an opportunity to buy at a lower price or sell shares at a higher price than the market price. The obvious disadvantage is that the limit orders may never be executed if the price never reaches the limit price. A limit order does not guarantee that your order will be executed, whereas with a market order you are assured of the execution, but you are not assured of the price of execution.

Stop Order

A *stop order* is an instruction to buy or sell a stock when the stock trades at or past a specified price, when it becomes a market order. The stop order may be used to protect existing profits or reduce losses. Although the stop order may appear similar to the limit order, there are some differences.

Stop orders cannot be used for over-the-counter stocks. However, they can be used for all stocks listed on the exchanges (NYSE, AMEX, and regional exchanges).

The stop order differs from the limit order in that once the stock's price reaches the stop order price, the stop order becomes a market order. For instance, assume you bought a stock at $20 per share and it is now trading at $30 per share. If you sell now, you would receive a $10 a share profit. To protect your profits from the stock falling rapidly in price, you could place a stop order to sell at $28 per share. If the stock drops to $28, your stop order will become a market order and will be executed at the prevailing market price. If the stock is sold at $27.75 a share, you have protected your profit of $7.75 per share. On the other hand, if the stock keeps going up from $30 a share when you place the stop order, it will lie dormant [if it has no time limit (GTC)] until the share price falls to $28.

Similarly, an investor can protect profits on a short sale by using a stop order to buy. Short-selling is explained in the next section of this chapter.

In addition to protecting profits, stop orders may be used to reduce or prevent losses. Suppose that a stock is bought at $10 in anticipation of a price increase. Soon after the purchase, news from the company suggests that the price may go down rapidly. The investor could place a stop order to sell at $9, which would limit the losses should the stock price decline.

Limiting losses on a short sale is the other use for stop orders. This is explained in the section on selling short.

Technical analysts use stop orders to get into a stock on strength or out of a stock on weakness. Technical analysis is discussed in Chapter 6.

Despite the advantages of the stop order, there are some disadvantages that should be noted. In volatile markets (in which the prices of stocks rise or fall rapidly), when the limit is reached, the stop order becomes a market order, and it may then be executed a few points away from the stop order price. Consequently, with a stop order you are never sure of the exact price you will obtain for your stock.

The second weakness is in the choice of the stop order price. If the stop order price is placed too close to the current price, a temporary surge or fall in the price of the stock to the stop order price will trigger the execution of the market order. Then, if the stock price moves back in the anticipated direction, you no longer have a position in that stock. On the other hand, if the stop order price is set further away from the current market price, then less profit will be protected or a greater loss will be incurred. The use of stop orders does not increase profits if the direction of the market price is not correctly anticipated. However, stop orders may limit losses.

There are other special types of orders, but they are not that widely used by small investors. The most popular types of orders placed by small investors are market orders, followed by limit orders. Understanding how these three frequently used orders work and what their risks are allows investors to place their orders more effectively.

HOW SHORT-SELLING WORKS

Most investors invest in common stocks by buying them first and then selling them at a later date. This is defined as taking a *long position*. The opposite of this process is the *short sale*, which is based on the expectation that the price of the security is going to decline. When stocks are expected to go up in price, investors can benefit from buying them. But investors can also benefit by selling short stocks that go down in price.

In a short sale, the investor borrows stocks to sell, hoping the price will decline so that the stock can be bought back later at a lower price and then returned to the lender. An example will better illustrate this process.

Ms. X thinks that the stock of Merck (the pharmaceutical company) is overvalued and is going to drop in price. She puts in an order with her broker to sell short 100 shares of Merck, which is transacted at $75 per share (the total proceeds are $7500, without taking commissions into account). The brokerage firm has three business days to deliver 100 shares of Merck to the buyer. The brokerage firm has several sources from which to borrow these securities. It may borrow the 100 shares of Merck from its own inventory of stocks, if it has any, or from another brokerage firm. Assume that the brokerage firm finds from its own inventory of street name securities the 100 shares of Merck, and that are held in a margin account belonging to Mr. Y. The brokerage firm will send these shares to the buyer who bought the shares sold short by Ms. X, and Merck will be notified of the new ownership.

All the parties in this transaction are satisfied. The buyer has acquired the shares. The short seller, Ms. X, has $7500, minus commissions, in her margin account, and the brokerage firm has received the commissions on the trade. The $7500 (minus commissions) is held in the margin account as protection should Ms. X default on the short sale. It cannot be withdrawn by Ms. X.

Mr. Y, who more than likely signed a loan consent form when he opened his margin account, is indifferent to the process. He still has all his rights to the ownership of the 100 shares of Merck. This process is illustrated in Figure 4-1.

The question that comes to mind is: Who pays the dividend? Before the short sale, the brokerage firm would have received the

FIGURE 4-1

Illustration of a Short Sale

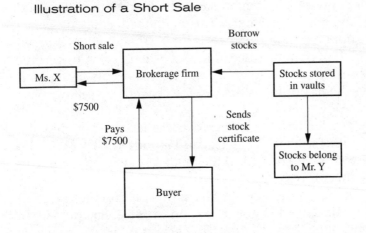

dividend on the 100 shares of Merck held in street name in Mr. Y's margin account, and this would then be paid into his account. However, those shares have been used in the short sale and forwarded to the new buyer, who receives the dividend from Merck. Mr. Y, however, is still entitled to his dividend. The short-seller, Ms. X, who borrowed his securities, is the one who will pay—via the brokerage firm—the amount equal to the dividend to Mr. Y.

If Merck declines to $59 per share, Ms. X puts in a buy order to cover her short position. The securities are returned to the brokerage firm, and Ms. X has made a profit of $16 per share, not counting the commissions on the trades and the dividend.

By using a margin account, the short-seller (Ms. X) has to leave the proceeds from the short sale in the account and is also required to pay in an additional amount of cash, known as the *margin requirement*. Assuming a margin requirement of 50 percent, the example in Table 4-2 illustrates the margin account of Ms. X:

Margin accounts provide greater leverage than cash accounts, as illustrated above. Ms. X put up $3700 and received a 38 percent return (1400 ÷ 3700). Cash transactions require the entire investment in the stock to be put up in cash, which reduces the rate of return. *Leverage*, which is the use of other people's money, is a double-edged sword, however. In the event of losses, the percentage loss would be greater on margin trading than on cash trades.

TABLE 4-2

Margin Account Illustrating a Short Sale

Proceeds from short sale of 100 shares of Merck at $75,	$7,500
Less commissions and fees	(100)
Net proceeds	7,400
Add total margin requirement (50%)	3,700
Balance	$11,100
Cost to purchase 100 shares of Merck at $59	$5,900
Add commission	100
Total cost	6,000
Balance	5,100
Less margin deposit	3,700
Profit	$1,400

What Are the Risks of Short-Selling?

Short-selling allows you to sell something that you do not own, which for virtually everything else besides stocks can land you in prison! If the stock price does go down below the sale price, the investor will make a profit.

If the stock goes up in price above the sale price, the investor will lose money. There is no limit to the loss because if the stock keeps going up, the amount of the loss increases. Suppose you thought a few months ago that some of the Internet stocks were overvalued and you decided to sell some of them short. You would have experienced tremendous losses. AOL has gone from $100 to about $400 per share on a presplit basis in a short period of time. If you had sold short at $100 and had not covered your position, you would have to buy it back at $400 to close out your position, a $300 loss per share.

With a long position, the most that you can lose is the amount of your investment. If you buy a stock at $12 per share and it goes down to $0 you lose $12 per share. With short-selling, there are no limits, the higher the price goes, the larger the losses.

There are other risks. Stocks can be sold short only if the price of the stock on its previous trade was traded on an *uptick* or *zero-plus tick.* An uptick means that the price of the existing trade must exceed the price of the previous trade. A zero-tick refers to the price of the existing trade being the same as the previous trade. Thus, if there is a precipitous decline in the price of a stock, your short sale might not be executed.

The short-seller is also required to pay any dividends due to the owner of the shorted securities. In addition, the proceeds of the short sale are held as collateral for the securities borrowed by the broker-age firm. The short-seller is also required to provide additional funds (the margin requirement of 50 percent set by the Federal Reserve). If the stock remains in a flat trading range, the short-seller's funds and the margin requirement are tied up in the account.

How to Use Stop Orders to Protect Profits on a Short Sale

Stop orders may be used to protect profits on a short sale. If an investor sells short a stock at $40 and the stock declines to $32, the investor may be reluctant to buy to cover the short position because he or she anticipates that the stock may decline further. To protect his or her profits against an unanticipated rise in price, the investor could place a stop order at $34 to preserve the $6 profit per share.

Similarly, the use of a stop order can reduce the amount of losses that can be incurred on a short sale. An investor who sells short a stock at $15 may place a stop order to cover a short position at $16. This limits the losses should there be a rise in the price of the stock. Without a stop order, if the stock kept going up in price, the investor could potentially face a large loss.

Beginning investors are not encouraged to use short-selling due to the speculative nature of the transaction: selling something you do not own.

Selling short may be risky for investors who do not have the stomach to watch the price of the stock turn in an unanticipated direction.

There are rules governing short sales on the New York and American exchanges as well as for stocks on the Nasdaq. Short sales may not be made when stocks are falling in price, because this will exacerbate the price declines. On the exchanges, short sales may be made for a higher price than that of the previous trade, on an uptick, or for a price which is equal to the previous trade but more than the trade prior to that, a zero-plus tick.

What Is Short Interest?

Short interest is the number of shares of a company's stock that have been sold short and have not been bought back. In other words, the shares borrowed have not been bought back and returned to the lenders. Both the New York and American Stock exchanges and Nasdaq publish figures of the short sales of listed companies. These are published in the financial newspapers monthly. See the short interest theory discussed in Chapter 6.

HOW THE SECURITY MARKETS WORK

The securities markets are where financial assets are traded. These are also referred to as the *secondary markets,* which are the markets for existing securities, as opposed to the *primary market,* which is the market for new issues of securities.

Primary Markets and Initial Public Offerings (IPOs)

New issues of stocks that are sold for the first time are called *initial public offerings* (IPOs). If a company that has already issued stock on the market wants to issue more stock, this also is referred to as a *new issue.* E-bay and Yahoo were two extremely hot IPOs on the market in the late 1990s.

With IPOs and new issues, the companies receive the proceeds from the sale of the stocks. These issues are marketed and sold through underwriters (brokerage firms). See Table 4-3 for a list of the top underwriting firms for 1998 (Reeves, p. 40). Commissions are not charged for the sale of these new shares. Instead, the brokerage firms that underwrite these issues receive their compensation from a fee included in the issue price. Companies issuing securities in the primary market, are required to provide investors with a legal document, called a *prospectus,* so that investors can make prudent decisions.

TABLE 4-3

Top Underwriters for 1998

| Lead Underwriter | Top 10 for 1998 | | |
	Number of Deals	U.S. Amount	1997 Rank
1. Morgan Stanley Dean Witter	23	$7392.8	2
2. Merrill Lynch	16	5313.2	3
3. Goldman Sachs	26	3249.4	1
4. Salomon Smith Barney	22	2434.2	9
5. Credit Suisse First Boston	15	1737.3	6
6. Warburg Dillon Reed	2	1681.5	19
7. Prudential Securities	12	1425.3	13
8. Donaldson Lufkin & Jenrette	15	1209.9	4
9. Bear Stearns	16	1124.0	10
10. J.P. Morgan	4	1057.1	5

| Lead Underwriter | Best Performance for 1998 | | |
	Average IPO Return	Best Performer	Return[*]
1. Goldman Sachs	82.4%	E-bay	914%
2. J.P. Morgan	52.7	Earth Web	136
3. Bank Boston Rob. Stephens	45.7	BebeStores	159
4. Morgan Stanley Dean Witter	37.1	Broadcom	288
5. Merrill Lynch	33.1	uBid	220
6. BT Alex Brown	24.0	Digital River	141
7. Nations Banc Montgomery	20.5	Ticketmaster	208
8. Prudential Securities	6.3	Mercury	120
9. Donaldson Lufkin & Jenrette	3.3	Duane Reade	134
10. Warburg Dillon Reed	2.5	Swisscom	42

[*]Returns through December 4.

In general, IPOs have provided investors with a wild ride with regard to returns. In September of 1998, E-bay, an Internet company, was brought to market at an issue price of $18 per share. Three and a half months later the stock was trading at $246. This is a 1267% return for a little over a single quarterly period.

Many investors have also been burned in the IPO market. One of the biggest losers for 1998 was USN Communications, which came to market at a price of $16 in February and ended the year at around $0.31 per share, resulting in a loss of 98 percent. Investors who placed market orders on the first day of trading for the new Internet issue Globe.Com were burned. The stock was offered at $9 and then rose to $97 a share before falling back down to close in the low double digits on the first day of trading. Investors who had their market orders filled at the loftier prices took a tremendous beating; at the end of December 1998, the stock was trading around $5 per share. The high closing price for this stock is around $16 per share.

Investors should not be blinded by the spectacular returns of some of the IPOs, because the long-term average returns of IPOs are not compelling. Investors who buy the shares in the aftermarket on the first day of trading do not generally earn the abnormal returns of those who are allocated the new shares from the issuing brokerage firms. There are several other disadvantages to the IPO market that individual investors should be aware of before trying to jump in:

- Institutional investors get very large allocations of shares, leaving only a small percentage available for individual investors.
- Institutional investors are privy to better information than individual investors. The latter rely on information primarily from a prospectus; institutional investors can attend road shows and meet company executives to obtain earnings projections not available in a prospectus. There also are *cheat sheets*, which are provided by brokerage firms to their preferred institutional clients. These cheat sheets provide management forecasts and income projections that are not part of the prospectus. For legal liability reasons, companies are reluctant to produce these for their prospectuses because if they miss their projections, they could be open to lawsuits. Hence this information is not made available to individual investors.
- Individual investors are penalized for selling their shares immediately after issue, whereas institutional investors are allowed to flip their shares. According to a study done by Christopher B. Barry and Robert H. Jennings in 1993, the

greatest returns on IPOs, on average, are earned on the first day. Professor Jay Ritter has concluded that the long-term performance of IPOs is very much poorer than that of companies trading on the secondary markets (existing shares traded on the markets). In light of these studies, the Wall Street practice of imposing penalties on brokers who sell their clients' shares immediately after issue is disadvantageous for small investors (Zweig, Nathans, Spiro, and Schroeder, pp. 84–90).

Currently, the IPO market favors the institutional investor. To rectify this situation, William Hambrecht, the former chief executive officer and founder of Hambrecht and Quist, has started a new company that will sell shares in IPOs over the Internet to individual investors. What is different is that these shares will be offered using the *Dutch auction* method to set both the offering price and the allocation of shares. The high bidders, not the preferred investors, will get the shares (Branstein and Wingfield, p. C1).

Individual investors who still want to participate in the IPO market should be aware of these disadvantages facing small investors. They might alternatively consider mutual funds that concentrate on IPOs. The next section shows how individual investors can do their homework to limit their risk of loss.

What You Can Do to Protect against the Risks in Choosing IPOs

For every successful IPO, there unfortunately have been many failures. This means that investors who are intent on investing in IPOs should take precautions to lower the risks of loss over the long term. Paying attention to the prospectus is not a sure way to ensure success, but it certainly is a good defensive measure.

Check the prospectus for the following:

- **The underwriters:** Are they well known? Generally, the large well-known underwriting firms (see Table 4-3) are busy enough to screen out the more speculative IPOs. Even so, there are still some new issues underwritten by the top underwriters whose stock prices have fallen into oblivion.

You can check the underwriter's record by asking the broker for a list of recent underwritings or through the Internet at *www.ipomaven.com.*

How many underwriters are there in the syndicate? Generally, the larger the number of underwriters, the more exposure the IPO will have, and the more firms to trade the stock to support the price (Barker, pp. 168–169).

- **Financial statements:** Look at the financial statements in the back of the prospectus. From the *balance sheet* you want to determine who has provided the capital for the assets. Is it primarily from the debtholders or shareholders? If total liabilities exceed shareholders' equity, it should be a red flag and you should investigate further. If the company has a downturn in revenues, will it still be able to service its debt?

  If the shareholders' equity is negative, you want to look carefully into this company. Companies that have posted losses that exceed the amount of their retained earnings will have negative retained earnings. If these negative retained earnings exceed the amounts in the capital accounts, there will be negative shareholders' equity. Can this company turn its losses into profits in the not-too-distant future in order to maintain its business? Related to the income or losses is the cash flow generated by the company. Friendly's Ice Cream, the restaurant chain, has chalked up losses from operations since 1992, but the company has had positive cash flows (Barker, p. 169). *Cash flow* can be calculated by taking the net income or loss and adding back the noncash items, such as depreciation and amortization.

  From the *income statement* you want to determine if there is growth in sales and earnings. If there is growth in sales but the company has losses, examine the prospectus to see if there are any comments about profits in the foreseeable future. If profits are not anticipated in the near future, this is another red flag. There is a note of irony here. If you had listened to this advice, you would never have bought any of the new Internet IPOs in October and

November of 1998, most of which went up with the same
trajectory as a rocket taking off for Mars. Most of these do
not have anticipated earnings for years to come, yet they
are trading at rich multiples of sales. The Internet is here to
stay, but many of the companies initially in this market
may not be the future beneficiaries. Internet IPO fever is
not typical even for IPOs, and when everything settles back
to the norm, investors should not continue with the
assumption that every stock with an idea and no earnings
will always be a tremendous success.

■ **Read the section of the prospectus called discussion and
analysis by management:** You want to read between the
lines to see if they are cushioning for any trouble ahead.
Take a step back and ask yourself what could go wrong
with this company? What are the risks of this company?
Who are their competitors? Who are their customers?
Assess these overall risks of the company. If it is too risky,
walk away from this IPO.

Secondary Markets

After new shares have been sold, investors can trade them on the
secondary markets. The company does not receive any proceeds on
these trades. Instead, the profits or losses on these trades are borne
by investors.

The secondary markets include the stocks listed on the
exchanges and the over-the-counter markets.

How Orders Are Executed for Stocks
Listed on the NYSE

An example can best illustrate the process of order execution on the
NYSE. Let's say Mr. X is interested in buying 200 shares of Exxon. He
calls his broker for a quote, which is $75 7/8 bid and $76 asked per
share. (The broker has on-line access to current quotes of listed
stocks on his television monitor.) The *bid* means that the specialist is
willing to buy Exxon shares at $75.875 per share, and the *asked* means
that the specialist is willing to sell Exxon shares at $76.00 per share.

Mr. X decides to buy 200 shares at the market price, which means that it should be transacted close to $76.00 per share if the order is put in after receiving the quote and if the market price of Exxon has not been fluctuating widely.

The broker fills out a buy order (see Figure 4-2), which is transmitted electronically to the floor of the exchange. There, the *commission broker* will take the order to the Exxon trading post to execute the buy order, either from another commission broker who has a sell order for 200 Exxon shares or from the *specialist*.

If Mr. X had placed a limit order to buy Exxon at $75³/₄ or better instead of a market order, the commission broker would see if the order could be filled from the "crowd" (other commission brokers). However, if the limit order does not fall within the quotes of the current bid and asked prices, the order will be given to the specialist. If it is not executed by the specialist, the limit order will be entered in the specialist's book for future execution. In this case, the specialist is acting as a broker for the commission broker. If the price of Exxon falls later in the day, the limit orders in the specialist's book will be executed in the order that they were entered (on a first-in, first-out (FIFO) basis). The specialist will receive part of the customer's commission for executing this limit order.

Besides acting as a broker, a specialist can act as a dealer by being allowed to trade the assigned stocks in his or her own account and to profit from these trades. However, specialists are required to maintain a fair and orderly market in the stocks assigned to them. For example, they are not allowed to compete with customer's orders. If there is a market order to buy, the specialist may not buy for his or her own account ahead of the unexecuted market order. Similarly, the specialist cannot sell from his or her account ahead of an unexecuted market order to sell. The purpose of allowing the specialist to act as a trader is to minimize the effects of imbalances in the supply and demand of assigned stocks. Specialists are prohibited from manipulating stock prices, which is also unlawful. The SEC monitors the trading activities of specialists, but even with numerous rules, maintaining an orderly market, given the profit motivations of specialists, is a gray area.

When Mr. X's order is executed, the price is reported on the ticker tape. The brokerage firm will send a confirmation of the execution on the next business day to Mr. X.

FIGURE 4-2

Example of a Buy and Sell Order

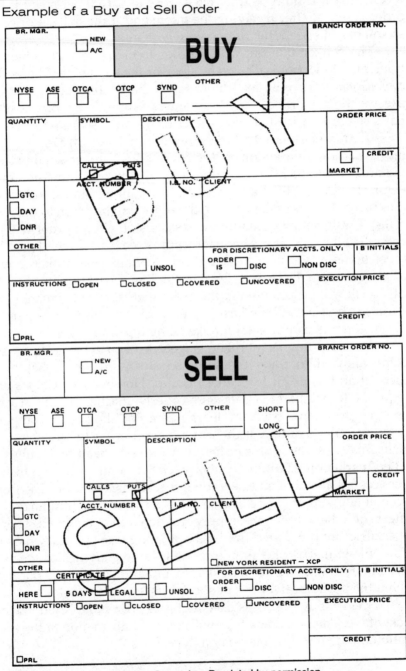

The NYSE is facing challenges from the trend toward electronic trading. In January 1999, the Pacific Exchange had its electronic system, OptiMark, ready to anonymously match the large trades of institutional investors. To counter this opposition, the NYSE has its own institutional system, Xpress, slated for introduction in the second half of 1999 to trade large orders electronically. Floor brokers will not be able to trade with an institutional Xpress order over 10,000 shares unless they can give a better price within 15 seconds. Other features of institutional Xpress are electronic dissemination of order imbalances and opening price indications (Ip, pp. C1, C18).

The SEC has approved new controls on the private electronic trading systems to ensure investor protection. The rules require that these systems publish their stock quotes for all to see. This would affect Reuters' *Instinet,* which places large trades in after-hours trading. Adherence to this rule should narrow the bid and ask spreads and lower prices for investors. Other rules would require that these private electronic trading systems register with the SEC and comply with the securities laws and regulations.

Many small orders are routed to the electronic computerized order execution system known as *Super-DOT* (Designated Order Turnaround). The subscribing brokerage firms send their orders directly to the specialist, where they can be executed within seconds.

At the opening each day, the expanded Super-DOT system pairs the buy and sell orders for specialists, which allows stocks to open more quickly than they would without the system.

The NYSE Circuit-Breaker System

In an attempt to reduce volatility and maintain investor confidence when the market goes up or down significantly, the NYSE instituted a circuit-breaker system of trading curbs. This was a consequence of the market crash of October 1987, which was blamed on *program trades.* Program trades are defined as a basket of 15 or more stocks from the S&P 500 Index valued at $1 million or more.

A 210-Point Move on the DJIA: A 210-point move up or down from the previous day's close on the Dow Jones Industrial Average will trigger the circuit breaker. This affects arbitrage or program trades on the component stocks of the S&P 500

Index. In an up market, arbitrage buy orders can only be executed on a minus or zero-minus tick. Similarly, in a down market, sell orders can only be executed on an uptick or zero-plus tick. When the Dow moves back to 100 points or less of the previous day's close, the circuit breakers are removed.

1050-Point Move: If the Dow goes down by 1050 points or more from the previous day's close, trading halts are instituted. The point levels for the trading halts are adjusted four times a year (Jan. 1, Apr. 1, July 1, and Oct. 1). The point levels are set at 10, 20, and 30 percent of the Dow's average closing values for the previous month, rounded to the nearest 50 points. The level in effect, as of the time of this writing, is for the third quarter of 1999. The trading halts are one hour if there is a drop of 1050-points or more before 2:00 p.m. Eastern Standard Time. If the downs occur between 2:00 and 2:30 p.m., trading is halted for 30 minutes. After 2:30 p.m., there is no trading halt unless the Dow drops 2150 points from the previous day's close.

2150-Point Move: If the Dow goes down by 2150 points or more (20 percent decline in the DJIA) before 1:00 p.m., this will cause a trading halt of two hours. Such a drop between 1:00 and 2:00 p.m. will trigger a trading halt of 1 hour. After 2:00 p.m., it will cause the NYSE to close for the day.

3200-Point Move: A drop of 3200 points or more (30 percent decline in the DJIA) from the previous day's close of the Dow will close the NYSE for the day.

How Stock Trades Are Executed
in the Over-the-Counter Markets

Transactions involving stocks listed on the over-the-counter (OTC) market are not executed on a central exchange floor, but entail the use of *dealers* who buy and sell securities out of their own inventories using an electronic computer system. The National Association of Securities Dealers (NASD) implemented the National Association of Securities Dealers Automated Quotation system

(Nasdaq), which allows subscribing brokerage firms to obtain price quotations on the stocks in the system.

The largest and most actively traded OTC stocks are listed in the financial newspapers under the Nasdaq National Market System (NMS). The rest of the OTC stocks are listed in the "Nasdaq Bid and Asked Quotations" or "Additional Nasdaq Quotes" sections of the financial newspapers. Many low-priced and foreign OTC stocks are listed in the pink sheets (available from brokerage firms), and their prices are not quoted in the financial newspapers.

Customer orders on OTC stocks are executed differently. A customer places an order with the brokerage firm, which writes up a buy order, or a sell order if the customer is selling stock (Figure 4-2). The order is sent to the brokerage firm's trading department, which then "shops" among that stock's market makers for the best price. When customers buy OTC stocks, a percentage amount is added to the price of the shares. This is known as the *markup*. Similarly, when selling OTC shares, a percentage amount is deducted from the proceeds of the sale, known as the *markdown*. This is illustrated in Table 4-4 (Lucchetti, p. C1). The difference between the bid and ask price is what the dealer keeps as a markup per share, which is compensation. The spread is $0.375 per share.

With the changes in the rules for Nasdaq trading implemented in 1997, the spreads have narrowed, which has caused many dealers to implement a different system for charging investors and portfolio managers for buying and selling stocks. This is a commission system in which the fees are negotiated. This is illustrated in Table 4-5. The

TABLE 4-4

Dealer Markup System

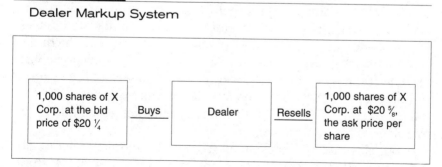

Source: *The Wall Street Journal*, November 5, 1998, p. C1.

TABLE 4-5

Dealer Commission System

1,000 shares of X Corp. at $20 ¼ per share + a commission	Buys	Dealer	Resells	1,000 shares of X Corp. at $20 ¼ per share + a commission

Source: *The Wall Street Journal,* November 5, 1998, p. C1.

dealer will buy and resell the shares at the same price but instead will charge a negotiated commission for each trade. Dealers will not be able to collect both a markup and a commission. It will be either a markup or a commission. The commission system is becoming more prevalent with the changes instituted by the SEC, which makes the markup system less profitable for dealers.

The amounts of the markups and markdowns are disclosed on the stocks listed on the National Market System. For the additional OTC stocks, the customer does not know what the markups and markdowns are. If the brokerage firm has acted as a principal in the trade (market maker or dealer), the brokerage firm may charge the customer either a commission or a markup (or markdown) but not both. The SEC periodically examines these markups and markdowns to see that they are reasonable.

Many criticisms have been leveled at the execution of trades on the OTC market. The fact that brokerage firms can simultaneously act as agents for their customers and self-interested dealers may be combining two incompatible ideas. As an agent, the broker should find the best price for the customer. This responsibility becomes blurred when the brokerage firm is also looking to profit from the deal. There is no need to look for more competitive prices if the brokerage firm can fill the order as a market maker and thereby fulfill its profit objective.

Spreads on OTC stocks tend to be wide, allowing a lot of latitude for market makers to take advantage of investors. A study done by two finance professors in 1994 suggested that Nasdaq dealers tacitly colluded on prices.

The existing dealer system of executing trades on OTC stocks was not conducive to the efficient handling of limit orders. They were frequently missed, which, needless to say, was frustrating for investors. Consequently, the SEC mandated that customers' limit orders be made public. To circumvent this, many money market makers send their limit orders to electronic trading systems rather than integrating them into their own quotes, which could lower their profits.

Electronic communications networks (ECNs) have grown in number and now account for roughly 35 percent of trades on the Nasdaq (Buckman and Lucchetti, p. C1). By matching the trades (buy and sell orders) electronically, ECNs can increase their volume by taking more trades away from the trading desks and lower the costs of trading. Much of the growth for ECNs has come from the SEC rule that limit orders be made public. To circumvent this rule, many market makers have diverted their limit orders to ECNs where the trades can be made anonymously. Critics of the ECNs complain that the electronic matching of orders without the same disclosure requirements of market makers will not simplify matters (Buckman and Lucchetti, p. 1).

The SEC's study of the securities markets (*Market 2000*) proposed some suggestions for addressing these and other shortcomings of the OTC markets:

- Moving toward pricing and recording stocks in decimals (tenths and hundredths), rather than the current pricing increments of one-eighth of a dollar.
- Giving nonmember firms access to the semiprivate computerized trading system, Selectnet.
- Disclosing the payments that brokers receive for directing their order flow to market makers.

The SEC's other proposals are two changes regarding customer limit orders and short-selling. The rule on customer limit orders would ban brokers from trading ahead of their clients' limit orders. The second change aims to restrict short sales on Nasdaq stocks during a falling market. In other words, a short sale could not be placed when the bid price is at or below the previous bid. This would prevent some of the volatility in a falling market.

Another development which will affect the markets is the proposal to extend trading hours. Nasdaq and the NYSE are contemplating this proposal.

REFERENCES

Barker, Robert: "Just How Juicy Is That IPO?" *Business Week*, October 6, 1997, pp. 168–169.

Branstein, Lisa, and Nick Wingfield: "New Company Aims to Shift IPO Playing Field," *The Wall Street Journal*, February 8, 1999, p. C1.

Brooker, Katrina: "Online Investing: It's Not Just for Geeks Anymore," *Fortune Investor's Guide, 1999*, December 21, 1998, pp. 89–98.

Buckman, Rebecca, and Aaron Lucchetti: "Electronic Networks Threaten Trading Desks on Street," *The Wall Street Journal*, December 23, 1998, p. C1.

Clareman, Lloyd S.: "Keep Your Broker Honest," *Fortune Investor's Guide, 1994*, Fall 1993, pp. 167–168.

Ip, Greg: "For Big Board's Floor, Many Challenges Loom From a Single Trend: Electronics," *The Wall Street Journal*, December 22, 1998, pp. C1, C18.

Lucchetti, Aaron: "In Rules' Wake, Nasdaq Dealers Add Fees," *The Wall Street Journal*, November 5, 1998, p. C1.

Reeves, Scott: "Egad! It's Crazy," *Barron's*, December 14, 1998, pp. 35–48.

Schroeder, Michael, and Anita Raghavan: "SEC to Fine Firms, Ending NASDAQ Probe," *The Wall Street Journal*, January 6, 1999, p. C1.

Zweig, Philip L., Leah Nathans Spiro, and Michael Schroeder: "Beware the IPO Market," *Business Week*, April 4, 1994, pp. 84–90.

CHAPTER 5

Fundamental Analysis

KEY CONCEPTS

- Economic analysis
- Industry analysis
- Company analysis
- Ratio analysis

There are two main methods for choosing stocks; fundamental analysis and technical analysis. Technical analysis is discussed in Chapter 6. This chapter discusses the fundamental approach to selecting stocks. Fundamental analysis uses the financial statements of a company to investigate the value of the company with regard to its potential growth in earnings. It starts with a broad analysis of the economy: economic growth, inflation, unemployment, and the level and direction of interest rates. By considering the indicators that affect the economy, financial analysts can then forecast future levels of GDP. These forecasts are used as a basis for projecting the future sales picture of different industries in the economy, which is then used to project the forecasted sales and earnings of companies within these industries. Fundamentalists then select common stocks within the favorable sectors of the economy. This method of forecasting sales and earnings is known as the *top-down approach* and is illustrated in Figure 5-1. Based on eco-

FIGURE 5-1

Fundamental Analysis Using the Top-Down Approach

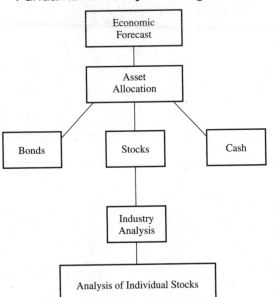

nomic analysis and other personal factors, the assets in the portfolio are allocated to the different types of financial assets, for example, 60 percent to stocks, 30 percent to bonds, and the remaining 10 percent to cash. An industry analysis will reveal which industries will benefit the most from predicted economic events, and then amounts are allocated to each of the different industry sectors. The final step is to analyze the different companies within the industries for those with the strongest potential growth in earnings.

The other approach financial analysts use is the *bottom-up approach*, which starts with sales and earnings projections for companies in different industries. The primary emphasis here is to use fundamental analysis to determine which stocks to purchase, regardless of the industries or sectors of the economy they are in. The analyst may be looking for certain characteristics of the companies as a basis for their stock selection, such as low sales-to-price-ratio stocks, low price-to-earnings-ratio stocks, or small- or mid-cap stocks. Peter Lynch, who used to manage the Fidelity Magellan Fund, and Warren Buffett of Bershire Hathaway are bottom-up stock pickers. The top-down and bottom-up approaches lead to different styles of management, which is discussed in Chapter 8.

ECONOMIC ANALYSIS AND HOW TO USE IT

Because companies operate in the larger economic environment, they are somewhat dependent on the state of the economy. Chapter 3 showed that economic analysis involves an examination of fiscal and monetary policies, expectations of inflation, business and consumer spending, and the stage of the economic cycle. Financial newspapers and business magazines publish the forecasts of leading economists on a periodic basis. These can be used to get a feeling for the state of the economy. Table 5-1 looks at some of the relationships between the economic variables and the stock market. These were discussed in more detail in Chapter 3.

During periods of prosperity, there are more people employed, which means that the nation's income is growing. With increased income, there will be more spending, which translates into greater sales. Companies will spend more on property, plant, and equipment to increase their capacity to produce more goods in order to share in the future increases in sales.

For individual companies, these higher sales translate into increased profits, leading to an increase in dividends and higher stock prices. Generally, even poorly run companies may see increased sales and profits.

The opposite occurs during a recession. There is a downturn in economic conditions, which leads to declining sales, earning, and stock prices.

Forecasting the direction of the economy may be a more important step than selecting individual stocks. This is not easy. Economists differ in their analyses and projections, which leaves little hope for the rest of us to challenge their conclusions. However, it is not the difference between economists' figures that is important to investors but any consensus as to the direction and change in the economy.

Currently, the U.S. economy has been expanding, with increased sales and earnings resulting in a bull (increasing) market for stocks that has lasted for the past four years and well into 1999.

TABLE 5-1

Relationships between Economic Variables and the
Stock Market

Economy	Stock Market
Consecutive-quarter real GDP growth	Positive effect on the stock market. Declining GDP is a negative for the stock market.
Increasing unemployment	This may indicate a downturn in business sales, which is a depressant to the market.
Decreasing unemployment	An indication that business is moving toward full employment, which is positive for the stock market.
Inflation	A high level of inflation is detrimental to the stock market, since it tends to erode price/earnings ratios.
Corporate profits	Increases in corporate profits relate to higher stock prices.
Interest rates	There is a strong correlation between interest rates and the stock market; low interest rates are a positive for the stock market; high or increasing interest rates are a downer to the stock market.
Money supply	An increasing money supply is good for the economy and the stock market, provided it is not inflationary. A tight money supply tends to curb both the economy and the stock market.
Dollar	A strong dollar is good for the stock market; it encourages foreign investment. A weak dollar has a negative impact on the stock market because it discourages foreign investors.

The Federal Reserve Bank has tended toward lower interest rates, which has fueled stock prices.

Rising interest rates not only dampen the stock and bond markets but also make the selection of sectors in the economy more critical in terms of future stock investments.

Once you have developed an outlook for the economy, you can use this information to determine which industries or sectors of the economy will be affected by anticipated events. For example, with the economic turmoil in Asia during 1998, many of the basic materials industries were affected. Oil, steel, and paper prices all fell to historic lows. However, with good potential for a pickup in economic activity in this region for 1999 on, these industries may see a turnaround. Analyzing these industries will give you a clearer picture as to whether you should invest in oil, steel, and paper stocks.

INDUSTRY ANALYSIS AND HOW IT CAN HELP YOU

Not all companies are affected by the economy in the same way; nevertheless, it is important to do industry analysis. This is because if a particular industry is anticipated to be in the doldrums, it is unlikely that companies within that industry will outperform the market. However, that is not to say the performance of companies within an industry will not vary widely. For example, stocks in the oil service industry came down significantly in 1998 when the price of oil fell to around $11 per barrel. Yet in the first few weeks of 1999, the largest of the oil service stocks, Schlumberger, rose roughly $13 from its low of $41 per share. This was a 31 percent increase, versus a 6.62 percent increase for the stocks within the industry group for the same period.

A definition of some of the industry groups as determined by Dow Jones can be found in Table 5-2. Two of the stocks within each of the industry groups are included along with their ticker symbols.

Should You Look at Cyclical Industries?

Based on your economic analysis, you can determine which industries will likely benefit in the future. Some industries are much more sensitive to the economy than others. Industries—and companies within those industries—that move in the same direction as the economy are referred to as *cyclical industries*. The stage in the business cycle of the economy becomes important in timing investments in these cyclical companies. For example, you would not want to invest in the stocks of automobile companies at the peak of an economic expansion, because their stock prices would be at

TABLE 5-2

Some of the Dow Jones Industry Groups

BASIC MATERIALS
  Aluminum
    Alcoa AA
    Reynolds Metals RLM
  Other Nonferrous
    Asarco AR
    Cyprus Amax Min. CYM
  Commodity Chemicals
    Dow Chemical DOW
    DuPont Co. DD
  Specialty Chemicals
    Engelhard Corp. EC
    Grace (W.R.) & Co. GRA
  Forest Products
    Georgia Pacific GP
    Weyerhaeuser Co. WY
  Paper Products
    Boise Cascade BCC
    Int'l Paper Co. IP
  Steel
    Bethlehem Steel BS
    USX-U.S. Steel Gp. X
CONGLOMERATES
    Allegheny Teledyne Inc
    ALT
    General Electric GE
CONSUMER CYCLICALS
  Advertising
    Interpublic Gp IPG
    Omnicom Gp. OMC
  Airlines
    AMR Corp. AMR
    Delta Air Lines DAL
  Apparel/Clothing
    Liz Claiborne LIZ
    VF Corp. VFC
  Apparel/Footwear
    Nike Inc. NKE
    Nine West Gr. NIN
  Auto Manufacturing
    Ford Motor F
    General Motors GM
  Auto Parts
    Johnson Controls JCI
    Lear Corp. LEA

Casinos
    MGM Grand MGG
    Mirage Resorts MIR
Home Constructions
    Champion Enterp. CHB
    Lennar Corp. LEN
Home Furnishings
    Black & Decker BDK
    Whirlpool Corp. WHR
Lodging
    Hilton Hotels HLT
    Marriott Int'l. MAR
Media/Broadcasting
    CBS Corp. CBS
    Comcast Corp
    CMCSA
Media/Publishing
    American Greetings AM
    New York Times NYT
Recreation/Entertain-
ment
    Time Warner Inc. TWX
    Viacom VIA
Recreation/Other
    Disney (Walt) DIS
    Eastman Kodak EK
Recreation/Toys
    Electronic Arts ERTS
    Mattel Inc. MAT
Restaurants
    McDonald's Corp. MCD
    Tricon Global Rest.
    YUM
Retailers/Apparel
    Gap Inc. GPS
    Nordstrom Inc. NOBE
Retailers/Broadline
    May Dept. Stores MAY
    Wal-Mart Stores WMT
Retailers/Drug Based
    CVS Corp. CVS
    McKesson Corp. MCK
Retailers/Specialty
    Amazon.com AMZN
    Lowe's Co. LOW

CONSUMER NON-
CYCLICALS
  Beverages
    Anheuser-Busch BUD
    PepsiCo Inc. PEP
  Consumer Services
    America Online AOL
    Block (H&R) Inc. HRB
  Cosmetic
    Avon Products AVP
    Gillette Co. G
  Food
    Dole Food Co. DOL
    General Mills Inc. GIS
  Food Retailers
    Albertson's Inc. ABS
    Safeway Inc. SWY
  Health Care
    Aetna Inc. AET
    Tenet Healthcare THC
  Household Durables
    Newell Co. NWL
    Rubbermaid RBD
  Household Nondurables
    Clorox Co. CLX
    Proctor & Gamble PG
  Medical Supplies
    Abbott Labs ABT
    Baxter Int'l BAX
  Pharmaceuticals
    Johnson & Johnson JNJ
    Merck & Co. MRK
  Tobacco
    Philip Morris Cos. MO
    UST Inc. UST
ENERGY
  Coal
    Arch Coal ACI
  Oil Drilling
    Diamond Offshore DO
    Transocean Offshore
    RIG
  Integrated Oils
    Chevron Corp. CHV
    Exxon Corp. XON

Secondary Oils
 Burlington Resources
 BR
 Noble Affiliates NBL
Oilfield Equip/Services
 Halliburton Co. HAL
 Schlumberger Ltd.
 SLB
Pipelines
 El Paso Energy EPG
 Enron Corp. ENE
FINANCIAL SERVICES
Banks/Money Center
 Bank America BAC
 Chase Manhattan
 CMB
Banks/Central
 Key Corp. KEY
 Wells Fargo WFC
Banks/East
 Bank New York BK
 Fleet Financial FLT
Banks/South
 Sun Trust Banks STI
 Wachovia Corp. WB
Banks/West
 Banc West Corp BWE
 U.S.Bancorp USB
Diversified Financial
 Associates First
 Capital AFS
 Citigroup C
Insurance/Full Line
 CIGNA CI
 CAN Financial CAN
Insurance/Life
 AFLAC Inc. AFL
 Equitable Cos. EQ
Insurance/Prop. & Cas.
 Allstate Corp ALL
 Chubb Corp. CB
Real Estate Investment
 Equity Office Prop. EOP
 Host Marriott HMT
Savings & Loan
 Golden West
 Financial GDW
 Washington Mutual WM

Securities Brokers
 Bear Stearns Cos. BSC
 Merrill Lynch & Co. MER
INDUSTRIAL
Air Freight
 Airborne Freight ABF
 FDX Corp. FDX
Building Materials
 Owens Corning OWC
 Sherwin-Williams SHW
Containers & Packaging
 Bemis Co. BMS
 Sealed Air SEE
Electrical Components
 AMP Inc. AMP
 Honeywell HON
Heavy Construction
 Fluor Corp. FLR
 Foster Wheeler FWC
Heavy Machinery
 Caterpillar Inc. CAT
 Deere & Co. DE
Indus./Com'l Svcs
 Equifax Inc. EFX
 Manpower Inc. MAN
Industrial Diversified
 Allied Signal Inc. ALD
 Ingersoll-Rand IR
Marine Transportation
 Overseas Shipholding
 OSG
 Tidewater Inc. TDW
Pollution/Waste Mgt.
 Allied Waste AW
 Browning-Ferris BFI
Railroads
 CSX Corp. CSX
 Union Pacific UNP
Transportation Equip
 Cummins Engine CUM
 Navistar Int'l NAV
Trucking
 Roadway Express ROAD
 Yellow Corp. YELL
TECHNOLOGY
Aerospace & Defense
 Boeing Co. BA
 General Dynamics GD

Communications
 Technology
 Cisco Systems CSCO
 Motorola Inc. MOT
Computers
 Apple Computer AAPL
 Compaq Computer
 CPQ
Diversified Technology
 Minnesota Mining & Mfg.
 MMM
 Rockwell International
 ROK
Industrial Technology
 Symbol Technology SBL
 UCAR Int'l UCR
Medical Biotechnology
 Amgen Inc. AMGN
 Chiron Corp CHIR
Medical Devices
 Guidant Corp. GDT
 Medtronic Inc. MDT
Office Equipment
 Pitney Bowes PBI
 Xerox Corp. XRX
Semiconductors
 Applied Materials AMAT
 Intel Corp. INTC
Software
 Microsoft Corp. MSFT
 Novell Inc. NOVL
UTILITIES
Telephone Systems
 AT&T
 SBC Communications
 SBC
Electronic Companies
 Duke Energy DUK
 Texas Utilities TXU
Gas Companies
 Columbia Energy CG
 Consolidated Natural
 Gas CNG
Water Companies
 California Water CWT
 Philadelphia Suburban
 PSC

their upper limits, and they could be facing a downturn in earnings if the economy slows down.

During an economic expansion, the stock prices of cyclical companies increase; during an economic recession, they decline. Cyclical companies are in such industries as automobiles, building and construction, aluminum, steel, chemicals, and lumber. Since these stocks are sensitive to changes in economic activity, investors should time their purchases of cyclical stocks to coincide with the early phases of an expansionary period. Figure 5-2 breaks down the cyclical industries into further categories: consumer durables, capital goods, and basic industries (Kuhn, p. 140).

Financial stocks tend to do well coming out of a recession because of lower interest rates. In an expansionary phase, consumer durables are the stocks to buy. This was evidenced in 1993 when the auto stocks—General Motors, Ford, and Chrysler—took off on a bull run, in part due to pent-up demand, that has continued into 1999. During a recession, consumers delay purchases of automobiles, large appliances, and houses. Cyclical stocks fluctuate with the state of the economy and are always hit hard by rising interest rates.

Into an expansionary phase, capital goods companies benefit from increased sales in the business sector. With increased business sales, there is an increase in the demand for raw materials and commodities (Kuhn, p. 140).

This is the typical pattern in most business cycles. By timing purchases into these different industries, investors may be able to improve their returns.

Stable Industries

Investors who are uncomfortable with the risks of cyclical stocks might prefer to invest in the stocks of companies in the stable industries, also referred to as *countercyclical industries*. These industries include the food, beverage, and retail companies, and certain public utilities. Sales and earnings in these companies do not fluctuate as much as cyclical companies, especially during recessions. Many of these companies' stocks tend to hold their market values.

The difference between cyclical and stable industry companies is that the latter will be less risky in terms of stock price fluc-

FIGURE 5-2

Industry Selections

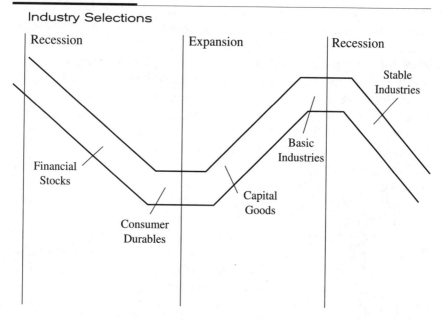

tuations. The other side of the coin is that cyclical stocks will generally outperform the stable industry stocks during an economic expansionary period. Over long periods of time, these fluctuations in stock prices will even out. Their overall growth will depend on the earnings of the individual companies.

Stocks that experience high rates of growth in sales and earnings are called *growth stocks.* A growth stock is one that has sustained high growth over a period of time—15 to 20 percent in earnings—relative to most other stocks, which see growth rates in the range of 5 percent. Because of their rapid growth, they also trade at high price/earnings multiples.

Identifying growth industries early on in their life cycle is difficult. It is only when they have established a growth record and matured somewhat that most investors become aware of their existence. Technology has been the main basis for the evolution of growth industries in the recent past. Pollution control, video games, and genetic engineering are examples. Currently, it is the computer-related and Internet stocks that seem to be in their early growth cycles. However, booming Internet companies may not all survive and profit over the long term. One is always reminded of the early gold miners, those first ones to dig. They were not the ones to benefit from the gold rush. It was the companies that supplied the industry with picks and shovels and other services that were the long-term winners. A less risky way to participate in the Internet revolution is to buy into companies that supply the growth in the Internet, such as the equipment suppliers and those companies that provide access to the Internet. Companies such as Cisco Systems, Lucent Technologies, AT&T, MCI Worldcom, and Sun Microsystems, to name a few, have all run up significantly thanks to their positioning with regard to the Internet. It seems likely that future growth industries will evolve as a result of a combination of changes in technology and the ever-changing need to satisfy consumer desires.

Using industry analysis, financial analysts attempt to identify those industries that will experience superior growth in sales and earnings. It is not always the industries with the greatest profit potential that consistently provide the greatest investment opportunities. Often the investments that do well are those that surpass the market's expectations. Therefore, investments in industries that may not look promising should not be ruled out. They could exceed market expectations.

Investors can use the Internet to find information on the various industry sectors of the economy. Different on-line brokers will also provide industry research. Some offer free research from S&P industry surveys and other on-line information services. By using these and other published sources of industry reports, investors can conclude which industries are better positioned to take advantage of anticipated changes in the economy.

COMPANY ANALYSIS

The basic premise of fundamental analysis is that a company's stock price is primarily influenced by the performance of the company. After identifying the attractive industries, the financial analyst will evaluate the financial conditions of the companies within those industries. Any perceived long-run changes in a company's earnings may have an effect on both dividends and stock price. If earnings are expected to be greater than the expectations on Wall

Street, more investors will want to buy the company's stock, pushing prices up. Similarly, if earnings fall short of the expectations for that company, investors may sell those stocks if they perceive this to be a long-term trend, putting downward pressure on the stock price. When the company's earnings increase steadily, there is also the expectation of increases in dividends, which often contributes to rising stock prices. The opposite is true with decreased earnings.

It is not an easy task to forecast whether companies will meet their expected sales and earnings projections, but there are a number of factors that should be considered in addition to the financial analysis.

COMPETITIVE ANALYSIS

Whether a company can achieve its sales and earnings objectives depends in part on how it competes within its industry. Industry sales and earnings may be growing, but if the company is not competitive enough, it may not capture a large enough portion of the increasing sales in the industry.

How a company can compete in an industry depends on many factors:

- The resources the company has in relation to its competitors
- The range of products versus the competition
- How successful the company's existing range of products is
- How innovative the company is with introducing new products
- The company's ability to diversify into new markets
- The strength of the company's competitors

These factors should be considered in determining the relative strength of the company in the industry.

Quality of Management

Access to a company's management is often difficult for financial analysts and virtually impossible for the general investing public. The most the average investor can do to determine the quality of management is to look at the company's past and read the financial newspapers for stories about management. For example, turnover of top and middle management indicates all is not well. Generally, it is assumed that a company with effective management will be more successful in meeting its sales and earnings objectives than a poorly managed company.

Exxon, for example, has managed to consistently increase its earnings, even during periods of declining oil prices. In addition, Exxon faced a negative climate in the early 1990s due to the Exxon *Valdez* oil spill. Exxon's management was not deterred and stuck to their original investment objectives, which were projects with high returns. This strategy supported their profits, in contrast to the frivolous investments made by many of the other oil companies during the same period.

The Internet has made access to information about companies and management a little easier for individual investors. The first stop for investors wanting more information is the company's home page on the Web. For Exxon, the Website is *www.exxon.com*. There you can read about the company's sales strategies and how it is positioning itself for the future. For example, Exxon announced a merger with Mobil Corporation at the end of 1998, and potential investors can look at the reasons for the merger and how management sees the meshing of the two organizations in the future. Investors can also read the annual reports and quarterly reports filed by the company. The section of these reports on "Management Discussion" should be read to assess any future trends or investments.

Investors can also e-mail questions that they might have to the investor relations staff of companies they are interested in. The speed and quality of the replies will tell much about how management views its shareholders.

Another Website for information about companies is the Securities and Exchange Commission's Edgar database at *www.edgar-online.com*. On this Website, you can read all of a company's financial filings with the SEC. This information is made available within 24 hours of being filed by companies. The financial statements of Exxon Corporation used in Figure 5-3 were from Exxon's 1998 Annual Report. These are also available through Edgar-online and Exxon's Website. The financial statements provide the basis for financial analysis to assess the company's future strength.

Financial Strength of the Company

Many investors do not have the time or inclination to study a company's financial statements to determine its financial strengths or weaknesses. For such investors, there are many sources of published information to choose from, such as Value Line, Standard & Poor's tear sheets, and brokerage reports. On-line brokers will provide some research free of charge to their on-line clients. The type and amount of research will vary among the on-line brokers.

For many investors, however, the starting point is the company's financial statements. These can be found in the annual reports and the 10K reports, which are filed with the Securities and Exchange Commission.

Annual financial statements are audited by independent certified public accountants (CPAs) and are distributed to shareholders and other interested parties. The four financial statements, the balance sheet, income statement, statement of changes in retained earnings, and the statement of changes in cash, all provide investors with their most important sources of information.

The Balance Sheet   The balance sheet is a statement that shows the financial position of a company at one point in time. It includes *assets* (all the resources that belong to the company), *liabilities* (the company's obligations), and *shareholders' equity* (the amount of the stockholders' capital).

Assets (resources) minus liabilities (obligations) equal stockholders' equity. From this equation, the reader of the balance sheet can see how much stockholders have contributed in relation to total assets. See Figure 5-3 for a copy of the consolidated financial statements of Exxon Corporation.

On the asset side, there are current assets and long-term assets. *Current assets* include, cash, marketable securities, accounts receivable, inventories, and other resources that can be converted into cash within one year. The cash generated from these assets generally provides for the day-to-day expenses of operation, or working capital.

FIGURE 5-3

Consolidated Statement of Income

CONSOLIDATED STATEMENT OF INCOME

	1998	1997	1996
	(millions of dollars)		
Revenue			
Sales and other operating revenue, including excise taxes	$ 115,417	$ 135,142	$ 131,543
Earnings from equity interests and other revenue	2,355	2,100	2,706
Total revenue	$ 117,772	$ 137,242	$ 134,249
Costs and other deductions			
Crude oil and product purchases	$ 45,020	$ 57,971	$ 56,406
Operating expenses	11,540	13,045	13,255
Selling, general and administrative expenses	8,372	8,406	7,961
Depreciation and depletion	5,340	5,474	5,329
Exploration expenses, including dry holes	863	753	763
Interest expense	100	415	464
Excise taxes	14,720	14,863	14,815
Other taxes and duties	22,576	23,111	22,956
Income applicable to minority and preferred interests	185	406	384
Total costs and other deductions	$ 108,716	$ 124,444	$ 122,333
Income before income taxes	$ 9,056	$ 12,798	$ 11,916
Income taxes	2,616	4,338	4,406
Income before cumulative effect of accounting change	$ 6,440	$ 8,460	$ 7,510
Cumulative effect of accounting change	(70)	–	–
Net income	$ 6,370	$ 8,460	$ 7,510
Net income per common share (dollars)			
Before cumulative effect of accounting change	$ 2.64	$ 3.41	$ 3.01
Cumulative effect of accounting change	(0.03)	–	–
Net income	$ 2.61	$ 3.41	$ 3.01
Net income per common share – assuming dilution (dollars)			
Before cumulative effect of accounting change	$ 2.61	$ 3.37	$ 2.99
Cumulative effect of accounting change	(0.03)	–	–
Net income	$ 2.58	$ 3.37	$ 2.99

The information on pages F15 through F25 is an integral part of these statements.

FIGURE 5-3

Consolidated Balance Sheet
CONSOLIDATED BALANCE SHEET

	Dec. 31 1998	Dec. 31 1997
	(millions of dollars)	
Assets		
Current assets		
Cash and cash equivalents	$ 1,441	$ 4,047
Other marketable securities	20	15
Notes and accounts receivable, less estimated doubtful amounts	9,512	10,702
Inventories		
Crude oil, products and merchandise	4,896	4,725
Materials and supplies	709	762
Prepaid taxes and expenses	1,015	941
Total current assets	$17,593	$21,192
Investments and advances	6,434	5,205
Property, plant and equipment, at cost, less accumulated depreciation and depletion	65,199	66,414
Other assets, including intangibles, net	3,404	3,253
Total assets	$92,630	$96,064
Liabilities		
Current liabilities		
Notes and loans payable	$ 4,248	$ 2,902
Accounts payable and accrued liabilities	13,825	14,683
Income taxes payable	1,339	2,069
Total current liabilities	$19,412	$19,654
Long-term debt	4,530	7,050
Annuity reserves and accrued liabilities	9,514	9,302
Deferred income tax liabilities	13,142	13,452
Deferred credits	475	575
Equity of minority and preferred shareholders in affiliated companies	1,807	2,371
Total liabilities	$48,880	$52,404
Shareholders' Equity		
Preferred stock without par value (authorized 200 million shares)	$ 105	$ 190
Guaranteed LESOP obligation	(125)	(225)
Common stock without par value (3,000 million shares authorized, 2,984 million shares issued)	2,323	2,323
Earnings reinvested	54,575	52,214
Accumulated other nonowner changes in equity		
Cumulative foreign exchange translation adjustment	(641)	(1,119)
Minimum pension liability adjustment	(282)	–
Common stock held in treasury (556 million shares in 1998 and 527 million shares in 1997)	(12,205)	(9,723)
Total shareholders' equity	$43,750	$43,660
Total liabilities and shareholders' equity	$92,630	$96,064

The information on pages F15 through F25 is an integral part of these statements.

FIGURE 5-3

Consolidated Statement of Shareholders Equity

CONSOLIDATED STATEMENT OF SHAREHOLDERS' EQUITY

	1998		1997		1996	
	Shareholders' Equity	Nonowner Changes in Equity	Shareholders' Equity	Nonowner Changes in Equity	Shareholders' Equity	Nonowner Changes in Equity
	(millions of dollars)					
Preferred stock outstanding at end of year	$ 105		$ 190		$ 303	
Guaranteed LESOP obligation	(125)		(225)		(345)	
Common stock issued at end of year (see note 11)	2,323		2,323		2,822	
Earnings reinvested						
At beginning of year	$ 52,214		$ 57,156		$ 53,539	
Net income for year	6,370	$6,370	8,460	$8,460	7,510	$7,510
Dividends – common and preferred shares	(4,009)		(4,032)		(3,893)	
Cancellation of common stock held in treasury	–		(9,370)		–	
At end of year	$ 54,575		$ 52,214		$ 57,156	
Accumulated other nonowner changes in equity						
At beginning of year	$ (1,119)		$ 1,126		$ 1,339	
Foreign exchange translation adjustment	478	478	(2,245)	(2,245)	(213)	(213)
Minimum pension liability adjustment	(282)	(282)	–	–	–	–
At end of year	$ (923)		$ (1,119)		$ 1,126	
Total		$6,566		$6,215		$7,297
Common stock held in treasury						
At beginning of year	$ (9,723)		$(17,520)		$(17,217)	
Acquisitions, at cost	(3,055)		(2,586)		(801)	
Dispositions	573		514		498	
Cancellation, returned to unissued	–		9,869		–	
At end of year	$ (12,205)		$ (9,723)		$(17,520)	
Shareholders' equity at end of year	$ 43,750		$ 43,660		$ 43,542	

	Share Activity		
	1998	1997	1996
	(millions of shares)		
Preferred stock outstanding at end of year	2	3	5
Common stock			
Issued at end of year (see note 11)	2,984	2,984	3,626
Held in treasury			
At beginning of year	(527)	(1,142)	(1,142)
Acquisitions	(45)	(43)	(18)
Dispositions	16	16	18
Cancellation, returned to unissued	–	642	–
At end of year	(556)	(527)	(1,142)
Common shares outstanding at end of year	2,428	2,457	2,484

The information on pages F15 through F25 is an integral part of these statements.

FIGURE 5-3

Consolidated Statement of Cash Flows

CONSOLIDATED STATEMENT OF CASH FLOWS

	1998	1997	1996
	(millions of dollars)		
Cash flows from operating activities			
Net income			
Accruing to Exxon shareholders	$ 6,370	$ 8,460	$ 7,510
Accruing to minority and preferred interests	185	406	384
Adjustments for non-cash transactions			
Depreciation and depletion	5,340	5,474	5,329
Deferred income tax charges	408	346	835
Annuity and accrued liability provisions	(296)	385	514
Dividends received greater than/(less than) equity in current earnings of equity companies	103	141	11
Changes in operational working capital, excluding cash and debt			
Reduction/(increase) – Notes and accounts receivable	1,321	120	(1,702)
– Inventories	6	(253)	246
– Prepaid taxes and expenses	(89)	(5)	(81)
Increase/(reduction) – Accounts and other payables	(2,060)	(833)	495
All other items – net	- (232)	435	(379)
Net cash provided by operating activities	$11,056	$14,676	$13,162
Cash flows from investing activities			
Additions to property, plant and equipment	$(8,359)	$(7,393)	$(7,209)
Sales of subsidiaries and property, plant and equipment	556	1,110	719
Additional investments and advances	(641)	(820)	(810)
Sales of investments and collection of advances	456	310	522
Additions to other marketable securities	(61)	(37)	(159)
Sales of other marketable securities	57	39	422
Net cash used in investing activities	$(7,992)	$(6,791)	$(6,515)
Net cash generation before financing activities	$ 3,064	$ 7,885	$ 6,647
Cash flows from financing activities			
Additions to long-term debt	$ 64	$ 589	$ 659
Reductions in long-term debt	(132)	(249)	(806)
Additions to short-term debt	270	531	261
Reductions in short-term debt	(1,136)	(991)	(607)
Additions/(reductions) in debt with less than 90 day maturity	2,110	128	239
Cash dividends to Exxon shareholders	(4,012)	(4,038)	(3,902)
Cash dividends to minority interests	(115)	(313)	(291)
Changes in minority interests and sales/(purchases) of affiliate stock	(95)	(123)	(338)
Common stock acquired	(3,055)	(2,586)	(801)
Common stock sold	403	340	347
Net cash used in financing activities	$(5,698)	$(6,712)	$(5,239)
Effects of exchange rate changes on cash	$ 28	$ (77)	$ 35
Increase/(decrease) in cash and cash equivalents	$(2,606)	$ 1,096	$ 1,443
Cash and cash equivalents at beginning of year	4,047	2,951	1,508
Cash and cash equivalents at end of year	$ 1,441	$ 4,047	$ 2,951

The information on pages F15 through F25 is an integral part of these statements.

Long-term assets consist of those resources with holding periods of greater than a year. These include long-term investments, property, plant, equipment, and intangible assets like goodwill and leasehold improvements. These assets are recorded at their historical costs, not their market values. The second feature is that property, plant, and equipment are depreciated over their useful lives, that is, a systematic charge is recorded against income for wear and tear.

Analysts check to see if there are any significantly undervalued assets. The historical cost concept used to account for long-term assets does not recognize any increases in market value of these assets until they are sold. Thus, property on the balance sheet that may have been bought many years ago at low prices may be significantly understated in terms of its market value.

The *liabilities* side of the balance sheet is also divided into two parts, current and long-term. *Current liabilities* are the obligations of the company that fall due within one year or less. These consist of account and trade payables, accrued (unrecorded) expenses, and other short-term debts.

It is important to compare the total current assets with the total current liabilities. The cash generated from the turnover of the current assets to cash will generally be used to pay the current obligations that fall due. In general, if current assets are equal to or less than current liabilities, the company may have a difficult time meeting its current obligations. The warning flags go up. In the same vein, if current assets are significantly lower than current liabilities, cash will have to come from selling off long-term assets or raising more debt to pay off current liabilities. This topic is explored further in the liquidity section later in the chapter.

Long-term liabilities are the debts of the company that have maturities beyond one year.

The *shareholders' equity* section of the balance sheet represents the claims of shareholders against the company's assets. The total assets minus the total liabilities of the company equal the amount shown in the shareholders' equity section. The three main parts of the equity section are the capital stock accounts, the paid-in capital accounts, and the retained earnings (or deficit).

- The *capital stock accounts* include both the common stock
  and preferred issues. The value of the common stock

account is determined by multiplying the stated (par) value of the stock by the number of shares issued.

- The *paid-in-capital accounts* represent the amounts that shareholders paid in excess of the stated (par) value in the capital accounts, when the shares were originally issued by the company.
- *Retained earnings* are the accumulated earnings that have been retained by the company, in other words, those earnings that have not been paid out in dividends. Companies accumulate earnings for various reasons, such as to acquire fixed assets or pay off liabilities. Retained earnings do not represent cash. Even though a company may have accumulated a large amount in retained earnings, it is still restricted by the amount of its cash in terms of spending for projects.

The balance sheet provides a picture at one point in time of the company's assets and liabilities. The balance sheet shows the amount of the assets that are financed by liabilities and the amounts provided by stockholders. *Leverage,* the amount of assets financed through debt, is discussed in the section on ratio analysis.

The Income Statement   The income statement provides a summary of the earnings of the company over a period of time (a year for annual statements; three months and six months for quarterly and semiannual income statements).

The income statement begins with the revenues (sales), from which various expenses are deducted: the cost of goods sold and selling, general, and administrative expenses. Interest expenses reflect the cost of the company's borrowing. After all the expenses and taxes are deducted, you are left with the "bottom line," which is the *net income.*

The income statement shows the profits (or losses, if expenses exceed revenues) over a period of time. These profits or losses can be compared with the profits or losses in previous periods.

Statement of Retained Earnings   The link between the income statement and the balance sheet is the company's net income (or loss), and it is shown in the statement of changes to retained earnings. Dividends on common and preferred stocks are paid out of net income, and the balance of the earnings is then added to the retained earnings in the equity section of the balance sheet. This is the third statement included in the financial statements of an annual report.

Statement of Changes in Cash   This statement analyzes the changes in the company's cash over the period by showing the sources and uses of cash. The first of three sections in this statement, *cash from operations,* shows how much cash was provided or used by the company's operations. The changes in the *investing* and *financing* sections summarize the uses and sources of cash from the changes in the assets, liabilities, and equity sections of the balance sheet.

The financial statements provide the data for an analysis of the company's financial position as well as for assessing its strengths and weaknesses. The financial position of the company in relation to its past data and in relation to other companies in the same industry provides a more meaningful picture than merely looking at one set of financial statements in isolation. In addition, the company's strengths and weaknesses can become more apparent through ratio analysis.

RATIO ANALYSIS

You don't have to have a master's degree in business administration or be a certified public accountant to be able to perform ratio analysis on a set of financial statements. Ratio analysis uses a company's financial information to predict whether it will meet its future projections of earnings.

Ratio analysis is simple to execute. It is the projections and extrapolations from these measures that become complex. Ratio analysis is a tool that can assist the investor in the selection of stocks. From financial ratio analysis, an investor is able to assess the present and past financial strength of a company. Armed with this information, an investor can project trends into the future for this company. There are many ratios that can be used, but they are all classified into one of four groups:

- *Liquidity ratios,* which determine the ease with which a company can meet its current obligations as they come due.

- *Activity ratios*, which show how quickly the assets flow through the company.
- *Profitability ratios*, which measure the performance of the company.
- *Leverage ratios*, which indicate the level of debt.

Not all the ratios in these groups are of concern to stockholders. Stockholders are primarily concerned with the company's ability to generate sales and earnings, which then affect the price of the stock.

Liquidity Ratios

Although liquidity is of greater concern to a company's creditors, this is a starting point for a potential investor in a company's common stock. Liquidity indicates the ease (or difficulty) with which a company can pay off its current obligations (debts) as they come due.

The *current ratio* shows the coverage of the company's current liabilities by its current assets, as computed below (figures from the financial statements in Figure 5-3):

$$\text{Current ratio} = \frac{\text{current assets}}{\text{current liabilities}}$$

$$\text{Exxon's current ratio for 1998} = \frac{\$17,593}{\$19,412} \qquad \text{for 1997} = \frac{\$21,192}{\$19,654}$$

$$= 0.91 \qquad\qquad\qquad = 1.0783$$

This ratio indicates that Exxon has $0.91 in current assets for each $1 in current liabilities, which is less than a one-to-one ratio in 1998. Looking at a longer trend, the current ratios for Exxon in 1997, 1996, 1995, 1994, and 1993 were 1.0783, 1.0208, 0.92, 0.84, and 0.8, respectively. This shows an improving trend in liquidity, except for the deterioration in 1998, when the current ratio slipped back below one.

Generally speaking, it is desirable for companies to have their current assets exceed their current liabilities so that if their current assets decline, they will still be able to pay off their liabilities. A low current ratio may indicate weakness. The company may not be able to borrow additional funds or sell off assets to raise enough cash to meet its current liabilities.

There are exceptions to a low current ratio, as we can see in Exxon's financial statements. Exxon is one of the strongest companies in the oil industry and, therefore, has the capacity to borrow on a short-term basis to pay off its current obligations. In fact, the notes to Exxon's 1998 financial statements showed that Exxon has unused lines of short-term financing with its banks and commercial paper. Potential investors should always read the footnotes in a financial statement, which contain additional information that can provide more insight into the figures on the financial statements.

Moreover, it is not a good idea to look at one ratio for one period in isolation. By examining the current ratio of the company for a few years and establishing a trend, it is easier to see whether the current ratio has deteriorated, stayed the same, or improved over this period.

What may be the norm for one industry may not hold for another. Utility companies tend to have current ratios of less than one-to-one, but the quality of their accounts receivable is so good that virtually all of them will be converted into cash. (Most people pay their utility bills; if they don't, they find themselves without power). Creditors of utility companies are therefore not as concerned with the low current ratios. Similarly, Exxon's liquidity is not significantly different from the rest of the oil industry. This then suggests that the oil industry also has a current ratio of around one-to-one or less of current assets to current liabilities.

Profitability Ratios

The profits of a company are important to investors because these earnings are either retained or paid out in dividends to shareholders, both of which affect the stock price. Many different measures of profitability indicate how much the company is earning relative to the base used, such as sales, assets, and shareholders' equity. The different profitability ratios are relative measures of the success of the company.

Using sales as a base, the income statement is the starting point. Compare the sales for the period with the sales figures for previous years to see whether there has been a growth or a decline in sales. For example, sales may have increased from the previous year, yet the company may report a net loss for the year. This indicates that expenses have risen significantly. The investor would then examine the income statement to see whether the additional expenses were nonrecurring (a one-time write-off) or increased operating costs incurred in the normal course of business. If the latter, the investor should question management's ability to contain these costs. Establishing a trend of these expenses over a period of time is useful in the valuation process.

There are several profitability ratios that use sales as a base: gross profit, operating profit, and net profit.

Gross Profit

Gross profit reflects not only the company's markup on its cost of goods sold but also management's ability to control these costs in relation to sales. The gross profit is computed as follows:

$$\text{Gross profit} = \frac{\text{gross profit}}{\text{net sales}}$$

$$\text{Exxon's gross profit for 1998} = \frac{\$70,397}{\$115,417} \qquad \text{for 1997} = \frac{\$77,171}{\$135,142}$$

$$= 61\% \qquad\qquad\qquad = 57.1\%$$

To obtain the gross profit figure of $70,397 (in thousands), you need to look for the figures in the income statement. The gross profit is sales minus cost of goods sold. Exxon does not list the cost-of-goods-sold figures. The cost of goods sold is obtained from the consolidated income statement in Figure 5-3, which includes the crude oil purchases of $45,020. Sales of $115,417 minus the cost of goods sold of $45,020 equals the gross profit of $70,397.

Gross profits for 1998, 1997, 1996, 1995, and 1993, respectively, were 61 percent, 57.1 percent, 57.12 percent, 58.69 percent, and 57.89 percent, indicating stable gross margins during this six-year period.

I have chosen to exclude the equity income of $2,355 from the total sales, concentrating on sales and gross profits from operations. Other revenues from nonoperations, such as equity income, are included as other income after the operating profit margin has been calculated.

Operating Profit
Operating profit is the income from operations (also known as the *earnings before interest and taxes* or EBIT) divided by sales. This includes the cost of goods sold and the selling, general, and administrative expenses. The total costs shown in Exxon's 1998 income statement are $108,716. When the interest costs of $100 are subtracted from this figure, the total operating costs become $108,616. This is subtracted from sales to give the operating profit of $6,801. This ratio shows the profitability of the company in its normal course of operations and provides a measure of the operating efficiency of the company.

$$\text{Operating profit} = \frac{\text{operating profits}}{\text{net sales}}$$

$$\text{Exxon's operating profit for 1998} = \frac{\$6,801}{\$115,417}$$

$$=5.89\%$$

$$\text{for 1997} = \frac{\$11,113}{\$135,142}$$

$$=8.22\%$$

The operating profit or loss often provides the truest indicator of a company's earning capacity, since it excludes the nonoperating income and expenses. Exxon's operating profits for 1998, 1997, 1996, 1995, and 1993, respectively, were 5.96 percent, 8.22 percent, 9.22 percent, 7.23 percent, and 6.44 percent. Except for 1998, this shows an increasing trend.

Net Profit
The net profit margin includes nonoperating income and expenses, such as taxes, interest expense, and extraordinary items. Net profit is calculated as follows:

$$\text{Net profit} = \frac{\text{net income}}{\text{net sales}}$$

$$\text{Exxon's net profit for 1998} = \frac{\$6,370}{\$115,417} \qquad \text{for 1997} = \frac{\$8,460}{\$135,142}$$

$$= 5.519\% \qquad\qquad\qquad = 6.26\%$$

To the lay investor, it may not seem that important to calculate all these profit ratios. Instead, there may be an emphasis on net profit margin only. This could be misleading, because if tax rates or interest expenses increase, or if there are some large extraordinary items in the year, there will be a significant change in the net profit, even though operating profits have not changed. The net profit margins for Exxon for 1998, 1997, 1996, 1995, and 1993, respectively, were 5.519 percent, 6.26 percent, 5.70 percent, 5.31 percent, and 4.82 percent. This shows an increasing net profit margin trend over the period through 1997, which indicates that management has had a tight handle on expenses. The price of oil during this period was declining, which makes these returns all the more impressive.

Other measures of profitability, which are more specific to common shareholders in that they measure the returns on the invested funds of the shareholders, are return on equity and return on common equity.

Return on Equity

This ratio indicates how well management is performing for the stockholders and is calculated as follows:

$$\text{Return on equity} = \frac{\text{net income}}{\text{equity}}$$

$$\text{Exxon's return on equity for 1998} = \frac{\$6,370}{\$43,750}$$

$$= 14.56\%$$

$$\text{for 1997} = \frac{\$8,460}{\$43,660}$$

$$= 19.377\%$$

In other words, Exxon is earning $0.1456 for every dollar invested in equity by shareholders in 1998. There is an upward trend in return on equity: the returns for 1997, 1996, 1995, and 1993 were 19.377 percent, 17.247 percent, 16 percent, and 15.17 percent, respectively.

Return on Common Equity

When a company has preferred stock, the common shareholders may be more concerned with the return attributable to common equity than to total equity. To determine this return, adjustments are made for the preferred dividends and preferred stock outstanding.

$$\text{Return on common equity} = \frac{\text{net income} - \text{preferred dividends}}{\text{equity} - \text{preferred stock}}$$

Exxon does not have any preferred stock, so this ratio is not meaningful in that case.

The Effects of Earnings on Stock Prices

Corporate earnings, under conventional stock price theory, are the most important determinant of the company's stock price. Analysts suggest buying those stocks whose earnings are expected to increase and selling the ones with anticipated downturns in earnings. This is evidenced on Wall Street when companies turn in earnings results that are shy of the analysts' estimates. The prices of these stocks usually get battered downwards.

However, there are short periods when stock prices appear to have no correlation to earnings. The prices of these stocks sometimes move in opposite directions to their earnings or increase more slowly than their earnings. There are occasions when stock prices go up ahead of their earnings.

So what is the beginning investor to do when analysts correctly forecast earnings and the stock price ends up going in the opposite direction?

These anomalies in the movement of stock prices and earnings can be explained by the *confidence theory*, which says that stock prices react more to trader and investor confidence than earnings. In other words, confidence or lack of confidence in a stock can drive its price up and down regardless of earnings. For example, Unisys Corporation reshaped its balance sheet and turned losses into profits, which made it the darling of many analysts in their buy recommendations. The euphoria ended when Unisys announced quarterly earnings slightly off from analysts' forecasts. This prompted many analysts to turn pessimistic on the stock, which resulted in the Unisys stock price plummeting over 40 percent. Thereafter, new management took over, and after many quarters of increasing revenues and diminishing losses, the investment community finally became convinced that Unisys had turned the corner. The stock price languished in the $5 to $6 a share range for quite some time before moving up to its current price of about $38 per share.

The difficulty of measuring and forecasting trader and investor confidence is even more nebulous than trying to forecast earnings. So where does all this leave the investor? Even an accurate forecast of a company's earnings does not mean the stock's price will follow. This leads to the realization that investors cannot rely on the relationship between stock prices and earnings over a short period of time. Over long periods of time, however, there appears to be a positive correlation between the movement of stock prices and earnings.

Exxon managed to increase profits in the face of declining oil prices over the five-year period shown, which means management has kept strict control of expenses. Exxon's share price has more than doubled in this period.

The Price-Earnings (P/E) Ratio

The most commonly used guide to the relationship between stock prices and earnings is the price-earnings (P/E) ratio. This is calculated as follows:

$$\text{Price/earnings ratio} = \frac{\text{market price of the stock}}{\text{earnings per share}}$$

The P/E ratio shows the number of times that a stock's price is trading relative to its earnings. The P/E ratios for listed common stocks are published daily in the financial newspapers. For example, the P/E ratio for Exxon Corporation as of January 26, 1999, was

27.68, and the closing price of the stock that day was $72.25 per share. This means that shareholders were willing to pay 27.68 times Exxon's earnings for its stock. Looked at another way, it would take 27.68 years of earnings at this rate to equal the invested amount of $72.25 per share.

By rearranging the formula, the earnings per share can be determined for Exxon:

$$\text{Earnings per share} = \frac{\text{market price of the stock}}{\text{P/E ratio}}$$

$$= \frac{72.25}{27.68}$$

$$= \$2.61$$

Investors who obtain company information from the service organizations, such as Standard & Poor's and Value Line, may find there are discrepancies between the P/E ratios reported in the newspapers and those reported by information services companies. This is because the financial newspapers quote the P/E ratio based on the annual earnings for the previous year, whereas the information services companies may quote the price/earnings based on earnings of the current quarter and projected future quarters.

Theoretically, if the earnings per share increase, the stock price should rise and the P/E ratio should stay much the same. In reality, this does not often happen. P/E ratios may be volatile and may fluctuate considerably. For example, the P/E ratios of the pharmaceutical companies dropped considerably in 1992 due to nervousness over the price controls of the proposed Clinton health plan. Merck had a P/E ratio around 24 in 1990–1991, but as of August 1994, it was trading at 13 times earnings. When the Clinton health-care plan was defeated, the stock prices of the pharmaceutical companies started to go up again as more investors sought safe haven in the anticipated sales growth of these companies (due to aging populations). Merck has a current P/E ratio of 32, which indicates that it is richly valued. The average market multiple is around 28, prompting many people to believe that the market is overvalued and ready for a correction.

As a rule of thumb, the P/E ratios of drug companies on average trade around the low 20s, while the P/E ratios of many small emerging growth companies, such as the biotech companies, may be greater than 50. P/E ratios of companies whose stock prices have been driven down due to pessimism may be very low. Unisys Corporation, for example, is currently trading at about 30 times earnings, while other computer companies are trading at much higher P/E multiples. Dell, for example, is trading around 79 times earnings.

In short, P/E ratios by themselves are not relied on very greatly in selecting stocks. For example, why would an investor pay 200 times earnings for the stock of a company that may or may not succeed when there are solid companies with steady earnings trading at low P/E multiples?

What Do P/E Ratios Tell Potential Investors?

The P/E ratio of a company shows how expensive the stock is relative to its earnings. High P/E ratios (above 20, as a rule of thumb) are characteristic of growth companies, although with the average market multiple currently around 28, a P/E ratio of 20 almost seems like a value stock, considering today's market. Investors may be optimistic about a company's potential growth and drive up the stock price in anticipation. This results in a high stock price relative to the company's current earnings. Some investors may be willing to pay a high price for a company's potential earnings; others may consider such stocks overpriced. Cisco Systems has seen a consistent rise in its stock price because investors think they see potential annual sales growth of 30 to 50 percent per year. Cisco's current P/E ratio is 110, making it an expensive stock to buy at these levels.

What becomes apparent, then, is that high P/E ratios indicate high risk. If the future anticipated growth of these high P/E ratio stocks is not achieved, their stock prices will be punished and they will fall very quickly. On the other hand, if they do live up to their promise, investors will benefit substantially.

Low P/E ratio stocks (under 10) are characteristic of either mature companies with low growth potential or companies that are undervalued or in financial difficulty.

By comparing the P/E ratio of a company with the averages in the industries and the markets, investors can get a feeling for the relative value of the stock. For example, the average P/E ratios for companies on the U.S. stock markets are currently around 28 times earnings. During bull markets, these ratios go up, and during bear markets, the average declines (perhaps to as low as six times earnings, which happened in 1974).

P/E ratios fluctuate considerably, differing among companies due to many factors, from growth rates and popularity to earnings and other financial characteristics.

Earnings Per Share (EPS)

Besides the market price of the stock, the other figure used to determine the P/E ratio is the earnings per share (EPS). The earnings per share indicate the amount of earnings allocated to each share of common stock outstanding. EPS figures can be used to compare the growth (or lack of growth) in earnings from year to year and to project future growth in earnings. Earnings per share is calculated as follows:

$$\text{Earnings per share} = \frac{\text{net income} - \text{preferred dividends}}{\text{number of common shares outstanding}}$$

The number of shares outstanding equals the number of shares issued minus the shares that the company has bought back, called *treasury stock*. In many cases, companies will report two sets of earnings per share figures; the regular earnings per share and the fully diluted earnings per share. For the beginning investor, this can be confusing.

When companies have convertible bonds, convertible preferred stock, rights, options, and/or warrants, their earnings per share figures could be diluted due to the increased number of common shares outstanding, if and when these securities are converted into common stocks. Companies are then required to disclose their fully diluted earnings per share figures as well.

It is the trend of earnings per share figures over a period of time that is important for investors. Exxon, for example, had an increasing trend of earnings per share for the years between 1993 and 1997, due primarily to increasing sales growth: $2.62 in 1998; $3.41 in 1997; $3.01 in 1996; $2.59 in 1995; $2.04 in 1994; and $2.10 in 1993. If earnings per share are increasing steadily due to growth in sales, this should translate into increasing stock prices. However, earnings per share can also increase through companies buying back their own shares. This reduces the number of shares outstanding, so if earnings stay the same, earnings per share will increase. Conceivably, earnings per share could increase even when sales and earnings decrease if a significant amount of stock is bought back. The astute investor examines the financial statements to determine whether the increase in earnings per share is due to growth in sales and earnings or to stock buybacks. If the increase is due to buybacks, the result could be a loss of confidence in the stock and a decline in the stock price.

Companies with poor fundamentals might try this tactic of buying their shares back to improve their earnings per share and ultimately their stock prices, but over the long term, this strategy could backfire.

Decreasing earnings per share over a period of time generally has a negative impact on stock prices. However, the reasons for the decrease are important. A decrease in EPS due to an increase in the number of shares outstanding from conversions of convertible bonds or preferred stock issues is not as negative as decreasing sales. If it is due to decreasing sales, further investigation is required to determine if this is a temporary or permanent phenomenon.

Consequently, when comparing earnings per share figures with those of previous periods, you need to examine the reasons for the changes in order to get a better fix on the potential changes in the stock price.

Dividends and Dividend Yields

Investors buy stocks for their potential capital gains and/or their dividend payments. Companies either share their profits with their shareholders by paying dividends, or they retain their earnings and reinvest them in different projects in order to boost their share prices. A company's dividend policy is typically made public. For example, there are growth companies and other companies that choose not to pay dividends, and there are the blue-chip, established companies, utility companies, and real estate investment trusts (REITs) that are well known for their dividend payments.

The amount of existing dividends that listed companies pay can be found in the stock listings in the newspapers. Generally, companies try to maintain these stated dividend payments even if they suffer declines in earnings. Similarly, increases in earnings do not always translate into increases in dividends. Certainly, there are many examples where companies experience earnings increases that result in increases in dividend payments, but this is not always the case. There is an imprecise relationship between dividends and earnings. There are times when increases in earnings exceed increases in dividends and other times when increases in dividends exceed increases in earnings. Thus, growth in dividends cannot be interpreted as a sign of a company's financial strength.

Dividends are important in that they represent tangible returns. The cash flow from dividends can be reinvested by shareholders. By contrast, investors in growth stocks that pay little or no dividends are betting on capital appreciation rather than current returns.

To determine the dividend yield, which shows the percentage return that dividends represent relative to the market price of the common stock, the calculation is as follows:

$$\text{Dividend yield} = \frac{\text{annual dividend}}{\text{market price of the stock}}$$

In the current bull market climate, many investors are nervous about growth stocks that either pay no or low dividends. Hence they are turning to high-dividend-yielding stocks. A strategy of buying high-dividend-yielding stocks may offer some protection against any fall in stock market prices due to rising interest rates. Dividend yields of many utility companies, REITS, and energy companies can be as high as 5 to 7 percent. High dividend yields are characteristic of a few blue-chip companies, large companies, and the utility companies.

It is risky, however, to choose stocks purely because of their high dividend yields. Dividends can be reduced, which usually puts downward pressure on the price of the stock.

When choosing high-dividend-yield stocks, you should look at the earnings to see that they are sufficient to support the dividend payments. According to Geraldine Weiss, editor of the newsletter *Investment Quality Trends*, earnings should be equal to at least 150 percent of the dividend payout (Gottschalk, p. C1). For example, Arco Chemical Company had a dividend yield of 5.5 percent, but its dividend payout ratio exceeded its earnings by 112 percent, suggesting an imminent dividend cut (Asinof, p. C1).

$$\text{Dividend payout ratio} = \frac{\text{dividend per share}}{\text{earnings per share}}$$

Exxon's dividends per share have been increasing as shown below:

1998	$1.640
1997	$1.625
1996	$1.560
1995	$1.500
1994	$1.455
1993	$1.440

The dividend payout ratio for Exxon during this same period was:

1998	63.00%
1997	48.39%
1996	51.83%
1995	57.92%
1994	71.32%
1993	68.57%

This shows a declining trend in the dividend payout ratio, except for 1998, which indicates that even if there is a downturn in Exxon's earnings, they would in all probability still be able to maintain the amounts of their dividends.

Besides earnings, you should look at the statement of changes in cash to see the sources and uses of cash. For example, if the major sources of cash are issuing debt and selling off assets, a company will not be able to maintain a high-dividend-yield policy.

Dividends and dividend yields are not good indicators of the intrinsic value of a stock because dividend payments fluctuate considerably over time, creating an imprecise relationship between the growth in dividends and the growth in earnings.

Book Value of the Stock

The *book value* of the stock is another statistic a potential investor can compare with the market value of the stock. The book value per share is the assets minus the liabilities divided by the outstanding common shares. In other words, if the company were to sell its tangible assets at the values stated on the balance sheet and pay off all its liabilities, the amount left over would be for shareholders. This is a simplistic scenario because certain assets, such as buildings and real estate, are recorded at their historical costs, while their market prices may be far greater (or less). Moreover, other assets, such as inventory, may sell for less than their balance sheet values if the company has to liquidate in a short period of time.

Many analysts look for companies whose stock prices are trading at less than their book values and interpret this as a buying signal. A small company quoted on the Nasdaq National Market System called Nuclear Metals, Inc., posted losses for the year, which caused its stock price to fall to around $8 per share, whereas its book value was around $18 per share. Six months later, Nuclear Metals, Inc., was trading at $17 per share.

Investors looking for value stocks would place more importance on finding stocks whose book values are greater than their market values. Growth stocks tend to have higher stock market prices than their book values.

Leverage Ratios

While leverage, or *debt financing*, is a major concern for bondholders, who use these ratios to determine the level of debt and the servicing of the contractual payments of interest and principal, it is also important for common stockholders.

By increasing the use of debt financing, a company can increase returns to shareholders. Table 5-3 shows how returns for a hypothetical company are increased through the use of leverage. This example shows how both the return on equity and the earnings per share can be increased from 14 percent to 21 percent and from $1.40 to $2.10, respectively, by increasing the debt financing from 0 percent to 50 percent of total assets.

There are two reasons for this increase. First, the company is able to earn more than the 10 percent cost of borrowing. Second, the interest cost is a tax-deductible expense. The federal government bears 30 percent (the rate used in this example) of the cost of the interest payments (30 percent of $50, which is $15).

TABLE 5-3

Financial Leverage and Earnings

Company with No Leverage

Balance Sheet		Income Statement	
Assets	**Liabilities**	Revenues	$1,000
		Cost of Goods Sold	500
$1,000	$0	Gross Profit	500
		Expenses	300
	Equity	Earnings before Taxes	200
		Taxes(30%) =	60
	$1,000*	Net Income	140
$1,000	$1,000		

*100 shares outstanding

Return on equity = 140/1000 = <u>14%</u>

Earnings per share = 140/100 = <u>$1.40</u>

Company with 50% Leverage

Balance Sheet		Income Statement	
Assets	**Liabilities**	Revenues	$1,000
		Cost of Goods Sold	500
$1,000	$500	Gross Profit	500
		Expenses	300
	Equity	Earnings before Interest and Taxes	200
	*500		
		Interest (10% x $500) =	50
$1,000	$1,000	Earnings before Taxes	150
		Taxes (30%) =	45
*50 shares outstanding		Net Income	105

Return on equity = 105/500   = 21%

Earnings per share = 105/50   = $2.10

Since the use of debt increases the return to shareholders as well as the earnings per share, why should shareholders be so concerned about the level of debt a company uses to finance its assets? The answer is that the more debt a company takes on, the greater the financial risk and the cost of servicing the debt. For example, if there is a downturn in sales, the company might have difficulty covering the interest payments. This could lead not only to a default and ultimately to bankruptcy but also to significantly reduced returns to shareholders and the earnings per share. When a company increases the amount of its debt, the costs of raising additional debt issues increase, which means that the company will have to earn more than the cost of the borrowing or it will not see the benefits of leverage. When the level of debt reaches the point where the earnings on the assets are less than the costs of the debt, the return on equity and the earnings per share will decline.

For common stock investors, a highly leveraged company means there is great risk, and a greater rate of return is required to justify the risk. This increase in the required rate of return could have a negative impact on the share price.

Thus, the use of leverage can increase the value of the stock when the level of debt used is not perceived as adding a great amount of risk to the company.

What Is the Optimal Level of Leverage?

All companies use different amounts of leverage, but some industries typically use more than others. Industries that require large investments in fixed assets, such as oil companies, airlines, and utilities, will use a higher percentage of debt to finance their assets. Banks typically also use large amounts of debt because their assets are financed by deposits. This leverage results in large fluctuations in the banking industry's earnings when there are slight fluctuations in revenues.

When considering the leverage of one company, compare it to the typical leverage for that industry. Investors should look at the debt and coverage ratios of a company to see the extent of its borrowing and its ability to service the debt.

Debt Ratio

The debt ratio indicates how much of the financing of the total assets comes from debt. The ratio is calculated as follows:

$$\text{Debt ratio} = \frac{\text{total current and noncurrent liabilities}}{\text{total assets}}$$

For Exxon Corporation, the debt ratio in 1998 was 52.76 percent ($48,880 ÷ $92,630). This means Exxon financed 52.76 percent of its assets with debt. The debt ratio should be compared with the average of the industry to get a better feeling for the degree of the company's leverage.

A company with a large debt ratio becomes increasingly vulnerable if there is a downturn in sales and/or the economy, particularly in the latter case, and if it is a cyclical company.

When examining the financial statements of a company, you should always check the footnotes to see if there is any debt that has not been included on the balance sheet. If a company does not consolidate the financial subsidiaries into its financial statements, any debt that the parent company is responsible for will be reported in the footnotes to the financial statements.

Coverage Ratios

The coverage ratios measure the company's ability to cover the interest payments associated with its debt.

The *times interest earned* ratio shows the company's coverage of its interest payments. It is calculated as follows:

$$\text{Times interest earned ratio} = \frac{\text{earnings before interest and taxes}}{\text{annual interest expense}}$$

If a company has low coverage of its interest payments, a slight downturn in sales or an increase in costs could have disastrous consequences, since the company might not be able to meet its interest payments.

What about a Company's Cash?

Earnings are an important determinant of a company's value and stock price, but the company's cash position is another important way to assess value. The statement of changes in cash position is a good starting point to assess cash flow. See Figure 5-3 for Exxon's consolidated statement of cash.

This statement shows the changes in cash during the year. This figure is the difference in the cash balances obtained from the balance sheet, as illustrated below:

	1998	1997	Difference
Cash and cash equivalents	$1,441	$4,047	($2,606)

The statement shows the changes to the cash account, which end up with a decrease of $2,606 to cash and cash equivalents, shown in the third to last line of the statement of Exxon's cash flows for 1998.

The statement of changes in cash has three sections:

- Cash from Operating Activities
- Cash from Investing Activities
- Cash from Financing Activities

The first section, Cash from Operating Activities, shows the inflows and outflows of cash from operations for the period. The noncash expenses, such as depreciation, deferred income tax charges, and annuity and accrued liability provisions, are added back to the net income to provide the *cash flow* for Exxon. This was $11,056 in 1998, $14,676 for 1997, and $13,162 for 1996. This shows an increasing trend of cash flows from operations for 1996 and 1997, which means that Exxon has cash available for investing and financing activities. As to the former, Exxon recently announced a merger with Mobil, which as a combined company will make them the largest in the industry.

Another more refined measure is *free cash flow*. This is cash flow minus capital spending. Companies that do not generate strong cash flows have less flexibility, and this is most often reflected in their stock prices.

For 1998, Exxon generated $11,056 from operations (the last line in the first section), of which $7992 was used for investing activities (the last line in the second section). Cash provided from operations was also used toward financing activities, which included the payment of cash dividends of $4012 and the purchase of its own stock ($3055). The net decrease to cash was $2606, which was deducted from the ending cash balance for 1997 to produce a cash balance at the end of 1998 of $1441 in the balance sheet.

What about the Announced Exxon-Mobil Merger?

At the end of 1998, Exxon and Mobil Oil announced their $80 billion merger, a stock deal if the merger goes through. Mobil Oil shareholders will get their shares converted into Exxon shares at a 30 percent premium. What will Exxon shareholders get?

- Exxon will get Mobil's oil resources in different parts of the world, such as the Caspian Sea and Asia.
- The combined company is projected to produce annual savings of $2.8 billion, with expected profits to follow in the future (after 2000).
- The combined company will be a major force in three markets: oil exploration, refining, and the petrochemical markets.
- The combined company will have a strong balance sheet, with roughly 18 percent in debt, which would be significantly lower than the industry.
- If oil prices remain depressed, the cost savings from the combined company will help it maintain its leadership in the industry. If oil prices go up, it could have a slight impact on earnings in the near term and a larger impact longer term.

The potential value of the stock will depend on the successful integration of the two companies and the future price of oil. A short-term-growth-oriented investor would not be "instantly gratified" by buying this stock, but it might appeal to a value investor, who can appreciate the financial strength of the combined company and who has the patience to wait for a turnaround in the price of oil. In the meantime, the investor will receive a yearly dividend of $1.64 per share.

REFERENCES

Asinof, Lynn: "How to Find Good Stocks in a Dicey Market," *The Wall Street Journal*, April 29, 1994, p. C1.

Gottschalk, Earl C., Jr.: "Nervous About Growth Stocks? Try Some High-Dividend Ones," *The Wall Street Journal*, May 2, 1994, p. C1.

Kuhn, Susan E.: "Stocks Are Still Your Best Buy," *Fortune*, March 21, 1994, pp. 138–144.

CHAPTER 6

Using Technical Analysis to Buy Stocks

KEY CONCEPTS

- Technical analysis
- Charts and their patterns
- Market indicators
- Trend methods
- Structural theories
- Implications for investors

In the previous chapter, we saw that the fundamental analyst studies the forces outside of the market and then zeroes in on the fundamentals of those companies whose stocks are undervalued and are expected to increase in the future. For example, the fundamentalist would be interested in the forecasted number of computer sales in order to assess the market for semiconductor computer chips. In addition, the analyst would want to be able to project average semiconductor chip prices into the future and the gross margins for the chips in order to make an assessment of the future stock prices of the semiconductor computer chip manufacturers. This will then form the basis of the fundamental analyst's view of whether these companies will increase their future sales and earnings, the relative strength of their balance sheets, and future cash flows. An investment decision will then be made based on these assessments.

The *technical analyst*, on the other hand, is not all that concerned about the fundamental factors of the company and the economic environment. Instead, technical analysts focus on the company's historical stock price movements and the trading volume of the stock.

169

From this information, the technical analyst will predict future stock price behavior. The technician focuses on a shorter time horizon than the fundamental analyst.

Even though many dispute the value of technical analysis, it is a widely used method for selecting stocks. Most large brokerage firms have a technical analyst on staff, and many rely on the information provided by their technical analysts in the selection of stocks. In academic circles, however, technical analysis is not given much credibility. Despite the many shortcomings of technical analysis, which are pointed out in this chapter, investors should be aware of how technical analysis works.

Generally, technicians are aware of the fundamentals of the stocks they are interested in and fundamentalists are cognizant of the volume and trading range of the stocks that they are interested in.

It is important for investors to be aware of the contradictions between these approaches, which will make it easier for them to recognize the philosophies their brokers follow.

WHAT IS TECHNICAL ANALYSIS?

Technical analysis focuses on past price movements of stocks, using them as a basis for predicting future stock prices. The assumption is that these price movements will be repeated into the future. In other words, the behavior of investors will always be the same when faced with similar situations, enabling technical analysts to predict future stock prices and whether they should be bought or sold. Technical analysts use several different methods to predict future price movements, one of which is charts. These show the patterns of stock price movements, which are the basis for interpreting future price movements. In other words, investors determine the markets for stocks, and when the same price conditions recur, investors will react to them in the same way they did in the past. This repetition of previous patterns in stock prices then becomes the basis for technicians' buy and sell recommendations.

Technicians also consider trading volume, together with price, to be an important indicator of the supply and demand for the stock. For technicians, the combination of price movements and trading volume indicates the mood of the market, summarized in Table 6-1.

When both volume and stock price are increasing, investors are bullish because the increasing trading volume will continue to push prices up. However, the opposite occurs when trading volume is increasing but stock price is decreasing. This indicates bearish sentiment because there are more sellers than buyers, which is depressing the stock price.

Both decreasing price and volume indicates a mixed mood in the market. The decreasing volume shows that the market is bottoming out for this stock. When the price reaches a low enough point, more investors will start buying, which will push the price up.

Although decreasing volume and increasing price also describe a mixed market, this has a somewhat bearish tone, since the increasing price will not be supported due to declining volume. The price is topping out and will start to fall.

The approaches to technical analysis may be classified into the following categories:

- Charts
- Market indicators
- Trends
- Structural theories

There are so many technical approaches within each of these broad categories that only a few of the more popular examples in each category will be discussed.

CHARTS AND THEIR PATTERNS

Technical analysts use charts to obtain historic information about individual stocks and markets. From these, they study the patterns to determine future trends which will tell them when to buy and sell. It is not critical to know the company, the industry that it is in,

TABLE 6-1

Volume and Price Movements Which Indicate Market Mood

Volume	Price	Market Mood
Increasing	Increasing	Bullish sentiment
Increasing	Decreasing	Bearish sentiment
Decreasing	Decreasing	Somewhat bullish
Decreasing	Increasing	Somewhat bearish

or what it produces and sells. Everything is in the charts! The past price movements and patterns can be used to predict future price movements. Four types of charts used are described below:

- Line
- Bar
- Point and figure
- Candlestick charts

Line Charts

A line chart can be used to show the stock price of a company or market prices over a period of time. This type of chart is used to show, for example, hourly changes to the Dow Jones Industrial Average in a day of trading. Similarly, closing prices of stock may be plotted over a period of time to show the trading patterns for the Dow. See Figure 6-1 for an example of a line chart that shows the prices of a stock for the months July through January. This shows the historical price patterns for this company and, according to technical analysts, will show trading opportunities in a stock.

Bar Charts

A bar chart is similar to a line chart, but it incorporates more information. If charting stock prices on a daily basis, a bar chart would include the high, low, and closing prices of the stock. On a weekly basis, the chart would show the high, low, and closing price for the week. A vertical line shows the high and low price, and a horizontal line shows the closing price. Figure 6-2 shows the bar chart for the following daily prices for a stock for two weeks:

Price	Mon	Tues	Wed	Thur	Fri	Mon	Tues	Wed	Thur	Fri
High	15	$15^{1}/_{2}$	$14^{3}/_{4}$	$15^{3}/_{4}$	$17^{3}/_{4}$	$18^{1}/_{4}$	$18^{3}/_{4}$	19	21	$20^{3}/_{4}$
Low	14	$14^{1}/_{2}$	14	$14^{1}/_{4}$	$15^{1}/_{2}$	$17^{3}/_{4}$	18	$18^{1}/_{2}$	19	$20^{1}/_{2}$
Close	$14^{1}/_{2}$	$14^{3}/_{4}$	$14^{3}/_{4}$	$15^{1}/_{2}$	$17^{3}/_{4}$	$18^{1}/_{4}$	$18^{1}/_{2}$	$18^{1}/_{2}$	21	$20^{3}/_{4}$
Volume	10,200	10,900	11,100	12,400	12,600	12,700	12,600	12,850	13,000	12,900

FIGURE 6-1

Line Chart

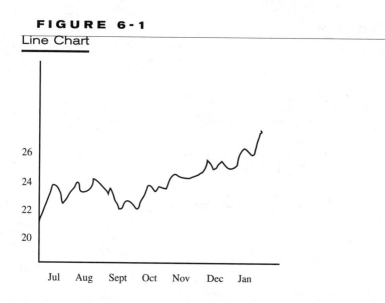

With more data plotted, a pattern would emerge which is studied by technicians. From this, trends can be determined as the upward trend line shows in Figure 6-2. Obviously, there is an art to drawing trend lines because there is no precise body of data on how to draw them. The trend line is drawn from the lowest points to the highest points. Once there is an established trend for a stock, the analysts will follow the stock for any changes to the trend. When the stock price falls below this upward trend line, technical analysts recommend selling it, because the trend has been broken. Similarly, crossing a downward trend would indicate a buy signal for that particular stock. Thus trend lines form the basis for buy and sell signals.

Point and Figure Charts

Point and figure charts differ from bar charts in a number of ways. Point and figure charts record only significant changes in the stock price. "Significant" is defined by the analyst drawing up the chart. For higher-priced stocks, above $50, there might be a two-point difference to activate recording the price (see Figure 6-3). For lower-priced stocks, the difference might be one point. The second major difference between point and figure charts and other charts is that

FIGURE 6-2

Bar Chart

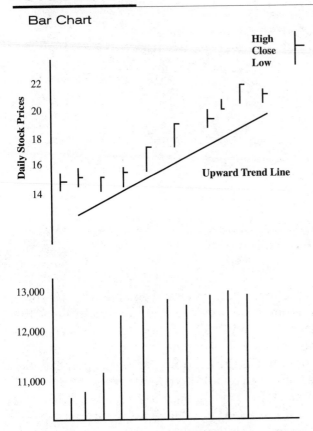

neither time nor trading volume is important with the former. This type of chart is used to draw attention to emerging price patterns.

The construction of a point and figure chart is relatively simple. The first step is to determine the fluctuations you consider significant. For a high-priced stock in the hundreds of dollars, three to five points might be appropriate, whereas a stock in the $10 price range might have a half- to one-point differential.

Assuming two points is decided on for a $50-range stock, the technician plots the changes in price as follows:

- An X is inserted on the chart when the price of the stock advances by at least two points.

FIGURE 6-3

Point and Figure Chart

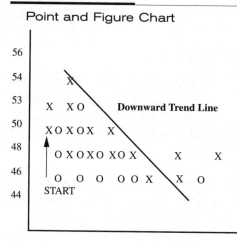

- An O is inserted when the stock declines by at least two points.

For example, the following prices would result in the point and figure chart shown in Figure 6-3:

First week	50	51	$51^{1}/_{2}$	$52^{1}/_{4}$	$52^{3}/_{4}$
Second week	50	$47^{3}/_{4}$	46	$47^{7}/_{8}$	$47^{1}/_{2}$
Third week	48	$49^{7}/_{8}$	$50^{1}/_{4}$	$51^{1}/_{8}$	53

The first X at $50 is plotted to begin the chart. The next two entries in the first week (51 and $51^{1}/_{2}$) are ignored because they are less than the $2 differential. The second X is placed at $52 to show the increase of the stock to $52^{1}/_{4}$, while the $52^{3}/_{4}$ is ignored.

In the second week, the stock price falls to $50, which necessitates putting an O next to $50 in the second column. The O signifies a decline in price. A second O is inserted at $48 to show the greater-than-two-point decline to $47^{3}/_{4}$, followed by a third O when the price falls to $46 per share. The third column shows the increase in price to $48, $50, and above $52. Each time the stock advances by more than $2, an X is inserted; and when it falls by more than $2, an O is inserted. Thus, at a glance, a point and figure chart will show price changes. Stock prices beyond the third week were plotted, and from this, a downward trend line emerged. Technical analysts would view the penetration (the upward crossing) of the downward trend line as a buy signal.

Candlestick Charts

The candlestick chart is the oldest type of charting method for determining prices of stocks. This method can be traced to Japan in the 1700s, where they were used for predicting the prices of rice. As a consequence, the different candlestick shapes and patterns have Japanese names, which adds some intrigue to the typical English-American investment terminology.

In addition to the high, low, and closing prices used by bar charts, candlestick charts use the opening price. Each of these four pieces of information is included in the candlestick diagram, as shown in Figure 6-4.

The data conveyed by the candlestick chart are:

- The real body represents the range between the opening and closing prices. If the closing price is lower than the opening price (normally a bearish factor), the body of the candlestick is filled in (black). When the closing price is higher than the opening price, the body of the candlestick is open or white (normally a bullish sign).
- The line above the candlestick body, called the upper shadow, represents the high price for the stock for the

FIGURE 6-4

Definition of the Components of the Candlestick

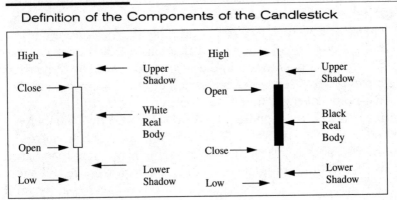

period. The line below the candlestick body represents the low price of the stock. A candlestick with no upper shadow indicates that the stock closed (or opened) at the high price; and a candlestick with no lower shadow means that the stock closed (or opened) at the same price as the low price for the period.

The candlestick chart makes it easy to spot the changes in opening and closing prices. When there is a filled-in real body (black body), you know that the stock closed at a lower price than the open for the day (week, month, or whatever period you choose). This indicates a weak close. Similarly, a long open body indicates that the stock closed at a higher price than the open for that day, a bullish close.

There are many different interpretations of the different candlestick patterns, which are beyond the scope of this book. Several books have been written on the topic should you want to explore this charting technique further. Figure 6-5 shows a five-day candlestick chart for the stock of Lockheed Martin Corporation, ticker symbol LMT. The three white candlesticks of the last three days

FIGURE 6-5

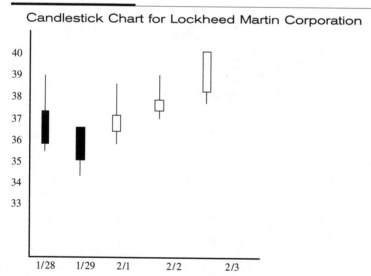

Candlestick Chart for Lockheed Martin Corporation

indicate a bullish pattern, and in the candlestick terminology, this is referred to as the "three white soldiers."

CHART PATTERNS

By plotting prices over a long period of time, many technicians believe they can predict how long a stock will advance or decline as well as identify the support and resistance levels. Once the type of chart has been decided on, the analyst will look for emerging formations (see Figure 6-6 for a few examples of common formations). From these volume and price chart patterns, trend lines, and support and resistance levels, technical analysts believe that they can predict the appropriate price at which to buy or sell a stock.

There are some difficulties for beginning chartists. First, in practice, the common patterns, such as those shown in Figure 6-6, may not emerge. Second, the buy and sell signals may not be obvi-

FIGURE 6-6

Chart Patterns

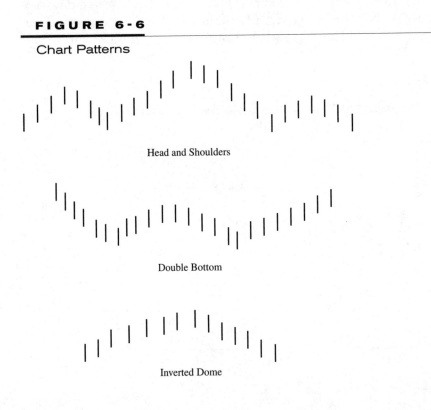

Head and Shoulders

Double Bottom

Inverted Dome

ous to the reader of the chart. Third, it is not of consequence to the technical analyst whether the double bottom formation chart belongs to Intel Corporation or Boeing Corporation. It all means the same for both corporations. This implies that stock-picking is a simplistic exercise and does not require any financial expertise other than reading financial newspapers to obtain price and volume information on stocks and the market.

Technicians plot their charts, and then the first thing they look for are trends in their charts. A *trend* is the direction of the movement of the stock's price or the market movement of prices. It could be in an upward, downward, or sideways direction. Generally, prices move in a jagged pattern. A succession of high and low points higher than the previous data signifies an upward trend. The opposite is true of a downward trend. These trends (upward and downward) are illustrated in Figure 6-7. There is the presumption that the momentum in the markets will continue to perpetuate these trends.

During an upward or sideways trend, a pricing point to which the stock rises, then repeatedly falls below without breaking through, is called a *resistance level.* An explanation for this level of resistance is that when the stock reaches its high side of this trading range, investors see a chance to make profits and sell. This prevents the stock from moving higher and breaking out of the resistance level.

Similarly, during a downward or sideways trend, there may be a lower level of trading, called a *support level.* This is the price level at which the stock will bottom out before increasing in price due to investors buying the stock. This is shown in Figure 6-8, where the stock rises to $30 per share only to fall back each time.

FIGURE 6-7

Trend Lines

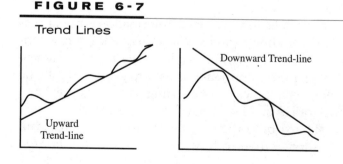

Upward
Trend-line

Downward Trend-line

FIGURE 6-8

Line Chart Showing Support and Resistance Levels

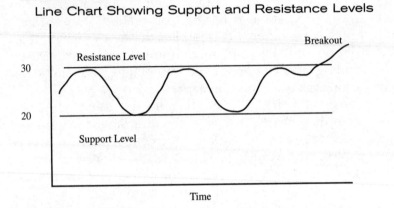

Finally, the stock surprises technical analysts by rising above the $30 level. For technical analysts, a *breakout* below a support level or above a resistance level (Figure 6-8) is significant. Technical analysts believe that when stocks break out of their support or resistance levels, the stock prices will continue to move lower or higher, respectively, which will establish new levels of support or resistance. Their explanations for this momentum appear to be twofold. When investors see that the price breaks through the resistance level, they will want to own this stock, which perpetuates further enthusiastic buying of this stock. Second, there may be some positive information which accounts for this breakout, and when the public hear about this information, the stock price has already reacted. This is when small investors will jump on the bandwagon to buy. The opposite is true for the breakout in the support levels, where selling momentum will push the stock lower.

Technical analysts believe that chasing information is not important. They identify the trading patterns as a consequence of reactions to the release of information. Charting is a lot easier than fundamental analysis, and stock price information is easy to get at virtually no additional cost. However, the value of charting as a method for predicting future stock prices and profits has been questioned.

Many chartists attribute their successes to their charts, but the crux of the matter—when to buy and sell—may lie more in the chartist's judgement than in the charts themselves. If it were that simple, the stock market would have been sewn up by now!

There are many free sources on the Internet for obtaining charting information. One such free Website is *www.askresearch.com*. You can obtain the line, bar, or candlestick charts along with moving average trend lines on the stocks of your choice.

MARKET INDICATORS

This group of technical indicators is used to determine the direction of the market.

Dow Theory

The oldest technical method of predicting the direction of market prices is the Dow Theory, developed by Charles Dow, the founder of the Dow Jones Company and the first editor of *The Wall Street Journal*.

The Dow theory is based on the premise that stock prices move together in patterns over a four-to-five-year period. According to the theory, there are three major movements in stock prices: primary, secondary, and daily, or tertiary, movements:

- *Primary price movements* are the long-term movements related to the stock's intrinsic values. These may be characterized as bullish or bearish.
- *Secondary price movements* are short-term fluctuations (weekly or monthly) based on current events, which, depending on the fluctuations, may indicate changes in the primary price trend (see Figure 6-9).
- *The tertiary, or daily, price movements* are inconsequential due to their erratic nature and volatility.

The Dow theory assumes that the primary trend will continue for an extended period of time (four years). The directional change can therefore be ascertained from observing the movement of the Dow Jones Industrial Average and the Dow Jones Transportation Average. According to the theory, a bull market is confirmed when the industrial average and the transportation average are moving upwards together. Similarly, a decline in both the industrial and transportation averages indicates a bear mar-

FIGURE 6-9

Dow Theory

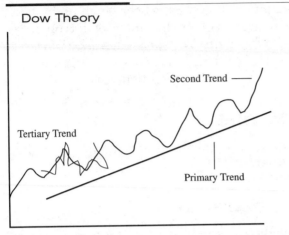

ket. When the averages move in opposite directions, it is an indication of uncertainty in the market, which may indicate a change in the primary trend.

Followers of the Dow theory use it to determine trends in the market and to predict changes in those trends. Two questions can be raised about the Dow theory. Why should the movement of the two averages be indicative of the market as a whole? Which leads to the second question: How accurate is the Dow theory in predicting changes to the direction of the market?

Many analysts believe that the Dow Jones Industrial Average is hardly representative of the market, since it consists of only 30 stocks which are mainly industrial-based stocks. In other words, the Dow is not reflective of the growth and importance of technology and service companies in the market, which makes it difficult for the Dow to represent the trend in the market. Research to test the reliability of the Dow theory in predicting trends and turning points have shown the following:

- The Dow theory can be used successfully to forecast market trends (Glickstein and Wubbels, pp. 28–32).
- The Dow theory is not very accurate and has missed more buy and sell signals than it has correctly predicted (Wright, pp. 312–317). Thus, the Dow theory is not given much credence in predicting changes in the primary trend.

Volume, Breadth, and New Highs and Lows

Many technicians gauge the short- and-intermediate-term directions of the market by looking at the following indicators:

- Daily volume
- Breadth
- New highs and lows

Volume Technical analysts consider volume as an indicator of future price changes. When the daily volume on the New York Stock Exchange increases and the indexes (prices as measured by the Dow Jones Industrial Average, S&P 500 Index, etc.) are up, this is considered bullish. This means there are more buyers than sellers. Similarly, if the volume on a stock is rising and the price of the stock has also risen, this is considered to be a bullish signal for the future price of that stock.

In a bear market, volume increases, while prices decrease due to increased selling. In a weak market, prices may increase but volume declines. When both prices and volume decline, this is a somewhat optimistic sign, interpreted to mean that stockowners are reluctant to sell.

In practical terms, daily price and volume changes may be difficult to correlate to determine a trend in the market.

Breadth Many technical analysts look at the *breadth* of the market, which is the number of issues traded. By examining the number of stocks that have advanced, declined, and remained the same on a particular day of trading, analysts feel they can determine the relative strength or weakness of the market.

For instance, of the roughly 3577 issues traded on the NYSE, if 1104 advanced, 1943 declined, and 530 remain unchanged on a particular day, a negative picture of the NYSE is presented for that day. In other words, for every 11 stocks that advanced in price, there were 19 that declined in price, while 5 remained unchanged. A stronger picture of the market would be presented by a greater number of advancing stocks over declining stocks, a favorable sign indicating a rising market.

The financial newspapers list these daily statistics for the markets, and many technicians use this data to calculate the *advance/decline indicator.* This is calculated by subtracting the number of declining issues from the advancing issues and then dividing this difference by the total number of issues traded for the day. This indicator is plotted on a daily basis, and the results can be combined to create an *advance/decline line,* which is used to indicate the trend of the market. When the advance/decline line is going up and the market is falling, this is a bullish short-term signal for the market, and when the advance/decline line is falling as the market is going up, this is viewed as a bearish signal. There does not appear to be any research to prove any consistent predictive reliability of the advance/decline line. Two more complex indexes are based on the advance/decline indicator. These are the ARMS Index and the Trading Index.

New Highs and Lows   Many technicians monitor the daily new highs and new lows on the NYSE. When a sizable number of stocks reach their 52-week highs and they outnumber the stocks that reach their 52-week lows, and this pattern persists over a period of time, technicians are bullish on the market.

Many technicians place importance on the signals given by volume, market breadth, and the new highs and lows. However, these signals are not foolproof, and possibly they are given too much importance as predictors of future market activity.

Short Interest Theory

Technical analysts use the information on short interest as a sign of weakness or strength in the market. For instance, when they anticipate that prices will go lower, investors and speculators sell stocks short so they can then buy them back at lower prices. Analysts monitor short interest figures, and they contend that when short interest positions are large, this is a bullish indicator. This is because when there are large short positions open, short-sellers will eventually have to buy back the stocks, which will drive the prices up. Small amounts of short interest are considered of no consequence to future market activity.

The short interest theory may not be all that reliable an indicator of future market sentiment because the amount of stocks sold short is a very small percentage of the shares outstanding on the NYSE. Moreover, investors sometimes sell short for tax purposes rather than in anticipation of lower prices. This is referred to as *short-selling against the box.* An investor can defer the tax consequences of selling appreciated stock into the next year by using this short-selling strategy.

For instance, let's say an investor who owns 100 shares which was purchased at $20 a share and is currently trading at $35 wants to sell but does not want to pay the taxes that year. To defer the taxes, the investor sells short 100 shares of the stock at $35 per share and now has two positions in this stock, a long position (purchased at $20 per share) and a short position (short sale at $35 per share).

If the stock goes up in price, the gain on the long position is offset by the loss on the short position. Similarly, if the stock declines in price, the gain on the short position offsets the losses on the long position. The investor has locked in the capital appreciation of $15 per share ($1500), and because the investor has open positions both long and short, the taxes on the gain are deferred for this year. The next year, the investor can use the 100 shares from the long position to replace the stock borrowed for the short sale, and of course pay the taxes on the gains. Congress has been talking about eliminating this incentive to defer taxes. Check with your accountant or tax advisor as to the status of short-selling against the box before you use this planning technique.

Many technicians are interested in the relationship of short sales to the total number of shares traded, known as the *short interest ratio.* The short interest ratio for the NYSE is calculated by dividing the short interest of the NYSE by the average daily volume on the NYSE for the same period. This ratio can also be calculated for other markets and for individual stocks:

$$\text{Short interest ratio} = \frac{\text{short interest}}{\text{average daily trading volume}}$$

Short interest figures are released in the middle of every month by each of the exchanges. For instance, if the short interest is 22 million for one month on the NYSE and the average daily trading volume in that same month for the NYSE is 20 million shares, the short interest ratio for that month is 1.1 (22 million divided by 20 million).

When the average daily volume is less than the short interest, the ratio is greater than 1. A short interest ratio of between 1 and 1.6 is considered neutral. Technicians regard a ratio greater than 1.6 as a bullish signal. They figure short-sellers will have to cover their positions and buy back the stocks. A ratio of less than 1 is considered bearish. There is some ambiguity to this indicator, since technical analysts believe that with a large short ratio, short-sellers will have to eventually buy back the stocks, which will send stock prices up. On the other hand, short-sellers have shorted the stocks because they think that the stocks are overvalued and will decline in price.

Although this is a popular indicator among technicians, it too is not infallible in predicting market directions, and there does not appear to be any research supporting the use of this technique as an accurate indicator of price movements.

Insider Transactions

Corporate directors, officers, and large shareholders, referred to as insiders, have access to privileged information about their companies and therefore are required by the Securities and Exchange Commission (SEC) to report their purchases and sales of stocks. Insiders know firsthand how the company is doing. If they are purchasing their company's stocks, this is a bullish signal for that stock. Conversely, if insiders sell their stocks, this is a bearish signal.

Insider transactions are reported in the financial newspapers on a weekly basis, and these can be followed using the Internet. On-line brokers may include insider trading transactions in their research.

Many technicians follow insider activity as a method for selecting stocks. Academic studies tend to lend more support to insider transactions as a means of correlating changes in stock prices than to other technical approaches (Jaffe, pp. 410–428 and Zweig, p. 5).

Odd-Lot Theory

The odd-lot theory is concerned with the purchase and sale of securities by small investors. An odd-lot trade consists of fewer than 100 shares, and they are generally placed by small investors. *The Wall Street Journal* reports odd-lot trading on a daily basis, and

Barron's reports it on a weekly basis. Technicians calculate the ratio of odd-lot purchases to odd-lot sales, which has a range from 0.6 to 1.4 (Reilly, p. 334):

$$\text{Odd-lot ratio} = \frac{\text{odd-lot purchases}}{\text{odd-lot sales}}$$

Technicians view small investors as unsophisticated and frequently wrong in their investment decisions. They are viewed to being uninformed about the workings of the market. According to the theory, these small investors are typically buying stocks at the peak of the bull market, which is the time for astute investors (advocates of this theory) to start selling. Similarly, after a stock market decline, the time to buy is when small investors are bailing out of their stock positions.

When the ratio approaches its upper limits (1.4), this means that small investors are buying more than they are selling. This indicates that the stock market is about to turn and become a bear market. In other words, small investors become enthusiastic about the stock market when the market has reached its highs and become disillusioned after a crash in the market, which gives a low reading on the ratio.

There appears to be no validity to the odd-lot theory. In fact, there were times in the mid-1970s and late 1980s when small investors outguessed many of the money managers (Hirt and Block, p. 272).

Investment Advisory Opinions

Technicians who follow the predictions of investment advisors take a contrarian view (do the opposite). When most of the advisors are bullish, technicians become bearish. Similarly, if the majority of advisors become bearish, for technicians this is a buy signal.

It seems strange to think that investment advisors who spend most of their working hours studying the market should be lumped in with the odd-lotters in their assessments of the market. However, with regard to individual stocks, there is some ambiguity because when analysts and advisors make their recommendations, the investing public may never be sure of their underlying reasons for those opinions.

Mutual Fund Cash Position

The cash position of mutual funds is another indicator. By monitoring the cash position of mutual funds, technical analysts can then assess their potential purchasing power. Equity mutual funds hold between 5 and 25 percent of their assets in cash. When mutual funds are fully invested or hold very little of their assets in cash, they have very little purchasing power in the market. However, when they hold larger percentages of their assets in cash (15 percent or higher), their potential purchasing power in the market is significant, which could trigger an upturn in the market (Hirt and Block, p. 278).

TREND METHODS

Some analysts subscribe to the belief that it is more important to identify a trend because trends are more likely to persevere. In other words, once a trend has been identified, you should move with it: in an up market you should be buying, and in a down market you should be selling.

Moving Average

The moving average is one of the most popular methods for determining a trend. An average is the sum of a set of figures divided by the number of figures used in the numerator. A moving average is an average over time. For example, using the closing prices of a stock for a 10-day period, the average is calculated as shown in Table 6-2.

A 10-day moving average would add the stock price for the 11th day and drop the stock price for the first day. For instance, if the closing price on the eleventh day is $18 per share, the new 10-day moving average will be:

10-day moving average =

$$\frac{\text{10-day average} + \text{11th day price} - \text{1st day's price}}{10}$$

$$= \frac{165 + 18 - 15^{3}/_{4}}{10}$$

$$= \$16.725$$

By continuing this method of adding the next day's price and dropping the oldest day's price, the moving average is calculated over time. This moving average can be plotted to show the graphical trend over time and how the moving average compares with the daily prices of the stocks. When the moving average line crosses the line of actual prices, this indicates a change in trend. The moving average line tends to smooth out any volatility in the actual daily stock prices.

You can choose any length of time for a moving average—10, 15, 30, or 200 days. The 200-day moving average is frequently used but can be tedious for the investor to calculate, particularly if a number of stocks are being followed. There would be the daily closing prices for 200 days to record and calculate as well as having to compute a moving average for each stock that is being followed. Many technical analysts provide charts for individual stocks with 200-day moving-average trend lines.

The length of time chosen for the moving average will have an effect on the trend line. A short duration moving average results in greater sensitivity to price changes than a longer duration moving average. With the former, an investor who religiously follows the signals indicated by the frequent crossing of the trend line and the price line will be encouraged to trade stocks after small changes in price. In other words, when the trend line goes up, the investor should buy, and when it turns down, the investor should sell. Thus, with a shorter period moving average, a volatile stock price would encourage the investor to enter and exit the stock frequently, which means both greater transaction costs and amounts paid in income taxes,which could eliminate any profits. With a longer duration moving average, the trend line will exhibit a greater lag behind the actual price line of these stocks.

A study done by James C. Van Horne and G. G. C. Parker (1967) suggests that the use of the moving average as a tool for buying and selling stocks does not produce superior results. Another study (James pp. 35–326) indicates that buying and selling strategies based on moving averages produced lower returns than a buy-and-hold strategy.

The fact that investors need to decide on the time period to use for the moving average and whether they should buy and sell when the lines cross suggests a somewhat arbitrary and simplistic approach to the complexities of buying and selling stocks. If there is a major uptrend in a stock, the investor will profit from it by buying early, and of course the opposite is also true. If a major downtrend is recognized early and the investor sells before the downturn, the investor is ahead of the game. For stocks that exhibit volatility, however, this method can give equivocal signs and encourage frequent trading, which is costly when transaction costs are taken into account.

The moving average for the Dow Jones Industrial Average is used by technicians to determine the trend for the market. Emphasis is placed on the crossover of the daily price to the moving average line as an indicator of a change in trend direction.

STRUCTURAL THEORIES

The structural theories of technical analysis are based on a repetition of previous price patterns. Price patterns are believed to be regular over long periods of time. There are many structural theories, some of which are quite esoteric and literally base their stock market predictions on lunar phases. Although these exotic theories may be colorful and interesting to the reader, the author will stick with the more down-to-earth theories.

Seasonal Patterns

Those who believe in seasonality in the stock market may find patterns, but the use of such knowledge may be limited. For example, in monitoring the Dow Jones Industrial Average on a monthly basis, the statistics show a slight seasonal pattern in December, January, July, and August. Some attribute the seasonal pattern in December and January to tax planning. By December, many investors sell stocks that are depressed in value to produce capital losses that can then be offset against other capital gains. This selling further depresses the prices of these stocks, which presents opportunities for investors to buy them back in January, which results in a surge in their stock prices. This is known as the *January effect*. Historically, the prices of small stocks have risen slightly in January. Gottschalk reported that since 1982, small stocks have increased by 4.2, percent as compared with 3.8 percent for larger stocks in January (pp. C1, C16).

TABLE 6-2

Moving Average

Day	Closing Price
1	$ 15$\frac{3}{4}$
2	16$\frac{1}{4}$
3	17$\frac{1}{2}$
4	15
5	16$\frac{1}{8}$
6	15$\frac{7}{8}$
7	16$\frac{1}{4}$
8	17
9	17$\frac{1}{4}$
10	18
Total	$165

$$\text{Average price} = \frac{165}{10}$$
$$= 16.5$$

The January effect should not be taken too seriously because there are some nagging questions. Which stocks will increase in January? Will these include the stocks in your portfolio?

Investors should not jump for joy over the January effect because the price increases may not cover the costs of trading and may not even involve the stocks that you choose for your portfolio.

The same questions can be asked about *summer rallies* in the markets. Research done by Hugh Johnson, chief investment officer at First Albany, has shown net gains in the Dow Jones Industrial Average from May 31 to August 31 for 21 of the past 33 years (Kansas, p. C1).

Birinyi Associates have found support for this premise with a longer study going back to 1915. There were only four time periods since 1915 when the Dow Jones Industrial Average reported losses in all three summer months—June, July, and August. On average, the gains on the industrial average were reported to be 0.41 percent, 1.31 percent, and 1.06 percent per year respectively, for June, July, and August, over the time period from 1915. Surprisingly, even in 1929, there was a summer rally in which the Dow Jones

Industrial Average surged 11.5 percent in June, 4.8 percent in July, and 9.4 percent in August (Kansas, p. C2).

There is also the *weekend effect:* Stocks peak on Fridays and fall back in price on Mondays. Research over decades shows some validity for this phenomenon (Hirt and Block, p. 475). According to this theory, investors should sell their stocks at the end of the week rather than at the beginning.

Elliott Wave Theory

The premise of this theory is that stock prices move in a five-wave sequence when following the major trend and in a three-wave sequence when moving against the major trend. Long waves can last longer than 100 years, while there are subwaves with rather short durations.

The Elliott Wave Theory gained a following after it was used by technicians to correctly forecast the bull market of the 1980s. However, it lost much of its following when it turned bearish in the late 1980s and early 1990s, missing out on the continuing bull market.

The problem with this structural theory, and with many of the others, is that what is considered to be a wave by some analysts would be considered a subwave by others. The Elliott Wave Theory may be too broadly defined to be conclusive. Its followers often tout the successes of the theory while discounting its failures.

WHAT ARE THE IMPLICATIONS OF TECHNICAL ANALYSIS FOR INVESTORS?

The methods used by technical analysts are an attempt to predict future prices of the markets and individual stocks as well as to determine when to buy and sell. The number of new methods touted by technical analysts keeps growing. Many of these, such as the hemline index, the Superbowl theory, and one day, the possibility of tying in the phases of the moon, have not made it into this book.

So, what is the explanation for technical analysis being successful in identifying future prices of stocks and the markets? First, technical analysts believe that the crowd of investors will always react in the same way. When there is a pattern of rising prices, investors will want to jump into the market (or individual stocks). This will then push prices higher as more investors jump on the bandwagon, causing a self-perpetuating increase in prices. As prices rise, so is there an increase in the enthusiasm and fervor with which the buy recommendations of the technical analysts are touted. This is because technical analysts recommend stocks only when there is a price trend. In essence, they are encouraging us to buy stocks when prices have already gone up, once there is an already established breakout or an upward trend. In other words, investors are being encouraged to buy stocks at high prices. If these stocks do not continue their upward trend, investors might find that they have bought stocks at high prices only to see them turn around and fall to prices below their purchase prices. On the downward trend, technical analysts then initiate their sell recommendations. This means that you are being encouraged to buy at high prices and sell at low prices. This does not sound like a winning formula to make money, let alone to get rich! The other problem is that stocks may take sudden turns in price, which could mean that technical analysts could miss the boat completely in their timed buys and sells.

Take the example of Intel Corporation over the past few months. Intel's stock price has gone up and down over the past six months, from roughly $47 down to the $32 range and then back to $73 on a post-split basis. During this period, technical analysts have come up with many published buy and sell recommendations. If investors were not very nimble in their trades, they might have missed the opportune points to get out of Intel and then get back in. In other words, if they wanted to get back into Intel stock, they might have had to buy the stock back at a higher price than the one at which they sold. By comparison, the buy-and-hold investor would have withstood the downturn in Intel and held it as it recovered from its low point around the mid $30s and ran up to an all-time high of $73 per share. Academic research shows that technical analysts have not been able to outperform the results of a buy-and-hold strategy in the market.

The astute reader might question this conclusion, because every brokerage firm employs not just one technical analyst on their staff, but in some cases many. What about that? There are very good reasons for having technical analysts on staff. Technical analysts read their charts and issue many buy and sell recommendations within short periods of time on the same stock, advocating the active trading of stocks. This generates commissions for brokers and brokerage firms. A buy-and-hold strategy generates only one commission per stock.

From the investor's point of view, a buy-and-hold strategy may not be exciting, but it does economize on taxes. The perpetual trader who is in and out of stocks in periods of less than one year pays taxes on capital gains at ordinary income tax rates. The investor whose holding period is longer than one year pays taxes on long-term capital gains at the lower capital gains rates. Currently, the top marginal ordinary income tax rate is 39.6 percent, whereas the maximum long-term capital gains rate is 20 percent. The buy-and-hold investor does not pay taxes on the gains until the stock is sold. By following the advice of technical analysts, you are bound to generate more commission costs and greater amounts of income taxes, hopefully some profits, too (after the transaction costs and income taxes are deducted).

Let's take a look at some of the holes in technical analysis. The argument put forward by technical analysts is that if there is an established upward trend in a stock, the momentum from buyers in the market will continue to fuel the stock upwards to even more dizzying heights. No attention is paid to the fundamentals of the stock or other reasons why the stock is rising in price or whether it is overvalued. In fact, it does not matter what the name of the stock is and what type of business the company is in. For example, if the stock prices of two different companies in two different industries have the same chart patterns with upward trends, there would be no differentiation in the buy recommendations. Yet we all know that the oil industry has not and generally does not perform in the same way as the health care industry, and that there could well be some fundamental factors which will even affect different companies in the same industry differently. What about the management of the companies? One management group may be more efficient and effective than the other. The charts and chart patterns do not take into account these factors. Neither do they take into account the possibility of change. People often react differently in the future from the way they have acted in the past. Events can change, too. If there is randomness in the market, past patterns will not be effective indicators of future prices.

Technical analysis encourages timing of stocks and the markets. To do so profitably requires a high degree of accuracy. There have been many famous technical analysts who have successfully called the tops and crashes in the markets, but they have not been able to do so consistently. Elaine Garzarelli successfully called the "Black Monday" crash of 1987, but she remained bearish thereafter while the markets went up. To get back into stocks and the market, the reentry points were very much higher than if investors had merely stayed in the market and held their positions during the crash. To successfully time stocks and the markets, you need to be accurate. This implies an intuition approaching clairvoyance, and of course when you have this, you will make so much money on the stock market, you should never have to trade again.

REFERENCES

Glickstein, David, and Rolf Wubbels: "Dow Theory Is Alive and Well," *Journal of Portfolio Management*, Spring 1983, pp. 28–32.

Hirt, Geoffrey A., and Stanley B. Block: *Fundamentals of Investment Management*, 3d ed., Irwin, Homewood, IL, 1990.

Gottschalk, Earl C.: "It's the `January Effect' but Will It Occur in January?," *The Wall Street Journal*, December 14, 1988, pp. C1, C16.

Jaffe, Jeffrey F.: "Special Information and Insider Trading," *Journal of Business*, July 1974, pp. 410–428.

James, Jr., F.E.: "Monthly Moving Averages—An Effective Investment Tool?" *Journal of Financial and Quantitative Analysis*, September 1968, pp. 315–326.

Kansas, Dave: "Analysts Expect Summer Rally, but Nothing Special," *The Wall Street Journal*, June 6, 1994, pp. C1, C2.

Reilly, Frank K.: *Investments*. Dryden Press, Hinsdale, IL, 1982.

Van Horne, James C., and G.G.C. Parker: "The Random Walk Theory: An Empirical Test," *Financial Analysts Journal*, November-December 1967.

Wright, Leonard T.: *Principles of Investments*, 2d ed., Grid, Inc., Columbus, OH, 1977.

Zweig, Martin E.: "Canny Insiders," *Barron's*, June 21, 1976, p. 5.

CHAPTER 7

Buying Strategies

KEY CONCEPTS

- Theories of stock prices
- Implications of the efficient market hypothesis
- Capital asset pricing model
- What about returns?
- Buy-and-hold strategy
- Active investment strategy
- Investment strategies to avoid timing the market
- Implications for investors
- Caveats

The fundamentalist is interested in what a stock is worth, whereas the technician looks only at the historical price and volume records. Fundamentalists look for stocks that are valued below their intrinsic values. They are also not concerned with the reactions of the crowds of investors, as technicians are. This chapter explores the different buying theories of stock prices and examines in greater detail the fundamental and technical approaches to buying stocks.

Many investors believe they can time the markets by buying stocks when the markets are moving up and then selling their stocks before the markets start to decline from their peaks. Many investment advisory newsletters are aimed at these investors, who are known as *market timers*. These newsletters advise their readers when to buy and when to sell their stocks.

Correctly anticipating a correction or a crash can certainly improve the rate of return for an investor. For instance, some newsletters correctly advised their readers to sell their stocks before the stock market crash in 1987, and to buy stocks after the Dow Jones Industrial Average had fallen to its lows for that year. Such a strategy would have increased investors' returns over those who had stayed invested during and after the market crash. However, the trouble with market timing is that if you exit the market at the wrong time, you may not only miss out on stock market gains but also greatly reduce your rate of return.

Over the long term, investors who stay fully invested in the stock market reduce the risk of mistiming the market. This strategy becomes evident in the next section, an examination of the different theories of stock prices.

THEORIES OF STOCK PRICES

In Chapter 5, the *fundamental theory* was discussed, which relates the movement of stock prices to earnings. Anticipating changes in earnings will precipitate changes in stock prices. According to this theory, the astute investor analyzes the fundamentals of the company and their possible effects on future earnings. When future earnings are expected to increase, the stock price will move up in advance of the actual changes in earnings. The belief is that by buying and selling stocks in advance of the actual changes in earnings, investors will increase their profits. In other words, it would be too late to buy stocks after the actual earnings increases are announced, or to sell them after decreases in earnings are announced, because the stock price has already reacted to this news. However, if earnings are expected to continue into the future, investors would continue to buy these stocks.

The fundamental analyst is concerned with the financial characteristics of different stocks in order to find those stocks that are undervalued. When the market price of the stock is less than its intrinsic value (a reflection of estimated earnings multiplied by a price/earnings ratio), the stock is said to be undervalued. If the market price is above the intrinsic value, the stock is overvalued. This theory then implies that the markets are inefficient, which allows large profits to be made from undervalued securities.

What are some of the possible reasons why fundamental analysis may not work? In his book *A Random Walk Down Wall Street*, Burton G. Malkiel, an economics professor at Princeton University, suggests three reasons (p. 124):

- The information collected by the analyst may be based on assumptions and bad information. The analyst may be overly optimistic about assumptions on future sales, cost containment, and earnings, which may not materialize, causing earnings disappointments.

- Second, the analyst may be missing the mark on "value." Analysts may agree that a stock is growing at a certain percentage into the future, but they may be incorrect in their perception of value. For example, there are analysts who agree that Cisco Systems is growing their sales in the double digits into the future with the growth of the Internet, but their assumptions on the future value of Cisco's stock may be incorrect.

- Third, the market may not value the stock in the same way as the analyst. For example, Cisco stock is currently trading at a P/E multiple of 120 times (its earnings), with a growth rate of around 30. The market might view the stock as overvalued, even though analysts still tout the value of Cisco. Instead of going up in price, Cisco may come down, which would bring its P/E multiple down from its current lofty levels.

Fundamental analysis may not always work, and it has been refuted by the efficient market hypothesis, which is discussed later in this section.

Since there are no assurances that stock prices always move in the same direction as earnings over short periods of time, investors may not be able to count on correctly forecasting stock price movements. Moreover, over and above the fundamentals, a multiplicity of conditions and factors affect stock prices.

Technical analysts believe that past price patterns will be repeated into the future, which forms the basis for their recommendations of when to buy and sell stocks. Besides defying logic, technical analysis has little support in the academic investment literature. Not only has the academic world not been kind to technical analysis, but there has also been disdain from supporters of the efficient market hypothesis.

These two theories (fundamental and technical analysis), put forward by the Wall Street investment community, have their limitations, as has been pointed out by various academic studies. Academicians, on the other hand, have their own theories, which they have advanced to explain the movement of stock prices. To recap, at the extremes of this out-and-out war, the Wall Street fundamental analysts believe that individual investors are totally lost without their recommendations and that investors will always underperform the analysts. Academicians, on the other hand, have come up with a number of hypotheses which relate to the dissemination of information, which in turn affects stock prices:

- If information is random, then a randomly selected portfolio chosen by throwing darts at stock companies would do as well as a portfolio carefully selected by analysts.
- If information about stocks is disseminated efficiently, then stock prices will always be fairly valued.
- The capital asset pricing model—another theory—holds that a security's expected return is directly related to its beta coefficient (which is its relationship to the market index).
- A fourth theory is that market information is disseminated inefficiently in the stock market and that stocks with low price-to-book ratios historically have shown greater returns than high price-to-book ratio stocks.

One implication of both fundamental analysis and technical analysis is that the markets are inefficient. By investing in stocks with low P/E ratios or high earnings yields or by purchasing stocks at the low end of their trading ranges, investors expect to receive higher returns. This may occur, but according to the efficient market hypothesis, investors will not be able to consistently outperform the markets by earning abnormally high returns.

Efficient Market Hypothesis

The basic premise of the *efficient market hypothesis* is that the stock markets are efficient. Information about stocks is disseminated throughout the investment community. Thus, if investors and analysts are all using the same public information on stocks, it becomes hard for anyone to generate superior returns. Stock price reflects all the available information, which implies there will be very few mispriced stocks. If a stock is undervalued, investors will quickly buy it, which will drive up the price and hence reduce the returns for subsequent investors. Similarly, overvalued stocks will be sold, which will reduce the price and increase returns for subsequent investors.

In other words, stocks will not be mispriced for long. Stocks will settle at their intrinsic values, which reflect the investment community's consensus about their earnings returns and risks.

The implication of efficient markets is that investors cannot expect to consistently outperform the markets or consistently underperform the markets. On average, investors will do no better or worse than the market averages over an extended period of time with a diversified portfolio of stocks. This is not to say that investors cannot find securities that earn abnormally high returns. For example, investors who bought MCI Corporation's stock at $7 per share in 1984 and sold it (now MCI-WorldCom) at $83 per share in 1999 would have outperformed the markets. The theory of efficient markets implies that investors will not be able to consistently buy stocks such as MCI and earn these kinds of returns over long periods of time.

The question most asked about the efficient market hypothesis is, What is the degree of efficiency in the markets? Obviously, if investors believe the markets are inefficient, they will continue using different techniques and analyses to select those stocks that will produce superior returns. However, if markets are efficient, the value of these techniques and analyses is diminished.

The Degree of Informational Efficiency

There is considerable debate about the degree of efficiency in the markets, and this centers on three forms of the efficient market hypothesis:

- The weak form
- The semistrong form
- The strong form

The degree of market efficiency has important ramifications for investors and the strategies chosen for the selection of their stocks.

The *weak form* of the efficient market hypothesis is not concerned with how the stock price was ascertained. Figure 7-1 illustrates the charts for two stocks, both of which have a current price of $20 per share. The stock of Company X rose from a low of $2 per share to $20, while the stock of Company Y fell from a high of $40 to $20. The weak form of the efficient market hypothesis maintains that past stock prices are independent of future stock prices. In other words, there is no relationship between past and future stock prices. This would make it futile to use the past prices in the chart in Figure 7-1 to determine which stock to buy. Technical analysts would argue that you would not want to buy a stock that has declined from $40 to $20 per share because of the downward trend. They would advocate buying Company X over Company Y because of its trend of going upward from $2 to $20 per share. According to the weak form of market efficiency, stock prices reflect all historical market data. The stock price already includes the price history of the stock, the trading volume, and all the other information that forms the basis for technical analysis.

The weak form suggests that if there is information out there that suggests a stock is undervalued and will increase in the near term, then the stock will react positively if it is indeed undervalued. In other words, stock prices will react to information to exploit any trading opportunities.

Studies testing the weak form of the efficient market hypothesis show that stock prices appear to move independently or in a random fashion due to the dissemination of information (Fama, pp. 34–105). This is also known as the *random walk hypothesis.*

FIGURE 7-1

Historical Price Information in the Weak Form of the Efficient
Market Hypothesis

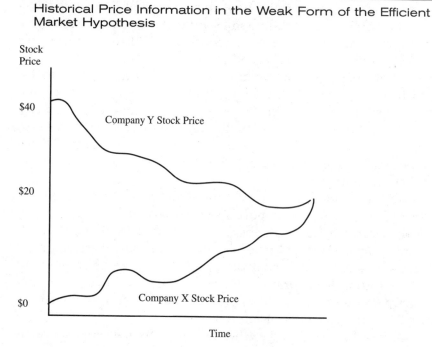

In *A Random Walk Down Wall Street,* Burton G. Malkiel supports the weak form of the efficient market theory by arguing that
investors would do no better or worse than the market averages if
they chose their investments by throwing darts at stock tables. This
is because information about stocks occurs randomly, and then the
stocks react to the news. Bad news will cause the stock to go down
immediately and good news will have an immediate positive effect
on the stock price. Good or bad news on a stock occurs randomly
and investors cannot accurately anticipate this news. This means
that stock prices will move randomly. According to Dremen (1991),
analysts were only accurate 40 percent of the time in forecasting the
next quarter's earnings for companies that they followed. Thus
stocks will react in advance of anticipated good or bad news, and by
the time news is announced, it is already reflected in the stock price.

Every six months, *The Wall Street Journal* publishes results that
compare stocks picked by dart throwers with those picked by

financial analysts. The stock picks of the analysts have outperformed those of the dart throwers to some extent. Does this mean
that the efficient market hypothesis has no validity? Absolutely
not, argue the academicians. According to Burton Malkiel and
Gilbert Metcalf, analysts picked stocks that were riskier than the
market (40 percent more volatile), as opposed to the dart picks,
which were only 6 percent more volatile. The second reason the
results are slanted toward the analysts is the favorable publicity
from the publicity of the competition, which drives up the prices of
the stocks picked by analysts (Dorfman, p. C1). If these advantages
of the analysts were taken away, then the competition would be on
an even footing.

Technical analysts and many on Wall Street dispute the findings of the studies that support the weak form of the efficient market hypothesis. After all, if there is no validity to the weak form,
technical analysts should be able to consistently earn superior
returns by charting and analyzing past stock price information to
predict future stock prices. The weak form, however, does not
directly refute the use of fundamental analysis in selecting stocks
that may produce superior returns.

The second form of the efficient market hypothesis is the *semistrong form*. According to this form, stock prices reflect all relevant
public information. This includes information in all published
reports; analysts' reports; analysts' and brokerage firms' recommendations; press, radio and television reports; and historical information. When a company announces new information, it will be reflected quickly in the stock price. Therefore, analysis of this information
may not produce superior returns. For example, when Dell
announced that its fourth quarter earnings for 1998 would be in line
with analysts' estimates but that its sales growth had dropped from
50 percent to 38 percent, its stock was severely punished. Dell's stock
price reacted quickly after the announcement in after-hours trading
on Instinet, where the stock fell more than 10 percent. In fact, Dell
stock had fallen in anticipation of the news that they would not meet
their expected earnings a few days before the announcement. This is
what the semistrong form of the efficient market hypothesis expects.
However, the door is not completely closed regarding superior
returns. The semistrong theory asserts that superior returns could be
achieved through the analysis of this information, but that over a

period of time, this will not consistently produce superior returns when transaction costs are taken into account.

This conclusion may be quite rational when you consider that analysts and investors are exposed to the same public information. In their competition with each other over changes in information, analysts and investors make the pricing of stocks much more efficient. If there is a perceived change in a stock's value, investors will buy it, moving the price up to its equilibrium value.

Many studies support the validity of the semistrong form of the efficient market hypothesis, which asserts that stock prices change very rapidly to reflect new public information and in many cases anticipate the announcements of the information to the public (Fama et al., pp. 1–21). This study questioned whether investors could earn higher profits from buying stocks that were about to split. The authors found that even though stocks went up in the weeks before the split, when the split was announced, the stocks did not go up any more. To profit from a split, investors would have to buy the stock months before the stock split is announced. This implies that investors could earn superior returns by anticipating any new information before it becomes public and is reflected in the stock price, in other words, by being clairvoyant.

If any institution could outperform the market averages, one would think that it would be the brokerage firms with their many analysts on their payrolls. Dorfman (p. C1) reported that only six of the sixteen major brokerage firms outperformed the 38 percent earned by the S&P 500 Index in 1995.

However, there are some anomalies in the research done on the semistrong form which suggest that some inefficiencies in the market can produce superior returns. These will be discussed after the strong form of market efficiency.

The *strong form* of the efficient market hypothesis reflects not only all public information, but all information that includes insider information. It assumes that the market is highly efficient and that stock prices react very quickly to insider information. If this is so, even corporate insiders will not have information that will benefit them because stock prices will have already reacted to this information. According to this form, no investors or groups of investors who are privy to monopolistic information (insider information) will benefit by earning superior returns because the markets are virtually perfect.

Research does not support the strong form of the efficient market hypothesis. This form has been studied and tested with regard to returns earned by specialists and by insiders using insider information. As discussed in Chapter 4, specialists have a book of orders waiting to be executed at different prices. The specialist buys and sells stocks from his or her own inventory, which means that the specialist has some very valuable information. For example, if there are many unfilled limit orders to buy a stock at $9 per share and the stock is trading at $12, the specialist knows the price will not fall below $9 per share. A study sponsored by the Securities and Exchange Commission reported that specialists earned on average a return of over 100 percent on their capital (SEC, 1971).

Corporate insiders are privy to special information that brings about superior returns. Studies show that insiders achieve greater returns than those expected of a perfect market (Lorie and Niederhoffer, pp. 35–53). Insiders are defined as officers and directors of a company and those shareholders who own at least 10 percent of a company's stock.

Insiders are privy to information that has not been made available to the public. Hence, there is a fine line distinguishing legal and illegal use of this information. Corporate insiders have access to privileged information but are not allowed to use this information to make profits or to engage in short-term trading (six months or less). They are allowed to trade and make profits on the stock on a long-term basis, and their trades must be reported to the SEC.

Despite the fact that specialists and insiders are able to earn superior returns, which refutes the strong form of the efficient market hypothesis, there is support for the strong form based on the performance of mutual fund managers. Mutual fund managers receive information faster than the investing public, yet they have not been able to consistently outperform the market averages (Hirt and Block, p. 285).

The difference can be summed up as follows: The use of privileged (monopolistic) information can help generate superior returns, but the use of publicly available information will not likely assist in earning superior returns on a consistent basis.

WHAT ARE THE IMPLICATIONS OF THE EFFICIENT MARKET HYPOTHESIS FOR INVESTORS?

The question for investors is how efficient is the market? If there are investment strategies that can consistently beat the market averages over long periods of time, then the markets are inefficient. The next logical question then is, What is the degree of inefficiency? If we start with the extremes of the theory, as shown in Figure 7-2, we can then move back toward the center of the argument with the more debatable aspects of the degrees of inefficiency.

If the market is truly efficient, then no information will be of any use to investors, not even monopolistic information. If this is the case, the only way investors will beat the markets is to watch for astrological signals of the alignment of the planets for cues on when to buy and sell stocks. From the many studies available, we know that the market is not absolutely efficient because there have been cases of investors beating the markets.

At the other extreme, if the market is totally inefficient, then all information is useful. We know this doesn't work, because all the analysts and investors who analyze all information have not been able to consistently earn returns in excess of the market averages. Thus, we are left with the question of how efficient the market is in processing information.

Readers who are averse to number crunching can give a sigh of relief that they can save all those hours given to analyzing financial statements for numbers on sales, earnings, and growth of a company. Readers who prefer the visual, pictorial information do

---

FIGURE 7-2

Degrees of Efficiency of Information in the Stock Market

Inefficient Market	Weakly Efficient	Semistrongly Efficient	Strongly Efficient	Totally Efficient
All information is useful.	Historic information is not useful.	Historic and public information is not useful.	Historic, public, and private information is not useful.	No information is useful.

not have to waste the gas in their cars by going out to buy graph paper to plot charts.

According to the weak and semistrong forms of the efficient market hypothesis, the use of technical and fundamental analysis will not produce superior returns on a consistent basis. This may be disconcerting to investors, but what about the technical and fundamental analysts, whose occupations are deemed worthless, null, and void? It is no wonder Wall Street has not embraced the efficient market hypothesis.

The two sure ways, it seems, to earn abnormal returns are to obtain insider information or to become a specialist. I am not suggesting by any means that you should break into the headquarters of various corporations to gain access to their privileged information! Neither should you throw up your existing profession to become a specialist.

The theory suggests that all information is incorporated into the price of the stock and that stocks with good fundamentals will be bid up in price to reflect this. Similarly, stocks that are in trouble will be sold. In other words, there will be no undervalued or overvalued stocks.

If there is an even chance of stocks rising and falling due to new information, it doesn't matter which stocks you choose, or for that matter which stocks anyone else chooses. The random walk theory implies pure luck in picking stocks.

The efficient market hypothesis is hotly debated and the jury of academicians is still undecided on the degree of efficiency of the market. Even though the efficient market hypothesis has not aroused the enthusiasm of most investors, the implications are important because they effectively challenge any thoughts of creating overnight wealth in the stock market.

The efficient market hypothesis suggests that few investors will consistently beat the market averages over a long period of time. For example, if the market increases by 10 percent over a one-year period, most investors will not earn more than 10 percent, on average. In fact, most investors will earn less than the market averages because of the transaction costs and fees charged. However, this does not mean there won't be investors who do very much worse than 10 percent or who earn abnormally high returns.

The following are some anomalies within the efficient market hypothesis in which investors have been able to generate superior returns to beat the market:

- **Small Stocks.** A study done by Arbel and Strebel suggests that the undervalued stocks of small companies that have been neglected by the investment community may provide greater returns than the market averages. Analysts do not cover many of the small firms due to the larger perceived risks for their portfolios. This lack of attention does not drive prices up on these neglected small companies, which then tend to outperform the larger company stocks. This suggests that the securities markets may not be equally efficient.

- **Low P/E Ratio Stocks.** Studies done by Basu show that portfolios of stocks with low P/E ratios have outperformed portfolios of stocks with high P/E ratios on a risk-adjusted and non-risk-adjusted basis. This refutes the semistrong form of the efficient market hypothesis because P/E ratios of stocks can be obtained from publicly available information.

  Benjamin Graham, who did the pioneering work that forms the basis of fundamental analysis, realized that markets were becoming more efficient, thus making it more difficult to find undervalued stocks. Table 7-1 lists Graham's guidelines for selecting stocks. (One of his guidelines was to select low P/E ratio stocks.) The greater the number of yes answers, the more ideal the stock choice, according to Graham's model.

- There are other possible market anomalies that suggest inefficiencies in the market which could result in superior returns. One of these is the *January effect*, which asserts that stocks that have done poorly in December may produce superior returns in January.

These anomalies should not lead investors to think that the markets are inefficient. Rather, they should be viewed as exceptions. Academic studies lend support for the weak and semistrong forms of the efficient market hypothesis, which in turn lends support to

TABLE 7-1

Benjamin Graham's Guidelines of Stocks to Buy

Rewards

1. Is the P/E ratio less than half the reciprocal of the AAA corporate bond yield? For example, the current AAA yield is 7.34 percent and the reciprocal is 13.62 percent (1 ÷ .0734). The P.E ratio of the stock would have to be less than 6.81 (1/2 × .1362) to be bought.
2. Is the P/E ratio less than 40 percent of the average P/E of the stock over the past five years?
3. Is the dividend yield equal to or more than two-thirds the AAA corporate bond yield? Two-thirds of the current AAA corporate bond yield of 7.34 percent is 4.88 percent. In order to rate the stock a buy, the dividend yield should equal or be greater than 4.88 percent.
4. Is the stock price less than two-thirds of the book value of the stock?
5. Is the price less than two-thirds of the net current asset value per share?

Risks

1. Is the debt-to-equity ratio less than one? The total debt of the company should be less than the total equity.
2. Is the current ratio equal to two or more? The total current assets divided by the total current liabilities should equal two or more.
3. Is the total debt less than twice the net current assets?
4. Is the 10-year average EPS growth rate greater than 7 percent?
5. Were there no more than two years out of the past 10 with earnings declines of greater than 5 percent?

Source: Paul Sturm, "What if Benjamin Graham Had a P.C.?" *Smart Money*, March 1994, p.32.

the conclusion that very few investors outperform the markets over long periods of time. For investors who feel the efficient market hypothesis is not equally efficient with regard to the pricing of the smaller, less-known stocks, there is a role for fundamental analysis.

CAPITAL ASSET PRICING MODEL (CAPM)

The 1990 Nobel Prize laureates for economics, Harry Markovitz and William Sharpe, have done work on the financial markets that has had a profound effect on investors.

Harry Markovitz's work pioneered what is now known as *modern portfolio theory*. Concerned with the composition of investments that investors would select for their portfolios, Markovitz determined that the major properties of an investment of concern to investors are risk and return. By choosing a range of different investments for a portfolio, investors are able to determine and control the total risk in that portfolio through variance analysis of each investment. In other words, in plain English, investors can assemble portfolios of risky stocks in which the risks of the whole portfolio are less than the risks of any of the individual stocks in the portfolio.

A simple example can illustrate this concept. Let's say we have a portfolio with equal amounts invested in two stocks, a computer-related technology stock and a food stock. In good economic times, when computer sales are growing, the technology stock is expected to go up in price by more than 50 percent, while the food stock has an expected return of 6 percent, including the dividend. During a recession, when computer sales are in the doldrums, the technology stock is expected to decline by 20 percent. The food stock, however, being in a defensive industry, is expected to go up by 40 percent. Thus, in a good economy, the investors will earn an average return of 28 percent [(50% + 6%) ÷ 2]. In a recession, the portfolio will earn an average return of 10% [(40% −20%) ÷ 2].

While the technology stock is more risky than the food stock, by diversifying into two different industries, the average returns are greater than if all the funds were invested in one stock. Besides reducing risk by increasing the number of stocks, risk can be further reduced by choosing stocks that react differently to economic conditions.

William Sharpe and John Lintner further developed Markovitz's approach into what they called the capital asset pricing model (CAPM). In this model, the risk of portfolio theory is broken down into two parts: systematic risk and unsystematic risk.

Sharpe's theory is that risk and return are related, but the total risk of a stock is not that important. The risks pertaining to the security itself (such as business and financial risk) can be reduced or eliminated through diversification. What remains is the systematic risk, which becomes important in the relationship between risk and return. In other words, by combining several different stocks in a portfolio, the *unsystematic* or *diversifiable* risk is reduced and all that is left is the systematic risk. *Systematic risk,* also known as *market risk,* is the relationship of the security's price to changes in security prices in the general market. Some stocks will go up and down more than the market, and other stocks might fluctuate less than the market as a whole. Systematic risk is measured by the Greek letter *beta.* A stock with a beta coefficient of one means that if the market rises by 20 percent, the stock will go up in price by 20 percent. Similarly, if the market falls by 20 percent, the stock will see a 20 percent decline in price. The market itself is assumed to have a beta coefficient of 1, which means that this stock is perfectly correlated with the market. A stock with a beta coefficient greater than one should produce above-average returns in a bull market and below-average returns in a bear market. A stock with a beta coefficient of less than one will be less responsive to market changes. Most stocks have beta coefficients ranging from 0.6 to 1.6 (Martin, p. 102). Investors who seek higher returns will, therefore, need to be willing to assume more risk.

Increased diversification into many different stocks in a portfolio will not eliminate the systematic risk. In other words, these stocks will not be immune to a downturn in the market. However, diversification into at least 20 different stocks can eliminate the unsystematic risks, which are the risks that pertain to the company itself. These are financial, business, and purchasing power risks.

The key to this model is that in a rising market, by investing in stocks with higher beta coefficients than the market, investors should increase their potential returns. In a down market, investors should invest in lower-than-market beta coefficient stocks to minimize their potential losses. In other words, you can beat the market averages by following this strategy. This theory was adopted enthusiastically on Wall Street, and now, investors can find beta coefficients quoted on stocks from Value Line and many of the Internet research Websites.

Sharpe's model has evoked much debate and controversy. One theory from the CAPM is that the selection of high beta stocks in a portfolio is likely to produce above-average returns in a bull market and below-average returns in a bear market. Studies done to test the validity of the CAPM showed the following (Malkiel, pp. 243–255):

- There was some unsystematic risk that caused zero-beta securities to have higher returns.

- The risk-return relationship turned out to be different from that of the CAPM theory. Low-risk stocks earned higher returns than expected, and high-risk stocks earned lower returns than expected.
- For shorter-term periods, there were deviations from the relationships predicted by the CAPM.
- There was a problem estimating beta coefficients based on past sensitivity to the market. These relationships change, and there are other factors that need to be considered in determining the beta coefficient.

There is no perfect measure of risk, which means that there is still an active search by academicians for ways to assess a measure of risk and to look for ways to correlate this to returns. The assumption from these tests of the CAPM is that investors cannot outperform the market, but through managing the risks of the stocks in the portfolio, they can forecast returns that may be correlated to the market.

WHAT ABOUT RETURNS?

Many studies have been conducted looking at the behavior of the market and those stocks with the greatest returns. A study done by professors Eugene Fama and Kenneth French turns upside down the axiom: *The greater the risk, the greater the return,* always taught in finance classes. Their study showed that low-risk stocks—which are value stocks, or those with high book values relative to their market values—which were expected to perform poorly, outperformed high-risk stocks over the 27-year period from 1963 to 1990. High-risk stocks—or growth stocks, which have low book values relative to their market values—underperformed low-risk stocks over the same 27-year period, contrary to accepted wisdom.

They classified the stocks in their study into 10 deciles according to their book-to-market ratios. Stocks with the highest book-to-market ratios had average monthly returns of 1.65 percent, while stocks with the lowest book-to-market ratios had average monthly returns of only 0.72 percent. This is akin to the value versus growth stock competition. Wall Street analysts expect growth stocks to out-perform value stocks, but this study negates that finding.

Looking at the performance of stocks over the three years from 1996 to 1998, we have seen the large growth stocks in the Standard & Poor's 500 Index outperform the value stocks over the same period. These growth stocks have had strong records of performance, and stock investors have bid them up to very high price levels. Dell Computer and Cisco Systems, for example, trade at lofty multiples of earnings, reflecting investors' high future price expectations. Dell announced that their fourth-quarter revenues for 1998 had fallen from 50 percent to 38 percent, which resulted in the stock being punished by more than a 10 percent drop. Value stocks have low expectations with regard to return on sales, return on equity, asset growth, equity growth, and market-to-book value. Consequently, total return expectations for these stocks are low. Clayman (p. 58) identified growth stocks and value stocks in 1980 and then tracked their performance in the years 1981 through 1985. What she found was that the rate of growth and book value fell by half for the growth stocks, while the value stocks showed substantial improvement. If investors had invested $100 each in the value and growth portfolios, they would have earned $297.50 in the value portfolio versus $181.60 in the growth portfolio for the 1981–1985 period.

This study provides the investor an alternative to chasing the overvalued growth stocks with their lofty multiples. Consequently, it might be a good time to sell some of these growth stocks, some of which are trading at 100-plus P/E multiples, and switch to value stocks, which are currently trading at below-market multiples, such as John Deere, with a P/E ratio of 7; Ford Motor, with a P/E of 12; and other low-expectation blue-chip stocks.

As might be expected, security analysts have not really embraced these academic theories, especially the efficient market hypothesis. Their view is that academicians are so immersed in their own research that they would not be able to recognize an undervalued stock, even if it was brought to their attention. The ongoing battle between the analysts and the academicians is of little importance. What is important to individual investors, however, is an awareness of these theories from the practical point of view.

The investor's view of the degree of efficiency of the market will determine the investor's strategy with regard to the selection of stocks and the length of time to hold these stocks. If the investor believes that the market is efficient and that all information is reflected in the price of the stock, the strategy might be to select quality stocks with good future earnings and hold these stocks for long periods of time (a buy-and-hold strategy). On the other end of the spectrum, if the investor believes that the markets are inefficient, he or she can use technical analysis to determine which stocks to buy and sell over shorter periods of time, and fundamental analysis to select undervalued stocks to buy and hold for longer periods of time. The degree of efficiency is debatable; the ultimate decision is the investor's.

The Capital Asset Pricing Model suggests that investors diversify their investments to eliminate unsystematic risk. The returns earned by most investments will be consistent with those earned by the market and the related amount of risk. Bearing this in mind, the investment strategy that is chosen should be in keeping with the investor's objectives.

There appear to be no sure ways to consistently beat the markets over long periods of time. There are many anomalies to the efficient market theories, but these have not consistently held up for long periods of time to earn abnormal returns. This is due to the competitive nature of the markets. The easy winners have already been bought and the money has been made. At the other extreme, an overwhelming support of the efficient market hypothesis paralyzes the investor into thinking that all research is of no consequence. Investors can make their own decisions regarding what they believe and what they think will work for them based on their philosophies, which will lead to their choice of portfolio management styles. It is probably the case that the markets are fairly efficient, but there are still opportunities to exploit certain stocks using a creative and intelligent approach.

ACTIVE VERSUS PASSIVE INVESTMENT STRATEGIES

The debate over the degree of efficiency of the markets has resulted in the following:

- *Passive* strategies, suggested by efficient markets
- *Active* strategies, suggested by inefficient markets

The Buy-and-Hold Investment Strategy

The buy-and-hold investment strategy is a passive strategy based on the premise that over long periods of time, the returns on common stocks will exceed the returns earned from other investments, such as bonds and money market securities, and on the fact that historically, stock markets have always increased in value. The object of a buy-and-hold strategy is to do as well as the market. There is no attempt to beat the market. By holding a broadly diversified portfolio, which reduces the unsystematic risks, you should be able to approximate the returns of the market. Stocks in the portfolio are selected and held for the long term. There are very few revisions made to the portfolio, and no attempts are made to time the markets. The success of this type of strategy depends on the state of the market.

During an upward trend in the market, such as the decade of the 1990s, a buy-and-hold strategy will benefit most investors. Of course, in a market correction or crash, prices of most stocks will decline. However, after most stock market declines, the markets historically have recovered and moved on to greater heights.

It is always wonderful to hear the feats of investors who are able to time the markets, sell their portfolios days before a stock market crash, and then move back into the market at a lower level. However, few investors like to tell the story of how they exited the market in anticipation of a crash that never materialized. This might mean sitting on the sidelines during a bull market or reentering the market at a higher level.

The buy-and-hold strategy avoids the need to time the markets or read the financial stock tables in the newspapers on a daily basis. With a long time horizon, there is no need to time the markets because the investor remains fully invested in stocks.

The second advantage of a buy-and-hold strategy is that transaction costs are minimized. Similarly, the cost of acquiring information is avoided. This does not mean stocks that are bought are forgotten about. With a buy-and-hold strategy, investors should still review from time to time (year to year) the performance of their stocks with regard to growth in sales and earnings, and get rid of those stocks that do not present future potential growth and earnings.

Indexing is a concept that embodies the buy-and-hold strategy, thereby minimizing the transaction costs due to the passive investment strategy. By choosing a market index, such as the S&P 500 or the Dow Jones Industrial Average, and choosing the same stocks in that index for the portfolio, an investor replicates the performance of the market index. It may be difficult for individual investors to replicate these indexes due to the large numbers of stocks in them (500 for the S&P Index) and hence the enormous dollar cost. There are index mutual funds, discussed in Chapter 9, which make it easier than to invest in all the stocks of the specific indexes. In fact, index mutual funds have outperformed the many actively managed mutual funds over the past four years. Longer periods of time show a more compelling result:

	Amount Invested 1982	Amount Jan. 1999
Vanguard S & P Index Fund	$10,000	$193,550
Actively Managed Equity Fund	$10,000	$114,300

Source: Anne Tergesen and Peter Coy, "Who Needs A Money Manager?" *Business Week,* February 22, 1999, p. 127.

Although the buy-and-hold strategy minimizes the timing decisions of when to buy and sell, investors still need to decide which stocks to select. By approximating an index, the types of stocks to choose becomes an easy matter. Which index to follow would depend on the investor's overall objectives. A conservative investor who is looking for income and capital preservation would consider blue-chip stocks, utility stocks, and some of the more established growth stocks. A more aggressive investor would include growth stocks and the small-capitalized company stocks.

Investors who believe the market to be efficient would choose stocks from various industries to form a diversified portfolio and hope to replicate the performance of the market. According to the efficient market hypothesis, these stocks could be randomly selected because if the markets are efficient, these stocks would be correctly valued (at their intrinsic value). Efficient markets support passive investment strategies; inefficient markets suggest actively managed investment strategies.

With a buy-and-hold strategy, investors can take advantage of the *dividend reinvestment plans* (DRIPs) that many companies offer. Companies with DRIPs allow their existing shareholders to choose whether they want to automatically reinvest their cash dividends in additional shares of the company's stock. Brokerage fees can be avoided this way, but some companies assess a handling fee (which is generally less than the brokerage fees). In order to encourage shareholders to sign up for these dividend reinvestment plans, many companies are willing to issue fractional shares as well as to sell their stock at small discounts to the current market price. It is important to examine the fees charged by companies. Some companies charge excessive fees, and their dividend reinvestment plans should be avoided.

The advantage of DRIPs to shareholders is that they act as a forced savings plan in that dividends are automatically reinvested to accumulate more shares. This is particularly good for investors who are not disciplined savers.

The disadvantage of a dividend reinvestment plan is that shareholders need to keep their records of the additional shares purchased for tax purposes. These dividends are taxable income to investors whether they are received in cash or automatically reinvested in additional shares. However, when the additional shares are sold, the cost (purchase price) will be used to determine whether there is a capital gain or loss for tax purposes.

Active Investment Strategy

Timing the market accurately will always produce superior returns. This strategy involves buying stocks before they go up in price. In other words, you would be fully invested in stocks in an increasing market and out of stocks in a decreasing market. There are many newsletters that advocate timing the market. In timing the markets, you have to be accurate not only in calling the top of the market but also the bottom, that is, when to get back into the market.

The greatest disadvantage to timing is that there is very little margin for error in the accuracy of your calls on the market. If you are correct 50 percent of the time, you will earn less than if you pursued a buy-and-hold strategy, according to a study done by T. Rowe Price and Associates in 1987 (Cheyney and Moses, p. 19). During the period from 1926 to 1983, investors who were 100 percent accurate in their timing decisions would have earned an average of 18.2 percent per year versus an 11.8 percent average yearly return for a buy-and-hold strategy. With a 50 percent accuracy rate in calling the market, the return was 8.1 percent. Thus, to earn returns in excess of the market, investors would have had to be accurate more than 70 percent of the time in calling the market during this period (Cheyney and Moses, p. 19).

Technical analysis charts the past price movements of stocks to time when to buy and sell stocks, and advocates timing the overall market and individual stocks.

Fundamental analysis also advocates timing but with a longer time horizon and a more critical eye concerning which stocks to buy and sell.

Inefficient or weakly efficient markets suggest that investors may be able to earn returns in excess of the markets by pursuing active investment strategies. The downside to timing the markets is that you could be on the sidelines during an increasing market if a wrong call is made.

INVESTMENT STRATEGIES THAT AVOID TIMING THE MARKETS

Many investors use formula plans to avoid having to time the markets. These plans eliminate the need for timing, but investors still need to select their stocks to buy and sell when using these plans. By buying shares of stocks over a period of time at different prices, investors will lessen the impact of price fluctuations. Bear in mind that if the markets plummet, these methods will not result in investors not losing money. These methods keep investors in the markets whether the market is going up or down.

Three plans are discussed below.

Dollar Cost Averaging

Dollar cost averaging is a method of investing the same amount of money at regular intervals over a long period of time. This strategy can be used for stocks, bonds, and mutual funds. Most people build their portfolios over time, which means that by investing amounts at different times, they are avoiding the risks of putting all their money into stocks at one point in time. By consistently investing the same amount in a security at regular periods of time, the average cost of the security will be lower than the high price of the security for the period and higher than the low price for the period. Table 7-2 shows the dollar cost averaging method when $1000 is invested every month to purchase the stocks of Company X. The example assumes that fractional shares may be purchased, and commissions are ignored.

In January, $1000 is invested at $7 per share, resulting in 142.86 shares being purchased. The price of the stock goes up in February to $8 per share, which means that the same amount ($1000) will buy fewer shares (125.00) than in January. Conversely, when the price of the stock goes down to $6.75 in May, more shares are purchased (148.15) with the same investment dollars ($1000).

Over the 12-month period, $12,000 is invested to purchase a total of 1467.36 shares. The average cost per share is $8.18. In this example, an investor would lose money if the price falls below $8.18 and would make money when the stock price is above the average cost per share when selling. This average cost per share is $0.09 less than the average price per share during the 12-month period. Part of the reason for this is that during the months when the price per share is low, more shares are purchased for the same dollar amount. Thus, with fluctuating stock prices, the average cost per share will always be lower than the average price per share.

This does not mean that investors will always make a profit by using dollar cost averaging. If the price of the stock keeps going down, the average cost per share will still be lower than the average price per share, but the investor will lose money if the shares are sold at a declining price.

Advantages of Dollar Cost Averaging

- Investors avoid having to time the market.
- Investors can use this method to systematically add to positions in a stock over a long period of time, which will average out the fluctuations in the stock's price.

TABLE 7-2

Dollar Cost Averaging

	Investment	Price per Share	Number of Shares Purchased
January	$1,000	$7.00	142.86
February	1,000	8.00	125.00
March	1,000	9.00	111.11
April	1,000	7.50	133.33
May	1,000	6.75	148.15
June	1,000	7.75	129.03
July	1,000	8.00	125.00
August	1,000	9.00	111.11
September	1,000	9.50	105.26
October	1,000	9.00	111.11
November	1,000	8.75	114.29
December	1,000	9.00	111.11
	Total Invested	**Average Price**	**Total Shares Bought**
	$12,000	$8.27	1467.36

Average cost per share = total invested ÷ total no. of shares bought
= $12,000/1467.36
= 8.18

- Participating in a dividend reinvestment plan in conjunction with dollar cost investing enhances the benefits over a long period of time.

Disadvantages of Dollar Cost Averaging

- Transaction costs are higher using dollar cost averaging to purchase shares on a systematic basis.
- The use of the dollar cost averaging method to buy stocks requires large amounts of money for the regular payments needed to receive the lower commissions of buying shares in round lots over 100 shares. By investing smaller amounts, investors buy shares in odd lots (less than 100

shares), which means that transaction costs are higher. The total transaction costs will also be larger than if the shares were purchased in one or two transactions rather than 12. Dollar cost averaging works well with no-load mutual funds where there are no transaction fees.

- With a rising stock price, the use of dollar cost averaging will result in a higher average cost per share than if the total amount was invested at the beginning of the period.

- When shares are sold, the calculation for the tax basis of the shares is complicated for most investors. This requires keeping records of all transactions and may require the use of a tax professional to compute the gains or losses for tax purposes. The success of dollar cost averaging requires sticking to the plan and investing, particularly when the stock price falls. However, from time to time, investors should evaluate the stock with regard to its overall performance. A stock that is going downhill with no bright prospects should be viewed as a sunk cost, and an investor should sell it rather than sink more money into a bad investment. Thus, dollar cost averaging does not alleviate the decision regarding which stocks to buy and sell.

Constant Dollar Plan

The constant dollar investment plan requires an investment of a fixed dollar amount in a portfolio of stocks, bonds, or mutual funds. The constant dollar plan works well when the total investment dollars available are split into two parts: an amount going to the more speculative portion of the portfolio and the rest invested in more conservative investments. This fixed dollar amount is maintained by either buying or selling stocks.

For example, assume you have a total portfolio of $100,000, of which you want to keep $50,000 invested in stocks and the rest in bonds and money market securities. When the value of the stock portfolio increases to an upper limit set by you, stocks would be sold off so that the stock portfolio is reduced to a total market value of $50,000. Assume that the upper limit is $60,000. When the value of the stock portfolio reaches $60,000, $10,000 in stocks would be sold to reduce the portfolio to $50,000. The $10,000 would be invested in bonds and money market securities. If the stock portfolio declines to the lower limit set, stocks will be added to increase the value of the portfolio to $50,000. This type of plan forces investors to take profits when the upper target amount is reached and to buy more shares when the lower target amount is reached.

This method of investing works well for investors who do not tolerate risk well. By maintaining a fixed dollar amount in stocks and transferring the excess profits from stocks into more conservative investments, conservative investors can still pursue the growth objective for their portfolios.

However, if stocks keep increasing in price, this plan will not do as well as a buy-and-hold strategy. The return will be lower for a constant dollar plan. Similarly, if the stocks chosen for a constant dollar plan do not fluctuate very much in price, they will not enhance the value of the total portfolio. This plan will do well with stocks that fluctuate in price along with those that have good long-term appreciation potential.

Thus, not only does the investor have to take care in selecting securities for this plan, he or she must also make decisions about how much to set for the target dollar amount, as well as for the upper and lower limits. A conservative investor might allocate too small an amount to stocks, which may result in that investor not being able to fulfill the growth objective set for the total investment portfolio. On the other hand, if a greater dollar amount is allocated to stocks, such an investor may have sleepless nights. A more aggressive, growth-oriented investor will allocate a greater dollar amount to the stock portfolio.

Setting the upper and lower limits mitigates the timing decisions of when to buy and sell the stocks, but should these upper and lower limits be 5, 10, 15, 20, or 30 percent of the dollar plan? If the percentages set are too small, investors may be churning their stocks without getting the benefits of large runups in the stocks or being able to average down when the stocks fall in price. If the percentage limits are too high, the portfolio will not turn over the excess profits generated to the more conservative investments. After a period of time, the upper and lower dollar limits should be reassessed.

There is also reinvestment risk to consider. The money from the excess profits from the stock portfolio can be reinvested in bonds or money market securities, but that may provide a lower return than if the money had been left in stocks.

Advantages of a Constant Dollar Plan

- The plan is beneficial to conservative, risk-averse types of investors who can afford to limit the amount of their total portfolio that is invested in stocks.
- The plan increases the value of the total portfolio when the prices of the stocks rise in value.
- Once the upper and lower limits are set, the timing decision of when to buy and sell stocks is alleviated.

Disadvantages of a Constant Dollar Plan

- In a bull market, the constant dollar plan will not do as well as a buy-and-hold strategy.
- Investors are faced with the risk of having to reinvest the proceeds from the sale of stocks into other investments that may produce lower returns.

The Constant Ratio Plan

The constant ratio plan is an asset allocation plan that establishes fixed percentages to the different types of securities. An example of a constant ratio plan is an allocation of, say, 50 percent to stocks, 40 percent to bonds, and 10 percent to cash (money market securities).

The percentages allocated to the different types of investments are determined by the investor's objectives and risk tolerance. A conservative, risk-averse investor who is approaching retirement and needs income might use the following allocation:

25 percent to stocks
70 percent to bonds
5 percent to money market securities

A younger investor, seeking growth in a portfolio, would allocate a greater percentage to stocks (for example, 80 percent to stocks, 15 percent to bonds, and 5 percent to money market securities).

Once the investor has decided on the percentages to apportion to the different types of investments, the next step is to determine the trigger points, or percentages, for when to rebalance the portfolio. For example, in a portfolio of $100,000, with 50 percent allocated to stocks and 50 percent to bonds, the amounts in the different portfolios will change over time and the investor will need to decide when to rebalance. If stocks increase to $60,000 and bonds decrease to $45,000, the constant ratio is no longer 50:50. The rebalancing decision can be on a timely basis—every quarter, every six months, or every year—based on percentage limits (10 percent, 20 percent, etc.). If the 20 percent limit is chosen for the stock portfolio, rebalancing will occur when the stock portfolio increases to $60,000 (20 percent of $50,000) or drops to $40,000 (80 percent of $50,000).

From a total portfolio standpoint, if the total value of the portfolio has increased to $105,000, with the stock portion accounting for $60,000, or 57 percent, the stock portion will need to be decreased. To rebalance the portfolio, the investor would sell $7500 of stocks to reduce the total stock value to $52,500, which is 50 percent of the total portfolio of $105,000. The $7500 would be added to the bond portfolio to bring that percentage back up to 50.

As with the constant dollar plan, the long-run expectation is that the stock portfolio will increase in value. When this occurs, stocks will be sold to rebalance the portfolio and increase the amounts invested in more conservative investment sectors.

If stocks in the portfolio decline while the bond portfolio appreciates, bonds will be sold off to provide funds to purchase more stock.

Advantages of the Constant Ratio Plan

- Investors can change their asset allocation plans to meet changes in personal objectives as well as changes in the state of the markets.

- Over the long term, when stocks and/or bonds increase, the value of the total portfolio will increase.
- Profits can be taken when the stocks and bonds appreciate to set limits or on a time basis.

Disadvantages of the Constant Ratio Plan

- A constant ratio plan may not produce the greatest returns. Losses may be realized in declining stock and bond markets.
- Investors need to select the stocks and bonds for these portfolios that will meet their objectives. However, this plan does eliminate the timing decision of when to buy and sell.
- Investors face reinvestment risk when securities are sold and reinvested in other securities to rebalance the portfolio.

IMPLICATIONS FOR INVESTORS

There are formula plans and investment strategies for buying and selling stocks, but there are no magic plans for beating the market. Some investment strategies have produced superior returns to those earned by the stock market as a whole over various time periods. However, over long periods of time, it becomes difficult to consistently beat the market.

Investors still need to decide which stocks to invest in, in addition to deciding when to buy and sell. Fundamental analysis provides an insight into the makeup of the company and the industry, which may be helpful in the selection of stocks for the long term. Technical analysis uses past price and volume information as well as charting to determine when to buy and sell stocks.

The efficient market hypothesis (EMH) renders technical analysis a waste of time because, according to the EMH, past stock prices reflect all available information. Therefore, the movements of past stock prices have no relationship to future prices. This version of the efficient market hypothesis is called the weak form.

The semistrong form of the EMH suggests that there are no undervalued or overvalued stocks because all *public* information is reflected in the stock price. This is a kick in the teeth for the fundamental analysts.

The strong form of the EMH implies that the markets are perfect. They have digested *all* information pertaining to the stock's value.

There is little evidence to support the strong form, but there is some evidence of inefficiencies in the market that support the semistrong form, particularly with regard to small stocks that have been ignored by the fundamental analysts. After all, competition among the fundamental analysts helps make the market more efficient, which lends support to the semistrong form.

The capital asset pricing model differentiates risk in a portfolio into two parts: systematic and unsystematic risk. A diversified portfolio of stocks will eliminate only the unsystematic risk, which leaves the portfolio exposed to systematic risk. Thus, in order to earn higher returns in the market, investors need to invest in stocks with higher beta factors (coefficients measuring the systematic, or market risk) than the market.

These theories are important for three reasons:

- Investors will not consistently earn superior returns over those of the stock market for long periods of time.
- Diversification of a portfolio can reduce the overall risks of the portfolio.
- The way to increase returns is to invest in riskier securities. However, if the market heads south, the riskier securities will decline by more than the averages of the market. Other studies, however, such as the one by Fama and French (1992), show the opposite, that the lowest-risk securities outperform the highest-risk securities.

This then emphasizes the importance of the construction of a portfolio of investments that is compatible with the investor's overall level of risk tolerance. This can be accomplished through diversification, which can eliminate some of the risk. Furthermore, returns can be improved through the reduction of taxes, investment fees, and commissions.

Tax planning can reduce taxes and increase returns to some extent. At present, long-term capital gains (securities held for longer than one year that are sold at more than their original purchase price) are taxed at lower rates than the higher marginal tax rates for ordinary income and gains (investments held for less than one year). Capital gains become much more important than ordinary income for high tax bracket investors.

Capital losses result when stocks are sold for less than their original purchase prices. For tax purposes, gains and losses are netted out. Net short-term capital gains are taxed at the same rates as ordinary income, and net capital losses of up to $3000 can be used to offset ordinary income. Net capital losses of greater than $3000 can be carried forward to offset future income.

The tax code has a regulation that prevents the abuse of the deduction of capital losses. Investors should be aware of it. It is known as the *wash sale*. Capital losses cannot be claimed for tax purposes if the security is sold at a loss and then repurchased within 30 days. Thus, in order to take capital losses on the sale of a stock, the investor would have to wait longer than 30 days to repurchase that same stock.

A way to get around this regulation is to use a tax swap strategy. Assume that an investor has 200 shares of Haliburton, which has been beaten down in price along with the other stocks in the oil service and drilling sector, and the investor would like to realize these losses to offset other capital gains. The investor can sell the 200 shares of Haliburton, realize the losses, and replace that stock with another oil service and drilling company, such as Schlumberger or Diamond Offshore.

Reducing or eliminating fees and sales commissions can increase returns significantly, as was pointed out in Chapter 4. Since many brokers make their money buying and selling securities, they have an incentive to advise their clients to trade more than they should. This is called *churning*, i.e., buying and selling stocks at a rate that is not justified by their returns.

One way to reduce the costs of churning is to tell your broker that you are a long-term investor with a buy-and-hold strategy. Another alternative is to invest in stock mutual funds, which are low in cost and tax efficient. They are discussed in Chapter 9.

CAVEATS FOR INVESTORS

There is a direct relationship between rates of return and risk. Before investing, you should keep in mind the following:

- Is the expected rate of return for the investment abnormally high compared with similar investments?

- Is this based on past performance?
- Is the investment based on sound business sense? (If not, forget the whole thing.)
- Is there pressure to invest immediately or put some money up? Be cautious of schemes that require you to act immediately.
- Who are the principals? If you do not know them, have them checked out, especially with regard to their previous operations. Check to see if they have ever been involved in a bankruptcy.
- Are there financial statements? If so, are they audited? Check the auditor's report for qualified or adverse opinions.
- Can you afford to lose the money you invest in this operation? If not, don't invest.
- Is there a guarantee? Can it be verified? Guaranteed by whom? Remember that "guaranteed" does not mean much if a company goes bankrupt and has no assets.
- Has this investment been offered to you over the phone by someone you don't know or don't know very well? Never invest on the basis of a telephone call.
- Never invest on the basis of recommendations from chat rooms or other sources on the Internet. Always check out the fundamentals of the investment before you invest.
- Always check every detail before you invest. If there is not enough time, look for something else to invest in.
- If you do invest, do not put additional money in to "help out" or for any other irrational reason.
- Be wary of investment tips from investment talk shows on the radio, tv, and the Internet. There have been a number of scams in which investors have lost money instead of "getting rich quickly."
- Carefully investigate stocks that have been suggested by bulletin board messages on the on-line computer services. If you know nothing about the stocks, don't buy them.

The trader's lament aptly sums up the investor's dilemma:

Buy and you'll be sorry.

Sell and you'll regret.

Hold and you'll worry.

Do nothing and you'll fret.

REFERENCES

Arbel, Avner, and Paul Strebel: "The Neglected and Small Firm Effects," *Financial Review*, November 1982, pp. 201–218.

Basu, S.: "The Information Content of Price-Earnings Ratios," *Financial Management*, Summer 1975, pp. 53–64.

———"Investment Performance of Common Stocks in Relation to their Price-Earnings Ratios: A Test of the Efficient Market Hypothesis," *Journal of Finance*, June 1977, pp. 663–682.

Cheney, John M., and Edward A. Moses: *Fundamentals of Investments*, West Publishing Co., St. Paul, MN, 1992, p. 19.

Clayman, M.: "In Search of Excellence: The Investor's Viewpoint," *Financial Analysts' Journal*, May-June 1987.

Dorfman, John R.: "Luck or Logic," *The Wall Street Journal*, November 4, 1993, p. C1.

Dremen, David: "Flawed Forecasts," *Forbes*, December 9, 1991, p. 342.

Fama, Eugene F.: "The Behavior of Stock Prices," *Journal of Business*, January 1965, pp. 34–105.

Fama, Eugene F.: Lawrence Fisher, Michael G. Jensen, and Richard Roll: "The Adjustment of Stock Prices to New Information," *International Economic Review*, February 1969, pp. 1–21.

Fama, Eugene F., and Kenneth French: "The Cross-Section of Expected Stock Returns," *The Journal of Finance*, vol. 47, June 1992, pp. 427–466.

Hirt, Geoffrey A., and Stanley B. Block: *Fundamentals of Investment Management*, 3rd ed., Irwin, Homewood, IL, 1990, p. 285.

Lorie, James H., and Victor Niederhoffer: "Predictive Statistical Properties of Insider Trading," *Journal of Law and Economics*, April 1966, pp. 35–53.

Malkiel, Burton G.: *A Random Walk Down Wall Street*, W.W. Norton, New York, 1990.

Martin, John D., J. William Petty, et al.: *Basic Financial Management*, 5th ed., Prentice Hall, Englewood Cliffs, NJ, 1991.

Securities and Exchange Commission, *Institutional Investor Study Report*, Government Printing Office, Washington D.C., 1971.

Sturm, Paul: "What If Ben Graham Had a PC?" *Smart Money*, March 1994, p. 32.

Tergesen, Anne, and Peter Coy: "Who Needs a Money Manager?" *Business Week*, February 22, 1999, pp. 127–132.

CHAPTER 8

Portfolio Construction and the Different Investment Styles

KEY CONCEPTS

- Portfolio objectives
- Asset allocation and diversification
- Investment style
- Selection of stocks using a value equity style
- Selection of stocks using a growth equity style
- Selection of stocks using a blend of growth and value styles

The guidelines for constructing a portfolio are discussed in this chapter. There are three basic steps. The first is establishing the portfolio objectives, which will influence the investment style, which will, in turn, determine the types of stocks chosen.

PORTFOLIO OBJECTIVES

The first step in building a portfolio is to determine the portfolio objectives. Ideally, investors would like to find stocks that will double or treble in a short period of time with no risk. In reality, it is difficult to almost impossible to find such an investment. The Internet initial public offering stocks issued in the last quarter of 1998 live up to part of the definition. Many increased their values by 300 to 400 percent in less than three months. However, these stocks hardly qualify as low-risk securities. Many of them are trading at such lofty multiples of revenues (most of them do not have earnings to use for a price-earnings ratio) that the slightest hesitation in the market could send them tumbling.

In conjunction with their portfolio objectives, investors should determine where they feel comfortable with regard to the risk/return tradeoff. The time horizon for these portfolios will impact the choice of objectives. The longer the time horizon of the portfolio, the greater can be the weighting to common stocks. The four basic portfolio objectives are:

- Stability of principal
- Income
- Growth and income
- Capital appreciation

Stability of Principal

This is the most conservative investment objective. It concentrates on preserving capital while earning income. Common stocks can hardly qualify as an appropriate investment vehicle to preserve capital, because there is always the possibility of loss of principal due to stock prices falling below their purchase prices.

The types of securities that preserve principal are certificates of deposit (CDs), money market securities, and money market mutual funds. Generally, the time horizon for the preservation of capital objective is short, and money market instruments fulfill the requirements. Investors who have longer time horizons (five years or more) and are risk averse might be persuaded to devote a small portion of their portfolio assets to the defensive blue-chip stocks, which could give some growth to the portfolio assets.

Income Objective

This objective shifts the focus away from preserving the amount of principal to earning income for the portfolio. It presents more lee-way in the choice of securities for the portfolio, allowing bonds (Treasuries, government agency, municipal, and corporate), pre-ferred stocks, and high dividend yielding common stocks. For example, U.S. Treasury bonds currently yield around 5.4 percent, as compared to 4 percent returns on CDs. In a portfolio seeking stability of principal, the investor would forgo the higher yield on Treasury bonds to invest in the lower-yielding CDs, with which there is no possibility of erosion in principal. If market rates of interest rise, bonds will fall. However, if bonds are held to maturity, any paper losses will disappear.

Currently, there are preferred stocks and some high-yielding dividend stocks that can match the returns of the various types of bonds. Texas Utilities (TXN) is yielding 5.5 percent (as of this writing). By including stocks such as the high-yielding utility stocks and other high-yielding blue-chip stocks in their portfolios, investors are also building in the potential for capital growth in a bull market and the opposite in a bear market (capital losses).

The income objective allows investors to own common stocks. The amount allocated to this category will depend on the investor's time horizon and risk tolerance.

Growth and Income Objective

This objective looks for investments that bring both capital growth and income, which means that a larger part of the investment funds can be allocated to stocks than in the two previous objectives discussed. The types of securities for this portfolio would include a mixture of debt and equity. The equity allocation would be divided up between dividend-yielding stocks and stocks with the potential for capital growth. The focus of the latter group of stocks is to provide growth in the portfolio rather than income.

Portfolio growth is important, particularly since people are living longer, which means they will need greater amounts to fund their longer retirement periods.

Capital Appreciation Objective

This fourth objective focuses on capital growth in the portfolio rather than income. It is pursued by investors who can forgo income in favor of capital appreciation. Investors in high marginal tax brackets prefer capital appreciation to income because long-term capital gains are currently taxed at lower rates than ordinary income, which includes dividends and interest. Paper gains on stocks are not taxed until the stocks are sold. The holding period for long-term capital gains is one year or longer. If stocks are held for less than one year, then they are currently classified as short-term and are taxed at the higher ordinary income rates of the individual.

To achieve capital appreciation, investors increase their level of risk by pursuing small- and mid-cap stocks with the potential for growth, in addition to the large-cap stocks.

There are some key points which form the basis for the choice of objectives for a portfolio. These are:

- The risks that investors can take depend on their financial situations.
- The risks and potential returns of the different types of investments are related.
- The longer the holding periods for stocks and bonds, the lower the risks.
- Diversification reduces some of the risks.

ASSET ALLOCATION AND DIVERSIFICATION

Once investors have determined their specific portfolio objectives, they can develop plans to divide their assets into the various investment asset classes, such as money market securities, stocks, and bonds. This is called *asset allocation*. The focus of asset allocation is to diversify among various asset classes. *Diversification* focuses on investing in different investments within an asset class.

The aim of asset allocation is to reduce the overall risk of investing. By distributing portfolio amounts among different asset classes, investors can protect against any negative developments in the financial markets. For example, the bond and stock markets do not always rise and fall in tandem. If the stock markets go down, the bond and money markets can sometimes protect against any losses to the total portfolio value by preserving capital. This is due to the fact that there appears to be a weak relationship between bonds and stocks and virtually no relationship between stocks and money market securities.

Investors can use fixed weightings, flexible weightings, or a timing approach for their asset allocation plans. A *fixed weighting* allocates a fixed percentage to each asset class. Generally, these fixed percentages do not change. The following example illustrates a fixed asset allocation plan:

Asset Class	% Allocation
Money market securities	10
Bonds	40
Common stocks	50
Total portfolio	100

Gitman and Joehnk (p. 681) report that equal 20 percent allocations to each of the five asset classes (U.S. stocks, foreign stocks, long-term bonds, cash, and real estate) outperformed the S&P 500 Index in both risk and return for the period from 1967 to 1988. This lends support for a fixed asset allocation plan. Table 8-1 shows various possible fixed asset allocation plans for the different portfolio objectives during the life cycle of a couple. These asset allocations will vary depending on the specific financial and personal circumstances of the individuals concerned.

A *flexible-weighted asset* allocation plan involves changing the weights from time to time on the basis of market timing or other market factors. This suggests a shorter holding period than a fixed asset allocation plan, which would focus on less frequent changes to the plan. With a flexible asset allocation plan, investors are hoping to benefit from changing their weightings, whereas with a fixed asset allocation plan, investors hope to benefit through a strategy of buying and holding their investments. Table 8-2 illustrates a flexible-weighted asset allocation plan based on the assumption that interest rates will decline further.

A *tactical timing* approach to asset allocation is used by sophisticated investors who use quantitative models to determine when to get in and out of the different types of investments. In addition, they use derivative investments (stock index futures and bond futures) to hedge their positions in the markets.

If you are confused as to which asset allocation plan and formula to use, you are not alone. Most professional investment managers do not agree on the weightings of the different asset classes and when to change. Some brokerage firms have been bullish on stocks and have suggested weightings of 70 percent stocks, 25

TABLE 8-1

Examples of Fixed Asset Allocation Plans

Couple in their early seventies—No risk tolerance, in bad health, and cannot afford any losses in principal:

Money market securities	95%
Short-term bonds	5%
Total	100%

Couple in their mid-sixties, retired—Some risk tolerance (but not much) and need to generate income to live on:

Money market securities	10%
Bonds	70%
Preferred stocks and common stocks	20%
Total	100%

Couple in their mid-thirties with young children—Can tolerate high risk, but they need income in addition to capital growth:

Money market securities	5%
Bonds	40%
Common stocks	55%
Total	100%

Couple in their late twenties with no children—Aggressive risk-takers seeking capital growth (they do not need income from their portfolio):

Money market securities	5%
Common stocks	95%
Total	100%

percent bonds, and 5 percent cash, while others have been bearish on both the stock and bond markets and have weightings of 30 percent stocks, 30 percent bonds, and 40 percent cash. But keep in mind that the asset allocation plans of these brokerage firms can change from month to month.

Investors cannot escape the volatility of the stock and bond markets, but by allocating greater portions of their investments to the different asset types, they can stabilize their returns and their risks. The issue is not whether you should allocate 5 percent or 10 percent more or less to stocks, bonds, or money market securities. It is to have a plan that is consistent with your portfolio objectives and your financial and personal circumstances.

TABLE 8-2

Example of a Flexible Weighted Asset Allocation Plan*

Asset Class	July	January
Money market securities	20%	5%
Bonds	40%	40%
Stocks	40%	55%
Total	100%	100%

*Weightings changed due to anticipated changes in market rates of interest.

Diversification is the other balancing tool. You can have a well-balanced asset allocation plan, but if all your stocks and bonds are in the same companies in the same sectors, you still have not insulated your portfolio from the risks of loss. Remember from Chapter 7 that investments can be broken down into two types of risk: diversifiable and nondiversifiable. By investing in the stocks of different companies, the diversifiable risk can be reduced. Some research has shown that investing in 8 to 15 different stocks can reduce diversifiable risks but other researchers have concluded that investors should invest in up to 40 different stocks to be total-ly diversified. The greater the number of stocks in a portfolio, the lower the volatility. However, by increasing the number of stocks in a portfolio, investors are also reducing the potential performance of that portfolio.

Following are some of the yardsticks to ensure diversification in a portfolio:

- No more than 5 to 10 percent should be invested in one stock.
- No more than 20 percent of the portfolio should be invested in one industry.
- The amount of turnover in the portfolio should be limited to 20 to 30 percent.

Limiting turnover in the portfolio implies that there are some *core holdings* of companies that investors will buy and hold. Stocks that are likely candidates as core holdings are the companies that are the leaders in their particular industries and that will deliver sustained sales and earnings growth into the foreseeable future. Current core holding stocks might include Intel, Cisco, Microsoft, Merck, Johnson & Johnson, AT & T, and MCI-Worldcom. Investors in common stocks need longer time horizons to earn larger returns than they would need with other financial investments. As pointed out in an earlier chapter, the risks of common stocks can be lessened with longer time horizons.

Clearly, the amount of trading that investors do in a portfolio is dependent on their investment style. An *active strategy* is one where the portfolio assets are dynamic. They are constantly being traded (bought and sold). A *passive strategy* is one where the portfolio assets are bought and held.

CHOOSING AN INVESTMENT STYLE

One question often asked by investors is, "What types of stocks should I buy?" Should you rush to buy the small number of growth stocks that have been responsible for the major moves in the Dow Jones Industrial Average and the S&P 500 Index for the four-year period from 1996 to 1999? Or should you look for value stocks that have not participated in the rally of the last four years? Related to this issue are the sizes of the companies. The rally has mainly included the large capitalization stocks, while the small-cap and mid-cap stocks have been excluded.

Studies have shown that stocks can be classified into categories that have similar patterns of performance and characteristics. In other words, the returns of the stocks within the categories were similar, whereas the returns of the stocks between the categories were not correlated (Farrell, pp. 50–62). Farrell found four categories for stocks, namely growth, cyclical, stable, and energy. Other studies measured stocks by their market capitalization or size, which was then translated into small-cap, mid-cap, and large-cap stocks. What portfolio managers found was that they could enhance their performance by moving their money into the different categories of stocks from time to time.

From these categories of stocks, two investment styles have emerged, namely value investing and growth investing. Figure 8-1 illustrates the common styles of equity investing. This originated

FIGURE 8-1

Types of Equity Styles

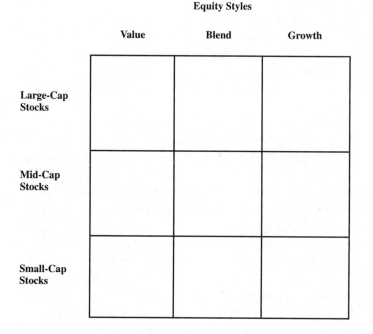

Equity Styles

	Value	Blend	Growth
Large-Cap Stocks			
Mid-Cap Stocks			
Small-Cap Stocks			

from Morningstar Mutual Funds for mutual fund investing, but it can also be used to determine individual equity portfolio holdings.

Investors can use this style box to determine the bulk of their equity investments that will suit their investment style as determined by their investment objectives. Value stocks have different financial characteristics and, as we have seen, different performance returns over the past four years than growth stocks. Value stocks generally pay some dividends and have low P/E ratios. Growth stocks generally have high P/E ratios and are expected to experience high sales growth for a period of time. A blend would include a mixture of growth and value stocks.

The size of the company is measured by market capitalization, which is the market value of the stock multiplied by the number of shares outstanding. Small-cap companies tend to be riskier than mid- or large-cap companies, but as the Ibbotson studies showed, over longer periods of time, the small-caps have surpassed the large-caps in terms of returns. This has not been the case over the past four years, however, in which large-cap growth stocks have outperformed the small- and mid-cap stocks quite handily. This runup does not apply to all the large stocks on the markets. In fact, more than half the stocks in the S&P 500 Index declined in share price or ended up with returns of 6.6 percent or less for the calendar year 1998; only a small number of stocks were responsible for the stellar returns (Tergesen, p. 110). This means that stock-picking becomes extremely important for individual portfolios, particularly if there is no benchmarking to an index.

For investors who chose the large, "nifty 50" stocks in the S&P 500 Index and most of the Dow Jones Industrial Average stocks, the returns for the four-year period in question were very rewarding, which might lead some to believe it is easy to make money in the stock market. However, in more broad-based markets, the choices are not so easy to make, and the average annual returns generally are not in the double digits, as has been the case lately.

The style box in Figure 8-1 illustrates the choices in terms of these dimensions. Investors can choose the current winners, the large-cap growth stocks, in which to invest more money. Alternatively, some investors might not want to pay the high prices for these types of stocks, and might look instead for the value stocks, which have not participated in the four-year rally. These could be in small-cap stocks, medium-cap, or large-cap stocks, or a combination of all three. Some investors might want to have a combination of growth and value stocks in the different size categories. The style box can also be used with international stocks.

Research has shown that value and growth stocks do not perform in the same manner within the same time periods. This is evidenced recently by the spectacular performance of the large-cap growth stocks, while the large-, mid-, and small-cap value stocks have underperformed the market. Some investors will choose to invest all their funds in the stocks that are performing well and then shift to other investment styles when they perceive that things are about to change. This is more conducive to an active management style, as opposed to a passive management style, in which investors would allocate their stocks among the different categories and then hold them for long periods of time. Active managers are more likely to be market timers; they will be more inclined to be fully invested in stocks when they perceive the market to be going up. When they think that the market is about to go down, they will exit the stock market. Passive investors tend to stay fully invested in stocks, regardless of the state of the markets.

Whether to manage actively or passively, or choose growth stocks over value stocks are decisions that every investor will ultimately have to make. The important thing is to know that having a plan and a strategy can make the stock selection much easier. The selection of individual stocks can also be made easier if direction is provided through an asset allocation model, which breaks down the different style categories of investment by asset class. Table 8-3 lists a few examples of the different portfolio possibilities. Investors might invest in a mixture of value and growth stocks, which could be allocated among domestic U.S stocks and international stocks. Following this, investors would then decide on the amounts to allocate to the different stock sizes, large-, mid-, and small-cap (see example 1 in Table 8-3).

TABLE 8-3

Asset Allocation of Stocks by Style

Example 1: Value/Growth Blend		Example 2: Value Stocks		Example 3: Growth Stocks	
Value Stocks					
Large-cap U.S. stocks	20%	Large-cap U.S stocks	25%	Large-cap U.S. stocks	25%
Mid-cap U.S. stocks	20%	Mid-cap U.S. stocks	25%	Mid-cap U.S. stocks	25%
International stocks	10%	Small-cap U.S. stocks	20%	Small-cap U.S. stocks	20%
Growth Stocks		International Large-cap	20%	Iternational Large-cap	20%
Large-cap U.S. stocks	20%	International Mid-cap	10%	International Mid-cap	10%
Mid-cap U.S. stocks	20%				
International stocks	10%				
Total Portfolio	**100%**	**Total Portfolio**	**100%**	**Total Portfolio**	**100%**

Examples 2 and 3 in the table show selections 100 percent weighted toward value and growth stocks, respectively. Diversification within the stock sector of an investor's portfolio offers protection against the downside risk of being fully invested in only one sector, such as large-cap value or growth stocks for example. If, in the near future, the tide turned against these stocks, investors would be protected by being able to participate in any price improvement in other sectors should the stock market rally become more broad-based.

Many investors may wonder whether they should take the time and effort to classify their stocks into these styles. That also depends, in part, on the risk tolerance of the investor. The following discussion on the relative performance of these styles may also help answer this question.

Active versus Passive Investment

Investors who believe in the efficient market hypothesis, which was discussed in Chapter 7, would likely argue on behalf of the passive investment style. If stock prices reflect all relevant information and stocks are always priced at their intrinsic values, it would be difficult for investors to beat the markets over long periods of time. Consequently, if investors cannot profit from insider information and there are no undervalued stocks, they have two alternatives: (1) invest in market indexes, or (2) choose individual stocks and hold them for long periods of time. These are known as *buy-and-hold strategies.*

Indexing

Those who subscribe to index investing believe that events affecting companies occur randomly. Therefore, investors have a 50-50 chance of being correct in picking stocks that will go up; hence, their odds of beating the market become more muted. Consequently, these investors are satisfied with the returns of the market and would invest in the stocks that make up the market indexes. This can be achieved in the following ways:

- Investing in the individual stocks in the index, for example, the 30 stocks in the Dow Jones Industrial Average.

However, investing in the 500 stocks of the S&P 500 Index is not practical for individual portfolios. Investors could invest in sectors of the S&P 500 Index, like the tech sector, the financial sector, or the nifty-50 stocks, or in the Dogs of the Dow.

- Investing in index tracking stocks, which underlie the indexes. Examples of these are the SPDRs, which track the S&P 500 Index, and the sector SPDRs of the S&P 500 Index; the DIAMONDs, which track the Dow Jones Industrial Average; and the Nasdaq 100 tracking stock, which invests in the largest 100 companies in the Nasdaq. These unit investment trust tracking stocks are discussed in Chapter 10.
- Investing in index mutual funds, discussed in Chapter 9.

By examining the results of index mutual funds versus actively managed mutual funds as a proxy for passive versus active investing, the case for indexing becomes more compelling. Tergesen (p. 110) reports that the average S&P 500 Index mutual fund earned around 18 percent annually over the past 10 years as compared with 16 percent annually for the actively managed equity mutual funds. This 2 percent annual difference may not seem all that significant, but when this difference is compounded over a period of time, the results point overwhelmingly toward indexing. Over a 10-year period, the compounded returns of index funds exceeded actively managed equity funds by about 80 percent (Tergesen, p. 108).

There are a number of reasons to explain these advantages of indexing over actively managed mutual funds:

1. Actively managed mutual funds may keep some money in cash anticipating a downturn in the market. If this does not materialize, then the index funds will earn more from their holdings, since they are always fully invested.
2. The annual expense ratios of index funds are considerably lower than those of the actively managed equity mutual fund counterparts. Index funds do not change their holdings unless the stocks in the indexes are changed. Actively managed funds can experience high turnover of their holdings, which means higher transaction costs.

3. Large-cap stocks, which are followed by many analysts, are probably efficiently priced, which gives the index fund an advantage over the stock-picker.

The opportunities for active managers and stock-pickers are in the small-cap and international stocks, which are followed less closely by the analysts. Similarly, in a market downturn, active managers can raise cash or invest in more defensive stocks, which might not go down as much as the fixed portfolios of the index funds. That is not to say that actively managed portfolios will not go down in a bear market. These portfolios will go down just like the index funds, but steps can be taken steps to reduce the amounts of the declines in their values. This can be seen in cases where small-cap equity managers have outpaced the Russell 2000 Index by including some large-cap stocks in their holdings. Other studies confirm that active managers do not consistently outperform indexing (Martin, pp. 17–20).

Buy-and-Hold Investing

Besides indexing, the other passive investment strategy for stock-pickers is to buy stocks for the long term and hold them. In other words, investors hold these stocks, making minimal changes over time. Performance between active and passive strategies is more difficult to evaluate since this depends on the composition of the stocks in both active and passive portfolios. However, using index funds as the basis for buy-and-hold investing, the results confirm that active portfolio managers do not outperform the buy-and-hold strategy. Jensen (pp. 389–416) surveyed 115 mutual fund managers during the period 1945–1964 and found that the average returns of these funds resulted in less than investments in a portfolio of T-bills and the market index would have returned.

Market timers often tout how they were able to successfully exit the market before a crash and then reenter at a lower point to increase their overall returns. This may be easier said than done. As was noted in the previous chapter, research done by T. Rowe Price showed that in order to do better than the buy-and-hold investor, market timers would need to be accurate in more than 70 percent of their calls to enter and exit the market. A study done by Nejat Seyhun covering the period from 1963 to 1993 found that an investor who exited the market for just 1.2 percent of the market's best-performing days would have lost out on 95 percent of the total returns (Strong, p. 363).

There certainly appears to be a disconnect between the research results reported from the ivory towers of academia and the communications and hype reported from many on Wall Street. The growth of newsletters forecasting the precise future movements of the markets and how to time them is on the rise, as more investors enter the stock markets hoping to double or treble their money over a short period of time. As of this writing, the clairvoyant with a 100 percent accuracy in calling the markets has yet to emerge. Until such time, the odds are stacked against timing the markets; they favor the buy-and-hold investor.

Yet the numbers and importance of technical analysts appear to be on the increase as judged by their fame and notoriety from the financial media. It is easy to see why many lay investors jump into technical analysis. Using the Internet, investors can easily come up with all the charts that they desire. According to technical analysis, these charts provide easy and definitive answers, and so do the multitudes of other technical analysts' tools. However, the academic studies done on charting and many of the other methods followed by technical analysis do not come up with positive results as far as beating the markets.

What becomes apparent is that it is difficult to beat the markets consistently over long periods of time, regardless of the method. This certainly lends support for the buy-and-hold strategies over the market timers. In addition to those already discussed, several reasons put forth for the underperformance of active investing over passive investing are:

- Active trading means higher transaction (commission) costs.
- If the holding period for stocks is not one year or longer, the gains incurred are taxed at the higher ordinary federal tax rates than the longer-term holding periods of the buy-hold investors.

Value versus Growth Investing

Although large-cap growth stocks have outperformed value stocks of all market capitalizations over the past four years (since 1996), this trend has not always prevailed, especially over longer periods of time. So, should investors continue to choose the leadership in the large-cap growth stock sector and ignore the other lagging sectors of the market? Over the long term, the answer is no. In the short term, it is more of a guessing game. There is currently a large amount of money moving into the leading growth stocks, such as Cisco Systems (CSCO), Sun Microsystems (SUNW), Intel (INTC), Microsoft (MSFT), AOL (AOL), Yahoo (YHOO), Johnson & Johnson (JNJ), and General Electric (GE), to name a few, all of which are trading at or near their historic highs at the time of this writing. This is known as *momentum investing*, which is to jump into those stocks that have been going up in price. The major problem with momentum investing is that the turning point can never be accurately predicted. These leadership stocks will eventually become laggards, and the rotation will shift into the other sectors of stocks. If one is investing in these leadership stocks at the top of their price cycles, the returns may not be positive for some time before they come back into favor. Over the long term, investors who have diversified portfolios of stocks among the different sectors (small-, mid-, and large-cap value and growth stocks) will see steadier returns.

An analysis of the stock market substantiates this premise. Over the 19 year period from 1979 to 1998, there have been periods where value stocks have outperformed growth stocks, and vice versa (Table 8-4).

Which stocks over a long-term period would have returned more to investors? The answer may be surprising. A study done by David Leineweber et al., reported that $1 invested in both value and growth stocks, as followed by the price-to-book value of the S&P 500 Index stocks during the period from 1975 to 1995, would have yielded $23 for value stocks versus $14 for growth stocks (Coggin et al, p. 188). These results have also been confirmed by studies done on foreign stocks. A study done by Capaul, Rowley, and Sharpe (p. 34) determined that value stocks outperformed growth stocks abroad (France, Germany, Switzerland, Japan, and the United Kingdom) during the period January 1981 through June 1992. Jeremy Siegel, a professor at the University of Pennsylvania, found that value stocks outperformed growth stocks over the 35-year period between July 1963 and December 1998. Value stock

TABLE 8-4

Performance of U.S. Stocks over the Period 1979–1998

Value Stocks Outperform Growth Stocks	Growth Stocks Outperform Value Stocks
1981	1980
1983–1984	1982
1986	1985
1987–1988	1987
1992–1993	1989–1991
1995	1992–1994
	1996–March 1999

earned 13.4 percent annually, while growth stocks earned 12 percent annually (Tam and McGeeham, pp. C1 and C19).

In short, this phenomenon—value stocks outperforming growth stocks over long periods of time—should have some significance in the choice of stocks for investment portfolios. The evidence shows that winning stocks do not keep their positions over time; they revert to the mean. Similarly, losing stocks do not remain losers over periods of time because they too rise to the average. In other words, the high-flying growth stocks of today will not be able to sustain their abnormally high returns, and they will turn into lower returns, and the low returns of the value stocks of today will eventually surprise with higher returns.

This phenomenon of returns reverting to the mean over time can be applied to both the small-cap and large-cap stocks. Small-cap stocks outperformed large-cap stocks during the periods 1979 to 1983 and 1991 to 1992. However, investing in small-cap and mid-cap stocks within the past four years would probably have resulted either in below-market returns or negative returns. Inevitably, though, small company stocks will eventually turn, and there will be some undiscovered bargains, since their current valuations are currently so low.

This underlines the overall advantages of diversifying into the different sectors of the market in order to reduce the risks of volatility. Many market timers consider that this style of investing across different sectors weakens the returns they could have achieved by moving with the top-performing sectors. Obviously, a diversified portfolio will not gain as much as the strongest performing sector or fall as much as the weakest performing sector. The results for market timers depend on their accuracy in timing their calls to move in and out of the different sectors. Your overall choice of whether to be an active or a passive investor and your motivation for the choice of equity style will ultimately depend on your outlook for the market and your specific makeup with regard to risk and return.

HOW TO COMPOSE A VALUE PORTFOLIO

Value investing relies on fundamental analysis to determine when a stock is trading at less than its intrinsic value. This is the opposite of growth investing, where investors are willing to chase after the stocks that have good growth records and have already risen in value. Value investors look for companies that have good ideas or products or that have been performing poorly but have good long-term prospects. A good example of value stocks are the oil service companies and oil drillers, whose financial operations are linked to oil prices. Currently, oil is trading around $14 per barrel, which is slightly above the low point for the year. With low oil prices, these companies will turn in lower earnings, which have depressed their stock prices. If and when the price of oil rises, these stocks will also go up in price.

Value investors are generally patient and are willing to wait for oil prices to rise. This is because when stocks have lagged other stocks over long periods of time, the gap will, in all likelihood, narrow and the laggards will come around to outperform other stocks in the future. This is known as *regression to the mean*. The flip side of the coin is that stocks that have been outperforming the market will likely revert to the mean and underperform the market at some stage in the future. Thus, value investors are always looking for stocks that are considered to be trading below their expected long-term rates of return.

There is not unanimous agreement on the definition of value stocks. Some definitions center on low P/E multiples, or those that are below the market multiples. Others focus on low multiples of cash flow or low price-to-book ratios. The most conservative definition of a value stock is one that has an above-average dividend yield. Out-of-favor stocks are also classified by some as value stocks. For example, when Intel, Cisco, and many other growth stocks fell in value in the third quarter of 1998, many value fund managers bought these stocks as value stocks. Depending, then, on how you define value, many investors will come up with different sets of value stocks. Some of the bases for determining value stocks are discussed in greater detail.

Price-Earnings Ratio

The P/E ratio for a stock is calculated by dividing the current market price of the stock by its earnings per share. This can be done using the past four quarters' earnings, which gives you what is known as a *trailing P/E ratio*. Alternatively, the P/E calculation can use expected earnings, based on forecasts for the upcoming year's earnings. This *future P/E ratio* may be of greater significance to investors because it is an indication of the expectations for the stock in the future.

However, investors should not base their decisions on P/E multiples alone, because the type of industry and the capital structure also affect the P/E. Some industries have higher average P/E ratios than other industries, and it would not necessarily be a meaningful evaluation to compare the P/E ratios across industries. For example, the drug companies have had much higher multiples than the brokerage stocks. Comparing Merck, then, with a trailing P/E of 35, with Bear Stearns' P/E of 12 would be meaningless. Some industries require much greater investments in property, plant, and equipment than others, which means they are probably much more leveraged in terms of debt. Generally, companies with high debt ratios are much riskier than companies with low debt ratios, and these more highly leveraged companies will have lower P/E ratios.

A low price/earnings ratio is a relative measure. Some investors might consider Merck, with a multiple of 35, to be a growth stock, while others would consider it to be a value stock when compared with the high multiples of some of the S&P 500

Index stocks. The composition of the S&P 500 Index has changed, as more growth stocks have replaced some of the companies with depressed stock prices and poor earnings. This means that the S&P 500 Index is currently trading at its historically high P/E ratio.

Price-to-Book Ratio

This measure compares the market price to the book value. The book value per share is computed as assets minus liabilities divided by the number of outstanding shares. Value investors look for stocks with market values that are below their book values. Benjamin Graham, who did the pioneering work in fundamental analysis, has some guidelines for stock-pickers, which include buying a company's stock when the stock price is less than two-thirds of the book value per share. See Chapter 7 for the complete list of Graham's guidelines for picking stocks.

There are a number of reasons why a low price-to-book ratio is not reason enough, by itself, to buy a stock. The book value per share is an accounting measure, and it can be distorted by using different accounting methods within the generally accepted accounting principles (GAAP), such as the use of accelerated depreciation versus the use of straight line, or LIFO versus FIFO for valuing inventory. The discrepancy between the historical cost of the company's assets and their market values will make the book value per share diverge from the realizable value per share.

Thus, it is a good idea to use more than one measure of value to select value stocks.

Selecting a Value Portfolio

The first step is to select a universe of stocks that you are interested in. This can be done using the Internet to print up the financial information on the stocks of interest. Investors can then narrow the list down to those stocks that conform with their criteria of value, namely the specific price-to-book and price-to-earnings ratios and dividend yields. On-line brokerage accounts provide stock screen services which can be used to plug in criteria for screening different stocks to come up with a list of value stocks (see Table 8-5).

These are not recommendations for particular stocks, since over time, the financial fundamentals for these stocks will change.

Reasons for Selecting These Stocks

Using a stock screen on the Internet, the list of stocks in Table 8-5 was produced, with P/E multiples of less than 17. This list was then further reduced, based on price-book values of less than three times. From this list, we looked at the *fundamental growth stories* for each stock. Deere & Company was chosen because it is one of the largest agricultural equipment producers in the world and has fallen on hard times because of the economic turmoil in Asia and Latin America. However, as the economically depressed regions of the world come back on stream, Deere & Company will stand to benefit from increased sales as these economies start to flourish again. It requires patience, which is practically synonymous with value investing. If sales in the next few years increase as expected, earnings for Deere & Company should double from existing levels.

Low P/E multiple stocks were selected because these stocks are all trading at reasonable prices. From this list, we screened the stocks further, looking for growth situations which may not have been recognized by the market, such as stocks with good management that may have fallen on hard times due to adverse swings in the sector or other temporary conditions. Allstate Insurance Company is in the property and casualty area of the insurance industry. Prospects for the future look much rosier than the present, which is the kind of scenario conducive to buying.

The *beta coefficient* gives some idea of the volatility of the stock in relation to the market. According to this measure, the two most volatile stocks in our list are Borders Group and Neomagic. If the stock market continues to go up, these stocks have the potential to go up much more than the increase in the overall market. However, they also have the potential to go down much more when the market goes down.

Over longer periods of time, *earnings* drive the growth in stock prices. Look for companies that will be able to sustain increased earnings over the long haul. Neomagic has consistently been able

TABLE 8-5

Value Stocks, Based on P/E Ratios and Other Fundamental Factors*

Comany Name	Symbol	Sector	Price	Beta	P/E	Book Value	Price/ Book	Sales per Share	Div Yld	Return on Equity	Equity/ Debt
Deere & Company	DE	Capital goods	$41.25	1.15	11.57	$17.39	2.37	$ 56.14	2.13%	20.98%	2.27
Lockheed Martin	LMT	Capital goods	$41.50	0.61	15.84	$15.60	2.66	$ 68.69	2.12%	17.26%	1.77
NeoMagie Corporation	NMGC	Technology	$11.75	1.56	9.84	$ 3.63	1.19	$ 9.21	0	40.41%	0.01
Allstate Ins. Company	ALL	Financial	$38.81	0.93	9.45	$21.08	1.84	$ 31.76	1.55%	20.41%	0.10
Ford Motor Company	F	Consumer Cyclical	$63.75	0.95	12.36	$22.26	2.86	$117.70	2.89%	26.98%	5.51
Furniture Brands Int'l.	FBN	Consumer cyclical	$23.13	1.19	12.71	$ 7.99	2.89	$ 36.43	0	26.45%	1.43
Borders Group Inc.	BGP	Services	$14.56	1.85	12.95	$ 8.16	1.79	$ 31.94	0	14.88%	0.57
Texas Utilities Company	TXU	Utilities	$39.63	0.15	14.53	$31.12	1.27	$ 55.47	5.8%	9.64%	0.57
AMR Corp.	AMR	Transportation	$71.75	1.20	11.21	$41.51	1.73	$110.84	0	16.88%	0.66
CSX Corp.	CSX	Transportation	$41.75	0.84	16.83	$27.08	1.54	$ 45.62	2.87%	9.15%	1.14

*As of April 23, 1999

to increase its earnings over the past year, while the price of its stock has come down from its yearly high of $23.75. For the nine months ending on October 31, 1998, the company's net income rose by 76 percent over the same nine-month period for the previous year. Earnings are expected to increase into the future. This technology company produces high-performance multimedia solutions on a single chip for notebook computers. This is also one of the small-cap plays for the portfolio.

Sales per share is another interesting fundamental to look at when determining the value of stocks. By using sales per share and taking it one step further, investors can determine the sales of a company for each dollar invested. This is computed as follows:

Sales per dollar invested = sales per share ÷ stock price per share

The sales per dollar invested for Ford Motor, Borders Group, and Lockheed Martin, respectively, are $1.85, $2.19, and $1.66. For each dollar invested in Ford, the investor is getting $1.85 in sales. Obviously, the higher the sales per dollar invested, the cheaper the stock with regard to this measure.

The *dividend yield* is another measure of value. Texas Utilities has an above-average dividend yield of 5.8 percent, compared with an average Dow Jones Industrial dividend yield for March 1999 of 1.58 percent. Stocks with high dividend yields are attractive to value investors, who can collect the dividends while waiting for capital appreciation. Texas Utilities has been expanding its operations worldwide, and if there is a 5 to 10 percent appreciation in the stock price to go with the 5 percent dividend yield, you get a total return of 10 to 15 percent per year.

Value investors select stocks that they believe are undervalued relative to their fundamental intrinsic values. The measures just discussed are some of the ones used to determine and select value stocks.

HOW TO COMPOSE A GROWTH PORTFOLIO

Growth investors look for companies with above-average growth rates. This can be companies with consistent sales growth or earnings growth or more speculative companies that have sales or earnings momentum. This latter category includes many Internet stocks, for which there is the expectation for rapid growth in sales that hopefully will translate into future earnings. There are many Internet stocks trading at very high multiples of revenue—though not earnings—because they have yet to post any profits. This suggests two styles within growth investing. There are investors who have longer-term horizons and seek growth stocks that are expected to deliver above-average, long-term consistent sales and earnings growth, such companies as Cisco and Intel. Then there are the momentum investors who have shorter horizons. They are willing to jump into stocks that exhibit above-average growth in sales or earnings in order to share in the rising stock prices for as long as it lasts.

Growth stocks have had an incredibly good run of consistent earnings growth in the slow growth economic environment of the U.S. during the period from 1995 to the present. This is in part due to low inflation and declining interest rates. The P/E ratios of these large-capitalized growth stocks have been expanding to historically high levels, which suggests a definition of growth stocks: those stocks with above-average sales and/or earnings, high P/E ratios, and high price/book ratios. The high P/E multiples mean that investors will pay a high premium to buy these stocks. However, if there are disappointments in sales or earnings growth, these stocks get severely punished and are therefore considered to be more risky, with greater potential for losses. Investors have lower expectations for value stocks. Consequently, any sales or earnings disappointments will cause smaller losses. Generally, growth companies reinvest their earnings to fund more growth rather than paying them out in dividends. If they do pay dividends, they have relatively low dividend yields.

Growth Rates

There is no precise definition of the exact growth rate that distinguishes a growth stock from a value stock. Investors can choose any growth rate to determine their universe of growth stocks and then extrapolate their growth rates into the future.

There are a number of measures of growth. Investors can focus on revenue growth, earnings per share growth, return on equity growth, or cash flow per share growth from year to year.

Selecting a Growth Portfolio

The first step is to select a universe of stocks that you are interested in. This can be done using the stock screens provided by on-line brokerage firms or those provided by Yahoo or Netscape. You can screen stocks according to various growth rates. The stocks in Table 8-6 were chosen from a stock screen using earnings growth rates in excess of 25 percent. This discussion is not to be construed as a recommendation for these stocks, as information and financial conditions change over time.

Reasons for Selecting These Stocks

Industry Leadership

Growth stocks at the time of this writing are very richly valued, as can be seen from the extremely high P/E ratios in Table 8-6. Consequently, if an investor were to go out on a day like today and compose a growth portfolio, paying such high multiples for just any stock would be going against the grain of logic. Picking the industry leaders might be more justifiable under the circumstances. Intel, CitiGroup, Cisco, and Dell are the leaders in their respective industries, in which they have sustainable sales and earnings growth.

Growth

A growth investor needs some justification to purchase such a high P/E stock and that justification is growth rate. Generally, investors look for growth stocks with P/E multiples that are less than their growth rates. However, with the runup in the prices of growth stocks, the P/E multiples of these leaders are all in excess of their growth rates. Picking sectors with sustainable growth into the future might be a good place to start. For example, the major drug companies will see increasing demand for prescription drugs into the foreseeable future due to the aging of the baby boomer generation. Using Table 8-6, you can see that Warner Lambert came in with the highest growth rates of the large-cap drug companies. There are other measures to evaluate the drug companies, one of which is the number of new drugs in their pipelines for FDA approval.

TABLE 8-6

Growth Stock Portfolio, Based on Growth in Excess of 25%

Company	Symbol	Industry	P/E	Growth	Price	Return
Intel Corp.	INTC	Semiconductors	31.65	31%	$61.18	51.43%
CitiGroup	C	Insurance	30.99	40.8%	$74.87	24.38%
Cisco Systems	CSCO	Computer networks	138.09	26.4%	$114.06	133.58
Dell Computer	DELL	Computer hardware	78.01	39.1%	$41.18	104.02%
Tyco International	TYC	Security systems	46.27	45.4%	$81.25	48.74%
Warner Lambert	WLA	Major drugs	42.49	29.9%	$67.81	7.43%

The Internet is one of the fastest growing industries; its growth doubles about every 100 days. However, not all the Internet players will survive into the future, so the key question is, Which companies will be the survivors? One way to benefit from the growth of the Internet is to buy the network provider companies, such as Cisco Systems and Lucent Technologies, and Internet software providers like Sun Microsystems. It's like the Gold Rush in 1849. It was not the gold diggers who became wealthy but the companies providing the equipment and infrastructure to the gold mining industry which benefited the most.

Returns

When growth stocks are trading at such rich valuations, investors need to look at the returns to justify the lofty prices. For example, Amazon, the Internet bookseller, is growing rapidly and has a market capitalization that exceeds many large-cap companies with significant bricks and mortar assets, but Amazon has yet to post a yearly profit. For example, some of the Internet companies are growing their sales rapidly, but if each sales transaction results in a loss, rapid sales growth will translate into greater losses!

Look for stocks that have or will post superior returns into the future rather than those companies with half the picture, namely, tremendous growth but no returns.

HOW TO COMPOSE A BLENDED VALUE AND GROWTH STOCK PORTFOLIO

Instead of concentrating on only one style of investing, investors can choose a blend of value and growth stocks for their portfolios. Within this blend, there may be a bias toward one or the other style or a straight 50 percent allocation to each style.

The divergences in the returns of the different styles of investing over time suggest that for buy-and-hold investors, who are not willing to time the different sectors, a blended portfolio of value and growth stocks spread among the different stock sizes is the answer. As market conditions change, the leaders in the stock markets eventually become the laggards, and then, over time, this process reverses. By diversifying into the different sectors of the market, investors avoid timing and market performance decisions. By going for a blend of stocks from value and growth styles, investors may be sacrificing on short-term performance, but they reduce their risk of having all their stocks invested in one equity style. For example, when interest rates go up, this has a more devastating effect on growth stocks than value stocks. This is because growth stocks have higher price/earnings multiples, and with their high expectations, they are punished more severely than value stocks with their low P/E multiples and low expectations.

By investing in the underperforming sectors such as the value stocks—most notably the out-of-favor cyclical stocks—along with the hot growth stocks, investors are taking advantage of the disparity in the markets and creating opportunities. Examining what has happened to the S&P 500 Index is a case in point. The S&P 500 Index has a bias toward growth stocks, even though it is composed of many stocks in the value area, such as the utilities, basic metals, energy, and process industry stocks. Not surprisingly, the stellar performance of the S&P 500 Index over the four-year period from 1996 well into 1999 has come from a small number of growth stocks, namely Microsoft, General Electric, Lucent Technologies, Cisco Systems, Wal-Mart, Intel, IBM, Dell Computer, and Pfizer. With the higher valuations of these stocks in the S&P 500 Index, there are greater risks of increased volatility in the index. By broadening ownership into the stocks that have not contributed to this remarkable rise in performance, investors can seek a balance between the leaders and laggard stocks in the market.

Table 8-7 lists some of the stocks that are value stocks and some which can be classified as growth stocks. The stocks were selected based on growth, but with a bias toward value. Using a stock screen from the Website *www.wsrn.com*, stocks with a P/E ratio of between 10 and 39, a five-year growth rate in excess of 20 percent, and a debt to equity ratio of no more than 1:2 were chosen. From this screen of stocks, only those with P/E ratios less than their growth rates were chosen.

Reasons for Selecting These Stocks

In this blended portfolio of value and growth stocks, the emphasis was on finding stocks that were priced like value stocks but which also had greater growth rates. Stocks were screened and only those which had P/E ratios of less than their growth rates were chosen. Oracle Corporation is a borderline example. This stock made the list because it is the number-2 software company and is expected to record a few quarters of flat sales and earnings due to Y2K concerns. However, after the end of 1999, business companies will be back spending on e-commerce software, where Oracle is a major supplier.

A very different portfolio could also be assembled strictly on value and growth definitions. Fifty percent of the portfolio could be in low P/E value stocks which have good earnings expectations in the future, and the balance of the portfolio could be put into stocks that are the leaders in their fields and have experienced exceptional growth despite their high P/E multiples. Investors would use the same process described in the previous two sections for choosing a blend of value and growth stocks.

REFERENCES

Capaul, C., I. Rowley, and W. Sharpe: "International Value and Growth Stock Returns," *Financial Analysts' Journal*, January-February 1993.

Coggin, Daniel T., Frank J. Fabozzi, and Robert D. Arnott: *Handbook of Equity Style Management*, 2nd ed. Frank Fabozzi Associates, New Hope, Pennsylvania, 1997.

Farrell, James L., Jr.: "Homogeneous Stock Groupings: Implications for Portfolio Management," *Financial Analysts Journal*, May-June 1975, pp. 50–62.

Gitman, Lawrence J., and Michael D. Joehnk: *Fundamentals of Investing*, 6th ed., Harper Collins, New York, 1996.

TABLE 8-7

Portfolio of a Blend of Growth and Value Stocks Company

Company	Price	P/E	Yield	Return on Equity	Debt/ Equity	% Change EPS	Earnings Growth
Brunswick Corp.	$23.56	10.1	2.1%	14.2%	0.48	5.1%	20.1%
C.R. Bard, Inc.	$50.31	11	1.5%	44.5%	0.28	15.9%	23.9%
Oracle Corp.	$24.50	31	0	27.5%	0.10	33.3%	30.3%
Rohm & Haas Co.	$44.81	17.7	1.6%	30.4%	0.27	10.3%	25.1%
Texas Utilities	$41.31	14.4	5.6%	9.0%	1.84	27.4%	NC
UAL Corp.	$80.00	11.7	0	25.2%	1.52	29.4%	31.9%

*NC: cannot be calculated

259

Jensen, Michael C.: "The Performance of Mutual Funds in the Period 1945–1964," *Journal of Finance*, May 1968, pp. 389–416.

Martin, Larry L.: "The Evolution of Passive versus Active Equity Management," *Journal of Investing*, Spring 1993, pp. 17–20.

Strong, Robert A.: *Practical Investment Management*, Cincinnati, Ohio, 1998.

Tam, Pu-Wing, and Patrick McGeeham: "Finding the `Value' in Value Funds," *The Wall Street Journal*, April 16, 1999, pp. C1,C19.

Tergesen, Anne: "With Index Funds, Who Needs Gurus?" *Business Week*, January 18, 1999, pp. 108–110.

Tergesen, Anne: "Sifting for Clues," *Business Week*, March 29, 1999, pp. 110–111.

CHAPTER 9

Mutual Funds*

KEY CONCEPTS

- How do mutual funds work?
- The different types of funds
- How does performance affect the choice of a mutual fund?
- What is the significance of the prospectus?
- What are the tax consequences of buying and selling shares in mutual funds?
- What are the risks of mutual funds?
- How to buy and sell mutual funds
- What are the advantages of mutual funds?
- What are the disadvantages of mutual funds?
- Should you invest in stock mutual funds or individual stocks?

In some respects, mutual funds have come close to being the ideal investment for millions of investors. Many of these investors are able to move their money in and out of different types of mutual funds just as portfolio managers would when overseeing large portfolios. Mutual funds have allowed investors, who do not have the time, knowledge, or expertise of different financial instruments on the market, to invest their money in stocks, bonds, and money market funds.

---

*Portions of this chapter have been previously published by Esmé Faerber in *All About Bonds and Bond Mutual Funds* (McGraw-Hill, New York, 2000).

Since the early 1980s, the number of mutual funds has grown rapidly to the point where quotations of mutual fund prices now occupy more than four full pages in *The Wall Street Journal*. The fact that there are more mutual funds than companies listed on the New York Stock Exchange means that investors should be as careful in selecting mutual funds as they are in investing in individual stocks and bonds.

Moreover, the management companies of these mutual funds compete very aggressively for investors' dollars. This is evidenced by all the print advertising in newspapers and magazines as well as the use of television to ensure that the mutual funds are seen and heard.

The decision becomes more difficult for investors who take the advertising messages literally, without reading the fine print and stepping back to analyze the investment objectives of the fund.

According to the advertisements, there appear to be no loser funds, only funds that are "number one" in something, or funds that have had remarkable yields. If you read the fine print, you'll find that many of the funds achieved that yield on No. 1 status only for a one-week or one-month period in some limited way. This does not ensure the fund of a rosy future. For example, the number one position may have been achieved by an exceptional manager who is no longer with the fund. Results reported by Lipper Analytical Services Inc. show that even poor-performing funds can sometimes rank as number one at something for a short time. The editor of *Morningstar Mutual Funds*, a Chicago newsletter, supports this finding (Clements).

Nor do the advertisements include the fees charged by the funds. If investors pick a fund that is number one in something and had a wonderful yield once upon a time, they will assume that they have invested wisely. But the fund they chose could be a poor performer. Fees charged by that fund could be higher than those charged by other mutual funds in the same category of investments. Or the fund could rely on riskier investment assets, which typically make that fund's share price more volatile. In fact, investors should be suspicious of funds that post yields much greater than those posted by funds in the same category. This may mean that the fund is investing in derivative securities, which can enhance returns but can also pose greater risks of loss.

Many investors are so confused that they turn to one of the many newsletters on the market. But the hype from some of the advertisements of these advisory newsletters can further overwhelm them and make the choice of a newsletter even harder than the choice of a mutual fund. Some newsletters even go so far as to predict the future returns for certain funds (Savage).

The aim is to get investors to subscribe to the newsletter, so the messages promoted by many of them use a combination of hyperbole and fear to move investors in that direction. Implying that they will choose the wrong fund makes some investors even more unsure about choosing a fund.

For investors who are so confused that they are in a state of paralysis as to how to invest their money, there are *wrap accounts,* which are supposed to answer the concerns of investors who don't know how to manage their money. Major brokerage firms offer these accounts, and for an all-inclusive flat fee, they will manage your investments by diversifying into stocks, bonds, and money market accounts. Sounds ideal!

However, many investors have been jolted into reality by the fees charged for some of these wrap accounts. Some have high annual fees that are not all-inclusive. This means they do not include the management of their cash accounts. An additional fee is charged to manage money market and cash accounts, which in today's economic environment of low interest rates means investors are losing money on their cash funds. Not all investors like to be fully invested in stocks and bonds, and their money in cash accounts may be earning only 2.9 percent per annum. With a 2 percent annual management fee levied, investors will earn negative rates of return after paying taxes and adjusting for inflation.

Performance is another widely touted reason for investing in a brokerage firm's wrap accounts. However, many of the brokerage firms do not factor their fees into their performance equation. It can make quite a difference and can be disturbing to find you will be earning ±2 to 3 percent less than the advertised rate.

The high cost and the equivocal performance of many wrap accounts should make investors think twice before jumping into them without a careful analysis. Besides cost and performance, investors should also look at potential conflicts of interest in the management of the wrap accounts. For example, does the broker favor securities underwritten by the same brokerage firm when choosing investment securities (Schultz).

The SEC has voted to require that the sponsors of wrap accounts give investors more information about their costs, services, and performance (Harlan).

It is indeed confusing for investors to choose a mutual fund, especially when there are more than 7000 of them on the market. Moreover, investors may be equally confused by all the conflicting advice and predictions offered by many of the newsletters. So what do you do? Go back to the basics:

- Understand how mutual funds work.
- Understand the fundamentals of the investments the fund invests in.
- Evaluate the performance of the fund from the prospectus.

By following these steps, investors can narrow their field of funds to choose from. They will then be in a better position to make a final decision on a fund.

HOW DO MUTUAL FUNDS WORK?

All mutual funds work similarly. A mutual fund makes investments on behalf of the investors in that fund. The money from investors is pooled, which allows the fund to diversify its acquisition of different securities, such as stocks for stock funds and bonds for bond funds. The types of investments chosen are determined by the *objectives* of the mutual fund. For example, if a bond fund's objective is to provide tax-free income, the fund should invest in municipal bonds. The fund will buy different municipal bond issues to achieve a diversified portfolio, and this will also reduce the risk of loss due to default.

When these securities pay out their interest or dividends, fund holders get their proportional share. Thus, an investor who invests $1000 will get the same rate of return as another investor who invests $100,000 in the fund.

When the prices of the securities fluctuate up or down, the total value of the fund is affected. These fluctuations in price are due to many different factors, such as the intrinsic risk of the types of securities in the portfolio, and economic, market, and political factors. The objectives of the fund are important because they will indicate the type and quality of the investments the fund will choose. From these objectives, investors are better able to assess the risks the fund is willing to take to improve income (return) or capital gains. See Table 9-1 for a classification of mutual funds by investment objectives.

Investors invest their money in mutual funds by buying shares at the net asset value (NAV). The fund's net asset value price of shares equals the total assets minus the liabilities of the fund, divided by the number of outstanding shares.

It is easy for a fund to determine the market value of its assets at the end of each trading day. For instance, if the fund is a balanced fund, which means that it invests in both common stocks and bonds, the investment company would use the closing prices of the stocks and bonds for the day. These prices would be multiplied by the number of shares of stock and the number of bonds that the fund owns. The resulting totals are added up, and any liabilities that the fund has (accrued fees, for example) are subtracted. The total is then divided by the number of shares outstanding to give the net asset value price per share. A numerical example illustrates the process:

Market value of stocks and bonds	$5,000,000
Total liabilities	−150,000
Net worth	$4,850,000
Number of shares outstanding	750,000
Net asset value (4,850,000 ÷ 750,000)	$6.466

The net asset value changes daily due to the market fluctuations of stocks and bonds. The net asset value is important for two reasons:

- It is the price used to determine the value of the investor's holding in the mutual fund (number of shares held multiplied by the net asset value price per share).
- It is the price used when new shares are purchased or when shares in the fund are sold.

The net asset values of the different funds are quoted in the daily newspapers. Table 9-2 shows how mutual funds were listed in the newspapers several years ago. The current way of listing mutual funds is shown in Chapter 3. The details of the funds in the two families of funds here (Vanguard and Fidelity) help illustrate the impact of load funds.

TABLE 9-1

Mutual Funds

Funds	Objectives
Money market funds	Invest in money market securities with relatively short maturitites.
Equity Funds	
Equity aggressive growth funds	Seek maximum capital gains. Invest in stocks of companies in new industries and out of favor companies.
Growth funds	Seek increase in value through capital gains. Invest in stocks of growth companies and industries (which are more mainstream than those chosen by aggressive growth funds.)
Growth and income funds	Seek increase in value through capital gains and dividend income. Invest in stocks of companies with a more consistent track record than the companies selected for growth and aggressive growth funds.
Income equity funds	Invest in stocks of companies that pay dividends.
Index funds	Invest in the securities that make up the index.
International equity funds	Invest in stocks of companies outside the U.S.
Global equity funds	Invest in stocks of companies in the U.S. and outside the U.S.
Emerging market funds	Invest in stocks of companies in developing countries.
Sector funds	Invest in stocks of the sector of the economy stated in the objectives of the fund. Examples are stocks in the energy sector, health care sector, technology stocks, or precious metals.
Balanced funds	Seek to provide value through income and principal conservation; they invest in common stocks, preferred stocks, and bonds.
Asset allocation funds	Invest in different types of securities (stocks, bonds, and money market funds) according to either a fixed or variable formula.
Hedge funds	Invest in securities (stocks and bonds) and derivative securities to hedge against downturns in the market, changes in interest rates, and currency values.

TABLE 9-2

Mutual Fund Quotations

	Inv. Ovj.	NAV	Offer Price	NAV Change
		Vanguard Group		
STAR	S & B	13.08	NL	+0.02
Intl Gr	ITL	13.87	NL	+0.02
Wnds II	G & I	16.83	NL	+0.05
		Fidelity Investments Group		
Gro Inc	G & I	22.04	22.72	+0.02
Latin Amer r	Itl	13.74	14.16	+0.07

Source: *The Wall Street Journal*

In the Vanguard Group, the International Growth fund, which invests in international stocks (as opposed to the STAR fund, which invests in stocks and bonds) has a net asset value of $13.87 per share. The investment objective column indicates the types of investments a fund will invest in. NL in the offer price column signifies that the fund is a *no load* fund, which means that investors can buy and sell shares at the net asset value of $13.87. The net asset value change column signifies the change in price from the previous day's closing price. The Vanguard International Growth fund closed $0.02 up from the previous day's closing price.

The two fund examples in the Fidelity Investments Group are *load* funds, since they charge commissions to buy and sell their shares. This is evidenced by the offer price, which is different from the net asset value price. To buy shares in Fidelity's Growth and Income fund, investors would buy at the offer price of $22.72 per share and would sell their shares at the net asset value price, $22.04. The difference ($0.68 per share) between the offer price ($22.72) and the net asset value price ($22.04) represents the load or commission that investors will pay to buy or sell shares in this fund. The *r* after the Latin America fund indicates that there is a redemption charge over and above the load when investors sell their shares.

Investors earn money from their mutual funds in three ways:

- When interest or dividends earned on the fund's investments are passed through to shareholders.
- When the fund's management sells investment securities at a profit and the capital gains are passed through to shareholders. If these securities are sold at a loss, the capital loss is offset against the gains of the fund, and the net gain or loss is passed through to the shareholders.
- When the net asset value per share increases, the value of the shareholder's investment increases.

Investors in funds are given the option of having their interest and capital gains paid out to them in check form or reinvested in additional shares of the fund.

There are two types of mutual funds: open-end and closed-end. With open-end funds, the investment company of the fund issues an unlimited number of shares. Investors can buy more shares from the mutual fund company, or they can sell their shares back to the mutual fund company, which means that the overall number of shares will increase or decrease, respectively. Closed-end funds issue a fixed number of shares; after they are all sold, they do not issue any more. In other words, they have a fixed capital structure. Closed-end funds are discussed in Chapter 10.

Mutual funds pay no taxes on income derived from their investments. Under the Internal Revenue Code, mutual funds serve as conduits through which the income from the investments is passed to shareholders in the form of interest or dividends and capital gains or losses. Individual investors pay the tax on their income and capital gains from the mutual funds.

Shareholders receive monthly and annual statements showing the interest, dividends, capital gains and losses, and other relevant data that should be retained for tax purposes. In fact, not only is the interest and dividend income important for tax purposes, but when investing in different mutual funds, investors should also keep track of the net asset value prices of the shares purchased and sold. This information helps in the computation of gains and losses when shares are redeemed.

THE DIFFERENT TYPES OF FUNDS

There are many different types of funds, and their differences are significant. The overriding difference between the types is that they invest in different investments in the markets. There are stock funds, bond funds, money market funds, hybrid funds, and commodity funds.

Money market funds are the only funds that maintain constant share prices. These are mostly one dollar a share, and the investment company will keep the net asset value at one dollar per share. Any expenses or short-term losses from the sale of securities are deducted from the revenues to keep the share price constant. This is more easily accomplished for funds that invest in money market securities, which are short-term, and don't have that much volatility in the prices of their investment assets.

However, within the past few years, a few money market mutual funds have incurred some losses due to investments in derivative securities, which were aimed at increasing the yields of the funds. When interest rates unexpectedly changed direction, many of these funds incurred large losses. Instead of allowing the net asset values to fall below one dollar per share, the fund's families quietly propped up the losses of these money market funds.

Stock funds vary with regard to the types of stocks that the funds choose for their portfolios. The choice is guided by the fund's investment objectives. The Securities and Exchange Commission requires that funds disclose their objectives. For example, the objective could be to seek growth through maximum capital gains. Because of the speculative nature of the stocks of the unseasoned, small companies that the fund invests in, this type of fund would appeal to a more aggressive investor who can withstand the risks of loss.

A more conservative investor would choose a fund whose objectives are slated more toward capital preservation while providing current income. Such funds would invest in high-yielding, good-quality stocks, which would also provide for capital appreciation, even though this may not be a primary objective.

Combined *growth and income funds* seek a balance between long-term capital gains and providing current income. See Table 9-1 for a list of some of the types of stock funds.

In their pursuit of higher returns, many stock funds have deviated from their objectives and turned to riskier types of investments. According to Clements (p. C1) some blue-chip and U.S. stock funds were investing in small stocks and foreign stocks, respectively. During bull markets this strategy boosted the returns of these funds significantly, but during a downturn in the market, these share prices will become much more volatile. This trend reversed in the latter part of the 1990s, when it was a small portion of the large-cap stocks that participated in the stock market boom. Generally, the 30 stocks in the Dow Jones Industrial Average and the top 50 stocks of the S&P 500 Index were the ones that showed the roughly 30 percent annual returns between the years 1996 to early 1999. The small-cap and mid-cap stocks generally did not participate in the stock market rally. Consequently, many actively managed small-cap and mid-cap equity funds included some large-cap stocks in their holdings to boost their returns.

All investors, especially conservative ones, looking at income equity funds should examine the makeup of the fund's investments to see if the stocks are of well-established companies and that there is a broad diversification within different industries.

Investing in equity funds does not immunize investors from the volatility in the markets. The more speculative stocks in the funds' portfolios will decline more than the more established blue-chip stocks in a market downturn. This means that the share prices of the aggressive funds will be much more volatile than the share prices of the more conservative stock funds.

Generally, for all types of funds, including bond funds, the higher the risk of the securities, the greater the potential return and the greater the potential loss on the downside.

By understanding the characteristics of the types of investments in the fund, shareholders will be better able to gauge the extent of the fluctuations in the net asset value of the fund.

Index funds are the new kids on the block, so to speak. An index fund tracks a market index and seeks to match the returns of that particular index. The Vanguard Family of Funds pioneered many of the index funds, and it has seen tremendous growth in its S&P 500 Index fund.

An S&P 500 Index fund invests in the stocks of the S&P 500 Index. This does not require active management of the assets in the fund because turnover is very low. The stocks are held in the fund until they drop out of the index. Only then are changes made to the fund. This translates into lower expense ratios for index funds. Vanguard's average expense ratio for its index funds in 1998 was 0.2 percent as compared with the typical 1+ percent for the average actively managed mutual funds. This means that for every $100 invested, shareholders will pay $0.20 for index funds versus $1+ for actively managed funds. This difference may seem trivial, but over time, with the compounding of returns, it can grow to significant amounts (Tergesen and Coy, p. 129).

The enthusiasm for index funds has spurred their growth into other areas, such as mid-cap and small-cap stocks, emerging markets, Europe, and Asia/Pacific Rim, to name a few.

The performance of many of the index funds has been impressive. During the period from 1989 to 1998, the following index funds outperformed the actively managed funds (Tergesen and Coy, p. 129):

S&P 500 Index, with average annual returns of 19.47 percent versus Growth/Income Funds at 16.40 percent

S&P Mid-cap with average annual returns of 19.73 percent versus mid-cap funds at 18.16 percent

MSCI Europe, with average annual returns of 16.54 percent versus Europe funds at 12.44 percent

IFCI Composite, with average annual returns of 10.06 percent versus Emerging Mkts. Funds at 4.60 percent

Over the past 10 years, 84 percent of large actively managed funds have underperformed the S&P 500 Index, and 70 percent of smaller-cap funds have underperformed the Wilshire 5000. This does not mean that they will always be outperformed by the passive index funds. In bear markets, index funds have experienced losses like their actively managed counterparts, who have the advantage of being able to convert to cash. During the downturns in 1980-1982 and in 1987, the actively managed funds prevailed over the index funds. However, this was not true for the bear market of 1973-1974 (Tergesen and Coy, pp. 129–130).

Many analysts and portfolio managers claim that in the future, when the market becomes more broad-based to include the small- and mid-cap stocks, actively managed funds will beat the index funds. In other words, the stock market rally for the period from 1996 to 1999 has been mainly attributed to the largest 50 stocks in the S&P 500 (called the "Nifty 50") and most of the Dow Jones Industrial Average stocks. When the other 450 stocks in the S&P 500 start to go up in price, it will be a stock-pickers market, as opposed to a market of stocks which will take the advantages away from index funds.

The advantages of index funds are their lower costs and the ease of diversification. By investing in index funds, an investor is participating in the entire market, which includes the European, Asian, and Latin American markets. This also makes the decision of which funds to invest in much easier for beginning investors.

Much has been written about hedge funds since the disaster at Long Term Capital Management, a Connecticut hedge fund, that had to be bailed out by 14 financial institutions in September 1998. (Table 9-3 defines hedge funds.) Long Term Capital Management suffered heavy losses in their positions on Russian bonds due to adverse swings in prices on the currency markets. Other hedge funds have also experienced heavy losses (Scholl and Bary, p. 19).

HOW DOES PERFORMANCE AFFECT THE CHOICE OF A MUTUAL FUND?

The overall performance of a fund involves the following:

- Yield
- Total return
- Expenses

As mentioned at the beginning of the chapter, most funds can boast attaining the number one position in some area of performance at some point in time. Similarly, good past performance may not be indicative of good future performance. Some funds that have performed well in the past have had poor performance thereafter. In fact, there are some funds that did well in the past that no longer exist.

It is little wonder that with 7000 mutual funds on the market vying for investors' savings, many of the messages in their advertisements would lead you to believe that they have attained superior performance. Even if funds do well during good times, investors should also examine how these funds have performed during the down markets. Several business magazines track the overall performance records (during up and down markets) of many of the mutual funds, which is a better yardstick than the advertising messages of the mutual funds themselves. *Forbes* magazine publishes annual performance ratings of mutual funds. From this (or from other publications), investors can see how well funds have performed in up markets as well as how the funds protected their capital during periods of declining prices.

New funds do not have track records. Therefore, a yardstick on performance during a period of declining prices may not be available. This is especially true for funds that have come into existence during the recent bull market.

Some organizations, such as Morningstar, rate a mutual fund's performance relative to other funds with the same investment objectives, but this too can be misleading for investors trying to choose a fund. (Morningstar's Internet address is: *www.morningstar.com.*) First, even though they have similar objectives the funds may not be comparable. One may have riskier assets than another, so a comparison is not appropriate. Second, past performance may not be a reliable indicator of future performance.

In choosing a fund, investors are better off looking at what the fund invests in (as best as can be determined) and then trying to determine the volatility in terms of up and down markets.

Yield is one aspect of performance. Yield is defined as the interest and/or dividends paid to shareholders as a percentage of the net asset value price. Money market funds quote yields over a seven-day period. This is an average dividend yield for seven days, and it can be annualized. Long-term bond funds also quote an annualized average yield, but it is generally over 30 days.

This yield is a measure of the fund's dividend distribution over a 30-day period and is only one aspect of the fund's *total return.* Mutual funds pass on any gains or losses to shareholders, which can increase or decrease the fund's total return.

Another factor that affects total return is fluctuation in net asset value. When the share price increases by 6 percent, it effectively increases the total return by an additional 6 percent. Similarly, when the net asset value price of the fund declines, total return will decrease. This explains why funds can have a negative return. It is what happened when the Asian currencies went into turmoil in 1998 and affected share prices of Pacific Rim mutual funds. These funds had been doing well, but their returns were diminished by the steep declines in their net asset value prices.

The interest on reinvested dividends is another factor in the total return. When the interest or dividends paid out by the fund are reinvested to buy more shares, the yield earned on these reinvested shares will boost the overall return on the invested capital.

Therefore, when comparing the total returns quoted by the different funds, you need to make sure you are comparing the same type of total return. In short, the total return of a mutual fund includes the following three components:

- Dividends and capital gains or losses.
- Changes in net asset value.
- Dividends (interest) on reinvested dividends.

When total returns are quoted by funds, you should ask whether all of these are included in the computation.

Expenses are a key factor in differentiating the performance of the different funds. By painstakingly looking for funds with the highest yields, investors are only looking at half the picture. A fund with a high yield may also be the one that charges higher expenses, which could put that fund behind some of the lower-cost funds with lower yields. Fees reduce the total return earned by a fund.

The mutual fund industry has been criticized for the proliferation of fees and charges. Granted, these are all disclosed by the mutual funds, but besides the conspicuous charges, investors need to know where to look to find the less obvious fees.

Load Funds versus No-Load Funds

Some mutual funds are *no-load* funds in that the investor pays no commission or fee to buy or sell the shares of the fund. With an investment of $10,000 in a no-load fund, every cent of the $10,000 goes to buying shares in the fund. You can no longer easily identify no-load funds in the newspapers. However, you can easily find out whether the fund that you are interested in is a no-load fund by calling the mutual fund family, looking on its Website, or examining the prospectus.

A *load fund* charges a sales commission for buying shares in the fund. These fees can be quite substantial, as high as $8\frac{1}{2}$ percent of the purchase price of the shares. The amount of the sales (load) charge per share can be determined by deducting the net asset value price from the offer price. Some funds give quantity discounts on their loads to investors who buy shares in large blocks. For example, the sales load might be 5 percent for amounts under $100,000, $4\frac{1}{4}$ percent for investing between $100,000 to $200,000, and $3\frac{1}{2}$ percent for amounts in excess of $200,000. When buying load funds, you have to check to see whether they charge a load on reinvested dividends as well.

Some funds also charge a *back-load* or exit fee when you sell the shares in the fund. This can be a straight percentage, or the percentage charged may decline the longer the shares are held in the fund.

The ultimate effect of load charges is to reduce the total return. The impact of the load charge is felt more keenly if the fund is held for a short period of time. For instance, if a fund has a return of 6 percent and there is a 4 percent load to buy into the fund, the total return to the investor for the year is sharply reduced. If there is a back-end load to exit the fund, this could be even more expensive for the investor. If the share price has increased, the load percentage will be calculated on a larger amount.

Don't be fooled by some funds that tout themselves as no-load funds but by another name assess fees that come right out of the investor's investment dollars like a load. These fees are not called loads, but they work exactly the same. Their uses are to defray some of the costs of opening accounts or buying stocks for the fund's portfolio. They vary from 1 to 3 percent among the different fund groups.

From the investor's point of view, it should not matter how lofty the purpose for these fees. They reduce your investment. If you invest $10,000 and there is a 3 percent fee, only $9700 of your investment will go toward buying shares.

Why then would so many investors invest in load funds when these commissions eat away so much of their returns? One can only speculate on possible answers:

- Investors may not want to make decisions by themselves as to which funds to invest in, so they leave the decisions to their brokers and financial planners.
- Brokers and financial planners earn their livings from selling investments from which they are paid commissions. These include load funds.
- No-load funds do not pay commissions to brokers and financial planners.

Do Load Funds Outperform No-Load Funds?

There is no evidence to support the opinions expressed by many brokers and financial planners that load funds outperform no-load funds. According to CDA/Weisenberger, there was no difference between the performance of the average no-load fund and load

TABLE 9-3

What Is a Hedge Fund?

Before defining a hedge fund, it is important to say what it is not. A hedge fund is not a mutual fund. Hedge funds are not required to register with the Securities and Exchange Commission (SEC) if they have fewer than 99 investors. However, investors in a hedge fund must be accredited by the SEC. In other words, investors must have at least $375,000 in liquid assets and be able to withstand the risks. The minimum investment in a U.S. hedge fund is generally over a quarter of a million dollars (Strong, p.435)

U.S. hedge funds have been in existence for almost 50 years, and they typically take the form of limited partnerships. Hedge funds have numerous investment styles, including market neutral strategies, in addition to the high- and low-risk strategies. Because they are not as heavily regulated as mutual funds, hedge funds do not have the same limits on the types of investments they can make. However, there are limits on how investors can withdraw their funds. Many hedge funds allow investors to withdraw money only at the end of the year. Others may only allow investors to withdraw at the end of each quarter (Scholl and Bary, p.19).

Hedge funds are not allowed to advertise, but information on them can be obtained from a number of publications, among them Hedge Fund News, Lookout Mountain Hedge Fund Review, and Barclay Hedge Fund Report.

fund over a five-year period (Clements). In fact, when adjusting for sales commissions, investors would have been better off with no-load funds.

Less obvious than loads are *12 (b) 1 fees*. These are charged by many funds to recover expenses for marketing and distribution. These fees are assessed annually and can be quite steep when added together with load fees. Many no-load funds tout the absence of sales commissions but tack on 12 (b)-1 fees, in essence, a hidden load. A 1 percent 12 (b)-1 fee may not sound like very much, but it is $100 less per annum in your pocket on a $10,000 mutual fund investment.

In addition to the above-mentioned charges, funds have *management fees* that are paid to the managers who administer the fund's portfolio of investments. These can range from a 0.5 percent to 2 percent of assets. High management fees also take a toll on the investor's total return.

Thus, all fees bear watching, since they reduce yields and total returns. Critics of the mutual fund industry have cultivated a sense of awareness regarding the proliferation of all these charges. Indeed, investors should not be deceived by funds that claim to be what they are not. Lowering front-end loads or eliminating them altogether doesn't mean a fund can't add fees somewhere else.

Funds have to disclose their fees, which means that investors can find them in the fund's prospectus. Management fees, 12 (b)-1 fees, redemption fees (back-end loads), and any other fees charged are disclosed somewhere in the fund's prospectus. The financial newspapers also list the types of charges of the different funds in their periodic mutual fund performance reviews.

You may want to follow these guidelines to choose a fund:

- Examine the performance records of the funds that you are interested in.
- Compare their total expenses and fees.
- Narrow the field of funds you feel will be the best choice in terms of performance. If there is no difference in performance, go with the fund that has the lowest expenses.

WHAT IS THE SIGNIFICANCE
OF THE PROSPECTUS?

Besides information about the different funds that can be obtained
from business magazines, newspapers and advisory services, and
Internet Websites, essential information is provided by the mutual
fund's prospectus. Currently, funds are required to send a prospectus to a potential investor before accepting investment funds.
However, the SEC is testing a new proposal, so this may change.
This will allow mutual funds to dispense with sending a prospectus as long as the key points of the prospectus are included in their
advertisements. The information in the advertisements would be
legally binding. If there were any facts that were not true, investors
could sue. However, there is a vast gray area of puffery that has the
potential for causing tremendous confusion among investors.
Imagine the clever letters advertisers of mutual funds could dream
up to send as direct mail to potential investors:

Dear Potential Investor:
    The markets are going to tumble, in addition to....No need for
you to bear these hardships. Invest in XYZ Fund and reap the
rewards.

    Sincerely,

    E. Z. Prey
    Chairman,
    XYZ Fund

    Although prospectuses are written in a manner that ranks
them high on the list of cures for insomnia, they still provide
investors with essential information about the fund that may not
be obtainable anywhere else.
    You should look for the following in the prospectus.

Objectives

The objectives and policies of the fund generally appear near the
front of the prospectus. The objectives describe the type of securities the fund invests in as well as the risk factors associated with

them. For instance, if the prospectus states that the fund will buy growth securities, the investor should not be surprised to find that most of the stocks will have high price/earnings ratios and may include more risky small-cap stocks.

The investment policies will outline the latitude of the fund manager to invest in other types of securities. This could include trading futures contracts, writing options to hedge bets on the direction of interest rates or the market or investing in derivative securities to boost the yield of the fund. Many so-called conservative funds, which supposedly only hold blue-chip stocks, have on occasion resorted to small company and offshore stocks to boost returns. The greater the latitude in investing in these other types of securities, the greater the risks if events go awry.

Selected per Share Data and Ratios

The selected per share data and ratios table in the prospectus summarizes the fund's performance over the time period shown. Table 9-4 gives an example of such a table. Although these will vary in detail from fund to fund, the format will be similar.

The investment activities section shows the amount of investment income earned on the securities held by the fund; this income is passed on to the mutual fund shareholders. For instance, in 1999 all of the net investment income of $0.37 was distributed to the shareholders (line 4), but in 1998 only $0.30 of the $0.31 of net income was paid out to shareholders. In this year, the $0.01 which was not distributed to shareholders increased the net asset value (line 7) in the capital changes section. (The capital loss and distribution of gains was reduced by the $0.01 that was not distributed.)

Capital gains and losses also affect the net asset value. Funds distribute their realized capital gains (line 6), but the unrealized capital gains or losses will also increase or decrease the net asset value.

Changes in the net asset value from year to year give you some idea of the volatility in share price. For instance, for the year 1998, the net asset value decreased by $1.01, which is a 9.17 percent decrease. How comfortable would you feel in the short term if you invested $10,000 knowing it could decline to $9082.65 (a 9.17 percent decline)?

TABLE 9-4

Selected per Share Data and Ratios

		1999	1998	1997
Net asset value (NAV)				
Beginning of the year		$10.02	$11.01	$10.73
Investment Activities				
line 1	Income	.40	.35	.55
line 2	Expenses	(.03)	(.04)	(.05)
line 3	Net investment income	.37	.31	.50
line 4	Distribution of dividends	(.37)	(.30)	(.47)
Capital Changes				
line 5	Net realized and unrealized gains (losses) on investments	$1.00	(.75)	1.50
line 6	Distributions of realized gains	(.70)	(.25)	(1.25)
line 7	Net increase (decrease) to NAV	.30	(.99)	.28
	NAV beginning of the year	10.02	11.01	10.73
	NAV at end of year	10.32	10.02	11.01
	Ratio of operating expenses to average net assets	.53%	.56%	.58%
	Ratio of net investment income to average net assets	.45%	.46%	.84%
	Portfolio turnover rate	121%	135%	150%
	Shares outstanding (000s)	10,600	8,451	6,339

The portfolio turnover rate gives prospective investors an idea of how actively the assets in the fund will be traded. A turnover rate of 100 percent indicates that the assets will be sold once in the year. This is measured in the total value of the assets. For example, if the fund holds stocks with a value of $100 million, then $100 million of stocks will be traded once a year. According to Morningstar Mutual Funds, as reported by the Vanguard Group (March 11,1999) the average stock mutual fund turnover was 86 percent. High portfolio turnover (200 percent +) may not necessarily be bad for shareholders, since the fund may be generating high capital gains.

High turnover also is an indication for shareholders to expect to incur capital gains distributions, which will be taxed at the end of the year. This is so even if investors have chosen the reinvestment option, i.e., to buy more shares with the distribution in lieu of receiving the cash. In accounting terms, the net asset value of the shares in the fund is reduced by the amount of the distribution per share.

Index funds have extremely low turnover, around 5 percent (Vanguard Group). The advantages of lower turnover are decreased costs and greater tax efficiency. However, a fund may also have low turnover because it has been holding low-performing stocks for a long period of time in the hope of a turnaround. This has occurred with many value funds whose value stocks have not participated as fully in the stock market rally of the three years from 1996 to 1999.

The ratio of operating expenses to average net assets is fairly low in this hypothetical fund (close to one-half of 1 percent).

Investors can calculate an average total return, taking into account the three types of return (dividends distributed, capital gains distributed, and the changes in share price), by using the following formula:

$$\text{Average total return} = \frac{\left(\begin{array}{c}\text{dividend + capital}\\\text{gains distributions}\end{array}\right) + \dfrac{\text{ending NAV - beginning NAV}}{\text{year}}}{\dfrac{\text{ending NAV + beginning NAV}}{2}}$$

$$\text{Average total return for 1999} = \frac{(.37+.70)+\left(\dfrac{10.32-10.02}{1}\right)}{\left(\dfrac{10.32+10.02}{2}\right)}$$

$$=13.5\%$$

This simple yield of 13.5 percent indicates that an investor in this fund would have received double-digit returns due mainly to realized gains and increases in the NAV share price. The more volatile the net asset value of the fund, the greater the likelihood of unstable returns. Thus, when considering whether to invest in a particular fund, don't go by the advertised yield alone; look at the total return.

Annual Expenses

Although annual expenses are shown in the selected per share data and ratios section, mutual fund prospectuses will have a separate table with a breakdown of expenses. This typically shows the different load charges, redemption fees, shareholder accounting costs, 12 (b)-1 fees, distribution costs, and other expenses.

By examining the prospectuses of the funds you are interested in, you will be able to make a more informed choice than if you merely go by the advertised messages of the funds.

WHAT ARE THE TAX CONSEQUENCES OF BUYING AND SELLING SHARES IN MUTUAL FUNDS?

Tax reporting on mutual funds can be complicated. Even if you buy and hold shares in a mutual fund, there are tax consequences. Dividends paid to investors may have been automatically reinvested in the fund to buy more shares. At the end of the year, the mutual fund will send a Form 1099 to each mutual fund holder showing the amount of dividends and capital gains received for the year. Individual shareholders pay taxes on these dividends and capital gains. Therefore, these dividends and capital gains need to be added into the cost basis when the investor sells the shares in the fund.

For example, suppose an investor invested $10,000 in a fund two years ago and has received a total of $2000 in dividends and capital gains in the fund to date. The investor sells all the shares in the fund and receives $14,000. The investor's cost basis is $12,000 (not $10,000), and the gain on the sale of the shares is $2000 ($14,000 − $12,000).

When investors sell only a part of their total shares, the procedure is different and may be tricky. This is further complicated when investors actively buy and sell shares as if the fund were a checking account. In fact, many mutual funds encourage investors to operate their funds like a checking account by providing check-writing services. However, every time an investor writes a check against a bond or stock fund, there is a capital gain or loss tax consequence. (This does not pertain to money market funds, which have a stable share price of one dollar.) This action either causes a nightmare for the investor at tax time or produces extra revenue for the investor's accountant for the additional time spent calculating the gains and losses.

The most important thing in an actively traded mutual fund (or any mutual fund for that matter) is to keep good records. For each fund, keep a separate folder and store all the monthly statements showing purchases and sales of shares, dividends, and capital gains distributions.

By keeping records of all transactions, investors will be able to determine the cost basis of shares sold. This can be done using either an average cost method or a FIFO basis, or using the specific identification method. *FIFO* is first in, first out, which means that the cost of the first shares purchased in the fund will be used first as the shares sold. Table 9-5 illustrates the FIFO method of calculating capital gains or losses on the partial sale of shares in a mutual fund. The example shows that the earliest shares purchased are the first to be used in the sale of shares. After all the shares of the invested funds are sold, the basis of the dividends and capital gains shares will be used to determine any gains or losses.

Several funds provide the gains and losses on an *average cost basis* when investors sell shares. The average cost method allows shareholders to average the cost of the shares in the fund. There is the single-category method and the double-category method. The former includes all the shares held in the fund. The double-category method involves separating the shares in the fund into short-term and long-term holdings and calculating average prices for these two categories. Redemptions use the short-term or long-term average price. The average cost basis can get quite complex with additional sales and purchases of shares. Hence, some funds don't allow their shareholders to write checks against their accounts.

The *specific identification method* allows shareholders to identify the specific shares that they wish to sell. Investors can minimize their gains by choosing to sell first shares with the highest cost basis.

To minimize any potential tax hassles, investors are better off not writing checks from their stock funds for their short-term cash needs. This only creates gains or losses where the investor would have been better off investing the money needed for short-term purposes in a money market fund, which alleviates these tax problems.

TABLE 9-5

Calculation of Gains/Losses on the Sale of Shares

Summary of Growth and Income Fund					
Date	**Transaction**	**Dollar Amount**	**Share Price**	**No. of Shares**	**Total No.**
06/14	Invest	$10,000	$10.00	1,000	1,000
11/26	Invest	4,500	9.00	500	1,500
11/30	Redeem (sell)	12,000	10.00	1,200	300
12/31	Dividends	1,000	10.00	100	400

To Calculate Gain/Loss on a FIFO Basis

Sold   1,200 shares at $10.00 per share   **Sale Price** 12,000

Cost Basis

06/14	1,000 shares at	$10.00	$10,000	
11/26	200 shares at	$9.00	1,800	
Total Cost				11,800
Gain				200

Cost Basis of the Growth and Income Fund After Sale

Date	**Transaction**	**Dollar Amount**	**Share Price**	**No. of Shares**	**Total No.**
11/26	Invested	$2,700	9.00	300	300
12/31	Dividends	1,000	10.00	100	400

Whether you trade actively or not, the solution to tax computations is to keep good records. If you can't determine the cost basis of your shares, an accountant will be able to do so, provided you keep records. If you don't have all the records of your purchases and sales, you may not be able to prove your cost basis to the Internal Revenue Service if it's disputed.

WHAT ARE THE RISKS OF MUTUAL FUNDS?

The major risk with mutual funds is the *risk of loss of funds invested* due to a decline in net asset value. This can be caused by many factors, such as interest rate risk, market risk, and the quality of the securities, to name a few. When interest rates go up in the economy, it tends to depress both the stock and the bond markets. This causes the net asset values of bond and stock funds to go down in price. Similarly, when market rates of interest go down, bond and stock prices (and the net asset values of bond and stock funds) appreciate.

The *quality of the securities* will determine the volatility of the fund's price swings. Stock funds that invest in small company stocks and emerging growth stocks will see greater upward swings in price during bull markets and greater downward swings during bear markets than conservative income equity funds which invest in the stocks of larger, more established companies. Some small company funds have knowingly invested in small stocks of dubious value, which has caused some losses to their funds.

Standard & Poor's Ratings Services, known for their ratings of individual bonds, are introducing a rating service for mutual funds. The funds will be rated with a select rating or not rated at all. To be eligible for a select rating, mutual funds must provide:

- Three years of performance data and outperform their peers in terms of absolute returns and risk-adjusted returns.
- Interviews with fund managers.
- Assessments of current and historical asset holdings and reviews of the fund's stability.
- Releases of data regarding their asset holdings to S&P four times a year.

S&P has already released the names of 24 funds in the large-cap growth category that earned the select rating. The list is available on the Internet at *www.standardandpoor's.com/onfunds* (O'Brien, p. C12).

As a result of some bank failures and the shaky financial status of some of the country's savings and loan associations, some investors are naturally concerned about the *risk of insolvency* of mutual funds. There is always the risk that a mutual fund could go under, but the chance of this happening is small. The key distinction between banks and mutual funds is the way that mutual funds are set up, which reduces the risk of failure and loss due to fraud. Typically, mutual funds are corporations owned by shareholders. A separate management company is contracted by the shareholders to run the fund's daily operations. The management company oversees the investments of the fund, but it does not have possession of these assets (investments). The investments are held by a custodian, such as a bank. Thus, if the management company gets into financial trouble, it cannot get access to the investments of the fund. However, even with these checks and balances, there is always the possibility of fraud. It has come to light that two mutual funds, which were cleared by the Securities and Exchange Commission and whose prices were quoted in the financial newspapers along with all the other mutual funds, were in essence bogus funds.

Another safeguard is that shareholders' accounts are maintained by a transfer agent. The transfer agent keeps track of the purchases and redemptions of the shareholders. In addition, management companies carry fidelity bonds, a form of insurance to protect the investments of the fund against malfeasance or fraud perpetrated by employees.

Besides these safeguards, there are two other factors that differentiate mutual funds from corporations like banks and savings and loan associations:

- Mutual funds must be able to redeem shares on demand, which means that a portion of the investment assets must be liquid.
- Mutual funds must be able to price their investments at the end of each day, which is known as *marking to market*.

Hence, mutual funds cannot hide their financial difficulties as easily as banks and savings and loans.

Mutual funds are regulated by the SEC, but as noted earlier, fraudulent operators will always find a way into any industry. The risk of fraud is always present, but it is no greater in the mutual fund industry than in any other industry. Investors should be aware, however, that they can lose money by purchasing a fund whose investments perform poorly on the markets.

HOW TO BUY AND SELL MUTUAL FUNDS

Buying and selling shares in mutual funds can be accomplished in several ways, depending on whether the fund is a load or no-load fund. Investors buy into no-load mutual funds dealing directly with the mutual fund. Most, if not all, funds have toll-free telephone numbers. Mutual funds will send first-time investors a prospectus along with an application form to open an account. The prospectus and application form can also be downloaded from a fund's Website on the Internet. Once investors have opened accounts with the fund, they can purchase additional shares by sending a check along with a preprinted account stub detached from the account statement. As mentioned earlier, there are no sales commissions with no-load funds, so they are not sold by brokers. Shares in no-load funds are bought and sold at their net asset values.

Load funds are sold through brokers and salespeople who charge commissions every time new shares are bought. Some funds also charge a redemption fee, which is a back-end fee, or reverse load, for selling shares. If the percentage loads are the same (for front-end or back-end), it may be preferable to go for a reverse load rather than a front load because all the money is invested immediately with the back-end load (Faerber, p. 177).

Financial planners, brokers, and salespeople may try to convince you to buy load funds claiming they perform better than no-load funds. There is no evidence to support this premise for either stock or bond mutual funds. In fact, according to a study by Morningstar, a Chicago firm that tracks mutual funds, no-load bond funds consistently outperformed load funds over 3-, 5-, and 10-year periods through March 31, 1993 (McGough). However, there may be some truth to the claim that no-load bond and stock funds are much more volatile than load funds during expanding and contracting markets.

Banks and discount brokerage firms have also entered the mutual fund arena, and they too sell mutual funds. This, of course, further complicates the choice process, but investors who feel confident enough to choose their own funds are better off with no-load funds. The difference saved may be minimal over a short period of time, but this difference can grow substantially over a 10-year period due to the compounding of interest (time value of money). A study done by Morningstar on performance and expenses among diversified U.S. stock funds found that over a 10-year period ending in 1993, the 25 percent of funds with the lowest expenses increased on average by 13.4 percent as opposed to the highest-cost funds, which averaged only 11.5 percent after expenses (McGough).

Information can also be obtained from the individual mutual fund companies' Websites along with other Websites on the

Internet. One such Website is *www.fundsinteractive.com*.

Table 9-6 summarizes the information you should consider when selecting one mutual fund over another.

Investors can invest in mutual funds only, or they can use mutual funds along with individual investments in stocks and bonds to produce a broadly diversified portfolio. As mentioned in earlier chapters, your portfolio should be divided up into stocks, bonds, and money market securities in order to lower the overall risks of loss. Diversification within the asset class is another tool that reduces the overall risks of loss.

The equity style box in Figure 9-1 is a useful tool in choosing funds that will give investors broad diversification in the market. This style box can also be used for international equity funds. Value funds invest in stocks which are perceived to be trading below their intrinsic values. The fund may invest in small-cap stocks, or it may be a medium-cap or large-cap fund. Growth stock funds invest in stocks with high growth in sales and market share. These stocks tend to trade at high price multiples to their earnings. By diversifying into the different sectors of the equity markets, investors can reduce their risk of loss even though they may be sacrificing some on performance. This does not mean that investors should invest in funds for each of the nine styles. Some investors

TABLE 9-6

Criteria to Consider When Choosing Mutual Fund

- Select funds with low costs.
- Don't overrate past performance. Top performance funds can lose their edge over time.
- Use performance data to see the range of performance and the risks of the fund.
- Don't buy too many funds, as you will become overdiversified.
- Define your long-term objectives, time horizon, risk tolerance, and then stick with the funds over the long term.

FIGURE9-1

Style of Equity Mutual Funds

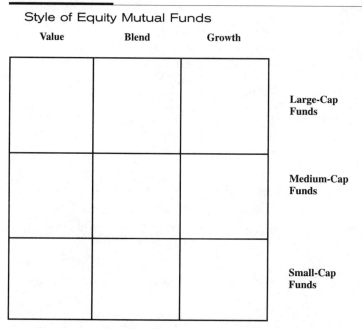

Source: Morningstar Mutual Funds as reported in "Measuring Mutual Fund Performance," *Plain Talk LIbrary*, Vanguard Group.

are more comfortable in value stocks, which have low P/Es, while others may prefer to hold a fund that invests in high-growth, high P/E stocks like Cisco Systems, Lucent Technologies, Yahoo, and Home Depot. Investors should choose the style of investment that they are most comfortable with and then diversify into domestic and foreign small-, mid-, or large-cap funds.

Index funds offer broad diversification in the different markets. By investing in the S&P 500 Index fund and a small-cap index fund, investors would have broad diversification in both large-cap stocks and small-cap stocks.

ADVANTAGES OF MUTUAL FUNDS

- Mutual funds offer investors the opportunity to own a fraction of a diversified portfolio. For instance, investing $2500 in a stock fund gives the investor a share of an excellent cross section of stocks. Investors would need to invest at least $50,000 in individual stocks to have a diversified portfolio of about 12 different stocks.

- Mutual funds provide administrative and custodial services; recordkeeping of all transactions, monthly statements, and information for tax purposes, as well as the safekeeping of all securities.
- Mutual funds are professionally managed. Many investors do not have the time or the expertise to manage their stock portfolios.
- Mutual fund companies redeem shares on demand. In the case of no-load funds, they are redeemed at net asset value.
- Investors have the option of reinvesting dividends and capital gains automatically for more shares in the fund or having them paid out to them in cash.
- Investors in a family of funds can switch from one fund to another as market conditions change. For example, when interest rates are going up, investors can switch money from their stock funds to money market funds.
- Levels of risk, return, and stability of income and principal vary with the type of fund chosen. Most families of mutual funds offer a range of different types of stock and bond funds with various characteristics.

DISADVANTAGES OF MUTUAL FUNDS

- Professional management does not guarantee superior performance. Many funds underperform the market over long periods of time.
- When load charges and fees are included, total returns may be significantly less than if investors bought individual stocks and bonds and held for long periods of time during bull markets.
- Investors have no control over the investment decisions that portfolio managers make.
- Investors have no control over the distribution of hidden capital gains, which can upset very careful tax planning.

Since investment companies do not pay taxes, income and capital gains are passed through to the shareholders.

CAVEATS

- Choose a mutual fund family with a wide range of different funds. This allows you greater flexibility to transfer from one fund type to another.
- Avoid funds with high sales charges, redemption fees, and management and expense ratios.
- Keep all the records of income and capital gains distributions, as well as the dates, amounts, and share prices of all purchases and redemptions of shares. This can alleviate a potential nightmare at tax time.
- Avoid buying into a mutual fund toward the end of the year because you could be increasing your tax burden. Before buying into a fund, investigate whether the fund has accumulated any capital gains distributions which have not yet been distributed to shareholders. This occurs when fund managers sell investments at higher prices than their purchase prices, which results in capital gains. These gains are passed onto shareholders at the end of the year through a capital gains distribution, even if the shareholders did not own the fund when the gains were incurred.

SHOULD YOU INVEST IN INDIVIDUAL SECURITIES OR MUTUAL FUNDS?

Stock and bond mutual funds have been very popular among investors, and record amounts have been invested in them over the years. The advantages of mutual funds, as stated earlier, are professional management, diversification, being able to invest small amounts of money, and the ease of buying and selling. For many investors, these advantages far outweigh the disadvantages of mutual funds. Mutual funds may be the most practical way for investors to buy many types of securities. Mutual funds, therefore, allow investors to own many different, complex types of bonds. Similarly, the decision of which individual stocks to select may be mind-boggling for many investors.

The diversification achieved by mutual funds minimizes the impact from any unexpected losses from individual stocks in the portfolio as well as the fact that professional managers of these funds have quicker access to information about the different issues. This means that they react sooner in buying or selling the securities in question.

However, in certain cases, there is a strong argument for buying individual securities over mutual funds. Rates of return on individual stocks and bonds may often be greater than those earned from mutual funds. This is true even for no-load funds because besides sales commissions, there are other fees (12 (b)-1 fees, operating fees) that eat into the returns of mutual funds. By investing in individual securities, investors avoid these fees.

If investors have small amounts of money to invest, mutual funds are a better alternative. A $2000 investment into a stock fund will buy a fraction of a diversified portfolio of stocks, whereas individually, this may allow for buying the shares of only one company.

Investing in mutual funds is good for investors who do not have enough money to diversify their investments and who also do not have the time, expertise, or inclination to select and manage individual securities. In addition, there is a wide range of funds offering investors the opportunity to invest in securities that would be difficult to buy on an individual basis.

REFERENCES

Clements, Jonathan: "The 25 Facts Every Fund Investor Should Know," *The Wall Street Journal*, March 5, 1993, p. C1.

——"Funds That Look Dull Can Be Real Daredevils," *The Wall Street Journal*, March 4, 1994, p. C1.

Faerber, Esmé: *Managing Your Investments, Savings and Credit*, McGraw-Hill, New York, 1992).

: *All About Bonds*, McGraw-Hill, New York, 1993.

Harlan, Christi: "SEC to Require More Wrap Account Data," *The Wall Street Journal*, April 20, 1994, p. C1.

Jereski, Laura: "What Price CMOs? Funds Have No Idea," *The Wall Street Journal*, April 12, 1993, p. C1.

O'Brien, Bridget: "Standard & Poor's Introduces Ratings for Mutual Funds," *The Wall Street Journal*, March 9, 1999, p. C12.

McGough, Robert: "Banks vs. Brokers: Who's Got the Best Funds?" *The Wall Street Journal,* May 7, 1993, p. C1.

————"Use Yardsticks to Weed Through Fees," *The Wall Street Journal,* July 7, 1994, p. R8.

Savage, Stephen: "Refrigerator Rules. ABCs for Today's Complex Fund Climate," *Barron's,* February 15, 1993, p. 43.

Scholl, Jaye, and Andrew Bary: "A Lousy New Year," *Barron's,* October 12, 1998, p. 19.

Schultz, Ellen: "How to Unwrap a Wrap Account," *The Wall Street Journal,* February 5, 1993, p. C1.

Strong, Robert A.: *Practical Investment Management,* Cincinnati, South-Western College Publishing Co., 1996.

Tergesen, Anne, and Peter Coy: "Who Needs a Money Manager," *Business Week,* February 22, 1999, pp. 127–132.

Thau, Annette: *The Bond Book,* McGraw-Hill, New York, 1992.

Vanguard Group 1999: "FUNDamentals: Turnover," *www.Vanguard.com,* March 11, 1999.

CHAPTER 10

Closed-End Funds*

KEY CONCEPTS:

- What are closed-end funds?
- What are unit investment trusts?
- What are index tracking stock unit investment trusts?
- What are the risks of closed-end funds and unit investment trusts?
- What are real estate investment trusts (REITs)?
- Guidelines for the selection of REITs
- How to buy and sell closed-end funds
- What are the advantages of closed-end funds and unit investment trusts?
- What are the disadvantages of closed-end funds and unit investment trusts?
- Are closed-end funds and unit investment trusts suitable for you?

WHAT ARE CLOSED-END FUNDS?

Closed-end funds bear certain similarities to open-end mutual funds, but there are some significant differences. Table 10-1 sum-

*Portions of this chapter have been previously published by Esmé Faerber in *All About Bonds and Bond Mutual Funds* (McGraw-Hill, New York, 2000).

marizes the differences. As pointed out in the previous chapter,
open-end mutual funds issue an unlimited number of shares, and
they will redeem shares from shareholders when they want to sell.
When investors buy more shares in an open-end fund, more money
is available to the fund manager to buy more investment assets.

Closed-end funds have a fixed number of shares outstanding,
and after these are sold, the fund does not issue any new shares.
Most closed-end funds are traded on the New York Stock
Exchange, some on the American Stock Exchange, and a few on the
over-the-counter market.

Since the number of shares in a closed-end fund is fixed,
investors who want to invest in an existing fund (as opposed to a
new fund) have to buy shares from shareholders who are willing to
sell their shares on the market. Consequently, the share price of the
closed-end fund fluctuates, depending on the supply and demand
for the shares and other factors, such as the return of the fund, the
average price of the stocks in the fund, the average maturity of the
assets of the fund (in the case of bonds), net asset value, and so forth.

Like open-end mutual funds, the net asset value is important
in the valuation of the share price. Unlike open-end funds, however,
share prices of closed-end funds can be above or below their net

TABLE 10-1

Closed-End Funds versus Open-End Funds

Closed-End Funds	Open-End Funds
1. Issues a fixed number of shares, which are sold to original shareholders.	1. Issues an unlimited number of shares.
2. Shares (after issue) are traded on the stock exchanges.	2. Shares (including new shares) may be bought from and sold to the fund.
3. Shares may trade at above, or below net asset values.	3. Shares trade at the net asset values.
4. Share prices depend not only on the fundamentals but also on the supply and demand for the shares.	4. Share prices depend on the fundamentals of the assets in the fund.
5. Closed-end funds do not mature. except for zero-coupon funds.	5. Open-end funds do not mature

asset values. For example, when market rates of interest decline, there may be heavy demand for closed-end funds, and that can drive their share prices above their net asset values. Hence, these funds would trade at premiums. During the currency crises in Asia and Latin America, many of the closed-end Asian and Latin American country funds fell in price and traded at significant discounts to their net asset values. For example, as of March 3, 1999, the Argentina Fund, (ticker symbol AF on the New York Stock Exchange) was trading at $8.63 per share, a 24 percent discount to its net asset value. At times, the discounts to net asset values of closed-end funds can be as much as 20 to 30 percent.

The type of assets held in the fund will affect the share price. The more risky the assets, the greater the volatility in share price.

As with open-end funds, there are many different types of closed-end funds. There are stock funds, bond funds, international funds, and specialized funds. There are also many different types of closed-end stock funds. There are diversified equity funds, specialized stock funds, and convertible funds. *Diversified stock funds* hold the stocks of companies from different industries and as the name suggests, provide the investor with a diversified portfolio of investments. *Specialized funds* concentrate on specific types of securities or industries, such as ASA Limited, which focuses on South African gold mining shares. Other examples are *country funds*, such as the Italy Fund, Turkey Fund, and Chile Fund, which focus on each country's investments, respectively.

Depending on the investment objectives of the closed-end fund, the professional managers (of the fund) will invest in different financial assets to make up a diversified portfolio. Even though closed-end funds do not issue new shares to expand their capital structure, their portfolio assets can and do change. Existing stock and bond issues may be sold and new ones bought for the portfolio. Closed-end funds, like open-end funds, never mature.

Net asset values for closed-end funds are calculated in much the same way as for open-end funds. The total assets minus any liabilities equals the net worth for the fund, which is divided by the fixed number of shares to give the net asset value per share.

Occasionally, closed-end funds become open-end mutual funds, and the net asset value becomes the price that the shares trade at through the mutual fund, that is, if it becomes a no-load fund. For a load fund, there will be an additional commission added to the net asset value.

There are closed-end funds that have a fixed maturity date, which are called *term trusts*. These term trusts invest in bonds which have the same maturity date, and at the termination date, the proceeds from the investments are returned to the unit holders. There are other types of closed-end funds that individual investors should be aware of: unit investment trusts (UITs), real estate investment trusts (REITs) and dual funds.

WHAT ARE UNIT INVESTMENT TRUSTS?

In the closed-end bond fund market, unit investment trusts have become very popular. Brokerage firms such as Merrill Lynch, Bear Stearns, Nuveen, and Van Kampen and Merritt all sponsor unit trusts.

Unit investment trusts have been seductively marketed as the investment that earns high current income as well as returning an investor's entire investment when the trust assets mature. Theoretically, this is possible, but in practice, it may not always be the case. By examining how unit trusts work, the difficulty of living up to these lofty promises becomes apparent.

A unit investment trust, like a closed-end fund, will sell a fixed number of shares. For instance, assume that the trust sells one million shares at $10 per share for a total of $10 million. Sales commissions of $500,000 would be deducted, leaving the unit trust $9.5 million to invest in different bond issues, (same for a closed-end bond fund). The trust will then remit the earnings on the investments, minus management fees, to the shareholders. When the different investments mature, the trust will pay back the proceeds from the investments to the shareholders. (Closed-end funds differ in that when issues mature, the proceeds are reinvested in other issues).

However, before looking at the factors that could make it difficult for the trust to live up to its promise of high income and the full return of principal, let's take a look at some of the differences between unit trusts and closed-end funds.

In general, with unit investment trusts, the portfolio of investments does not change after purchase. In other words, no new bonds are bought and no existing bonds are sold. Theoretically, as the bond issues approach maturity, the prices of the individual bonds will rise toward their par prices. So theoretically, management fees should be lower on unit investment trusts than on closed-end funds, since the portfolio remains unmanaged. Generally, the only time that bonds may be sold in a unit investment trust is when there is a severe decline in the quality of the issues. In fact, there should be no management fees on a unit investment trust, but in most instances, this is not the case. With closed-end bond funds, the portfolio changes as issues are bought and sold.

Shares of unit investment trusts, like those of closed-end bond funds, trade on the secondary markets. Under certain conditions, however, shares in unit investment trusts can become illiquid. This happens when interest rates are rising and new investors do not want to buy into a trust with bond investments that are locked into lower yields. Hence, existing unit trust shareholders might have difficulty selling their shares due to their illiquidity.

INDEX TRACKING STOCK UNIT INVESTMENT TRUSTS

Some new unit investment trusts, which come in the form of tracking stocks, have been introduced by the American Stock Exchange (Amex). In 1993, the Amex introduced *SPDRs* (spiders), an index tracking stock, which tracks the S&P 500 Index. In January of 1998, the Amex introduced *DIAMONDS*, which track the 30 stocks in the Dow Jones Industrial Average. In March of 1999, the Amex started trading a Nasdaq 100 tracking stock, which represents ownership in the 100 largest stocks in the Nasdaq. See Tables 10-2, 10-3, and 10-4, respectively, for descriptions of spiders, diamonds, and the Nasdaq 100 tracking stocks. More information on these investments can be obtained from the Nasdaq-Amex Website at *http://options.nasdaq-amex.com/indexshares/index_shares_spdrs.stm* or at *www.nasdaq100.com*.

THE ADVANTAGES OF INDEX TRACKING STOCK UNIT INVESTMENT TRUSTS

- These index tracking stocks offer investors diversification. Even though the stock prices that make up these indexes

TABLE 10-2

More about SPDRs (Spiders)

An investment trust based on the Standard & Poor's 500 Composite Stock Price Index, the SPDR Trust holds shares of all companies in the S&P 500 Index. The purchase of a single share in this trust gives the owner a share of the 500 large companies in the S&P 500 Index. There are several select specialized SPDRs which allow investors to track the financials in the S&P 500 Index, or the 79 tech stocks in the S&P, the utilities, industrials, and five other different sector SPDRs. These sector unit investment trusts are traded just like the main SPDRs which track the S&P 500 Index.

Ticker Symbol: SPY

Trading: Investors can buy and sell shares in Spiders on the American Stock Exchange

Trustee: State Street Bank and Trust Company

Life of the Trust: Throughout the 21st Century at a minimum

Approximate Share Price Ratio to S&P 500 Index: One-tenth S&P 500 Index

Dividends: Dividends are paid on a quarterly basis (Jan., April, July, Oct.)

Risks: Same risks as those experienced by other stocks, namely that there will be price fluctuations. There is also the risk that the trust may not replicate the exact performance of the S&P 500 Index because of expenses incurred by the trust.

Net Asset Value The net asset value per SPDR is calculated at the close of each business day. This value represents the market value of the stocks in the underlying index, plus any accrued dividends, minus any expenses on a per share basis.

Short Selling: Investors can sell Spiders short, and they can sell short on a downtick.

Source: Nasdaq Stock Market, Inc., 1999.

fluctuate when the markets are volatile, the impact of the fluctuations on each of the indexes may be more muted than those of a portfolio of individual stocks.

- Investing in these three unit investment trusts can give investors broad exposure to the blue-chip stocks through DIAMONDS, broad exposure to the 500 largest stocks on the markets through SPDRs, and exposure to the largest 100 Nasdaq stocks through the Nasdaq 100.
- Investors receive quarterly dividends. With the Nasdaq 100, dividends may be very small, since many of the stocks do not pay dividends.

TABLE 10-3

More About DIAMONDS

The DIAMOND trust is an investment trust based on the 30 stocks in the Dow Jones Industrial Average. The purchase of a single share in this trust gives the owner a share of the 30 Dow Jones Industrial Average stocks

Ticker Symbol: DIA

Trading: Investors can buy and sell shares in DIAMONDS on the American Stock Exchange

Life of the Trust: Throughout the 22nd century

Approximate Share Price Ratio to S&P 500 Index: 1/100th of the value of the DJIA

Dividends: Dividends are paid on a quarterly basis

Risks: Same risks as those experienced by other stocks, namely, that there will be price fluctuations. There is also the risk that the trust may not replicate the exact performance of the DJIA because of expenses incurred by the trust.

Net Asset Value: The net asset value per DIAMOND is calculated at the close of each business day. This value represents the market value of the stocks in the underlying index plus any accrued dividends, minus any expenses, on a per share basis.

Short Selling: Investors can sell DIAMONDS short.

Source: Nasdaq Stock Market, Inc., 1999. *www.nasdaq100.com*

- It's easy to buy and sell these tracking stocks. They are bought and sold just like any other stocks on the market.
- Investors do not need large amounts of money to buy these diversified trusts.

WHAT ARE THE RISKS OF CLOSED-END MUTUAL FUNDS AND UNIT INVESTMENT TRUSTS?

Both closed-end bond funds and unit investment trusts are subject to *interest rate risk*. When market rates of interest increase, generally, prices of the bond and stock issues held in both the portfolios of unit trusts and closed-end funds will go down. This, of course, means that the share prices will fall. Moreover, there is a double-edged sword effect, in that, if there is selling pressure on the shares, the decline in share prices will be even greater than the decline in the net

TABLE 10-4

More About Nasdaq100

This is an investment trust based on the 100 largest stocks in the Nasdaq market. The Nasdaq 100 trust holds the shares of the Nasdaq 100 stocks. The purchase of a single share in this trust gives the owner a share of all Nasdaq 100 stocks.

Ticker Symbol: QQQ

Trading: Investors can buy and sell shares in the Nasdaq 100 on the American Stock Exchange

Life of the Trust: Througout the 22nd Century

Trustee: Bank of New York

Approximate share price ratio to the Nasdaq 100: 1.20th of the value of the Nasdaq 100 Index

Dividends: Paid on a quarterly basis

Risks: Same risks as those experienced by other stocks, namely that there will be price fluctuations. The Nasdaq 100 tracking stock will be weighted more toward the fluctuations of Intel and Microsoft stocks due to their high concentrations in the index. There is also the risk that the trust may not replicate the exact performance of the Nasdaq 100 Index because of expenses incurred by the trust.

Net asset value: The net asset value per Nasdaq 100 tracking stock is calculated at the close of each business day. This value represents the market value of the stocks in the underlying index, plus any accrued dividends, minus any expenses on a per share basis.

Short Selling: Investors can sell Nasdaq 100 shares short and on a downtick.

Source: Nasdaq Stock Market, Inc., 1999. *www.nasdaq100.com*

asset values. The opposite is true in that if interest rates fall, there will be appreciation in the assets and, of course, in the share price.

For both closed-end funds and unit investment trusts, there is the risk that share prices will fall way below net asset values due to excess selling pressure in the stock markets. Then, of course, the danger arises of not being able, when selling, to recoup the original price paid for the shares. This is a common phenomenon experienced by closed-end funds and unit investment trusts.

In summary, investors in unit investment trusts should look beyond the advertised yield and scrutinize the makeup of the portfolio of investments. In reality, shareholders of unit investment trusts have no protection against either the deterioration of the quality of the investments in the portfolio or interest rate risk (Thau). Similarly, if there is an exodus of shareholders from unit investment trusts and closed-end funds, shareholders may find it difficult to sell their shares without taking large losses.

REAL ESTATE INVESTMENT TRUSTS (REITS)

Real estate investment trusts (REITs) offer individual investors the opportunity to invest in real estate without having to own and manage individual properties. REITs were popular during the middle of 1996 when the markets feared a surge in inflation, and investors turned to REITs as safe haven investments. A REIT is a form of closed-end mutual fund and it invests the proceeds received from the sale of shares to shareholders in real estate. REITs buy, develop, and manage real estate properties and pass on the income from the rent and mortgages to shareholders in the form of dividends.

REITs do not pay corporate income taxes, but in return, they must by law distribute 95 percent of their net income to their shareholders. What this also means is that there is not much income left to finance future real estate acquisitions.

There are three basic types of REITs:

- *Equity REITs,* which buy, operate, and sell real estate such as hotels, office buildings, apartments, and shopping centers.
- *Mortgage REITs,* which make construction and mortgage loans available to developers.
- *Hybrid REITs,* which are a combination of the equity and mortgage REITs. In other words, they may buy, develop, and manage real estate, in addition to providing financing through mortgage loans. Most hybrid REITs will have stronger positions in either equity or debt. There are very few well-balanced hybrid REITs.

These different types of REITs have different risks. They should be evaluated carefully before an investment is made in them. Generally, equity REITs tend to be less speculative than mortgage REITs, but the level of risk depends on the makeup of the assets in the trust. Mortgage REITs lend money to developers, which involves a greater risk of loss. Consequently, the shares of mortgage REITs tend to be more volatile than the shares of equity REITs.

Equity REITs have been the most popular type of REIT recently, and their performance of 5.31 percent (on average) outpaced the S&P average of a negative 3.9 percent for the first six months of 1994 (Zuckerman, p. 35). Equity REITs derive their income from rents received from the properties in their portfolios and from increasing property values.

Mortgage REITs are more sensitive to interest rate moves in the economy than equity REITs. This is because they hold mortgages, whose prices move in the opposite direction to interest rates. While equity REITs may be less sensitive to changes in interest rates, they too suffer the consequences of rising interest rates.

In the first six months of 1993, when interest rates were falling, mortgage REITs outpaced the S&P with a whopping 18 percent return versus 4.8 percent for the S&P.

Due to the different assets that mortgage and equity REITs hold, mortgage REITs tend to be more income-oriented, with the emphasis on current yields, whereas equity REITs offer the potential for capital gains in addition to current income.

REITs can either have finite or perpetual lives. Finite life real estate investment trusts, also known as FREITs, are self-liquidating. In the case of equity REITs, the properties will be sold at the end of a given time period. With mortgage REITs, when the mortgages are paid up, the profits are paid to the shareholders.

Guidelines for Selecting REITs

There are over 230 publicly listed REITs, making it difficult for investors to plow through them to find the better ones to invest in (Byrne, p. 32). Here are some guidelines that may be helpful:

- Investigate the REIT that you are interested in before you buy. Get an annual report from your broker or call the REIT directly and ask them to send you this information. Additional information can also be obtained from the National Association of Real Estate Investment Trusts, 1101 17th Street N.W., Washington D.C. 20036.

- Look to see how long the REIT has been in business. Directly related to this is how long the managers have been in the real estate business and how well they manage the assets. Select REIT investments with managers that have been in REITs for at least eight years (Dunnan, p. 181). Another question concerning management is how much of a personal stake they have in the REIT. According to Byrne, insiders should own at least 10 percent of the stock.
- Look at the level of debt of the REIT. The greater the level of debt, the greater the risk because more of the revenues will be needed to service the debt. If there is a downturn in revenues, the interest payments will become harder to service. Look for REITs with debt-to-equity ratios of less than 50 percent (Byrne, p. 32).
- Don't choose a REIT mainly because it has the highest yield. The higher the yield, the greater the risk. There have been cases where underwriters have raised the yield to hide poor fundamentals (Zuckerman, p. 35). On the other hand, too low a yield may mean the stock is overvalued.
- Select REITs that have low price-to-book values (1 to 1 or less).
- Check the dividend record of the REIT. There should be a history of dividends. Be wary of REITs that have recently cut their dividends. You should also check the source of cash for the payment of dividends. The cash for dividends should come from operations, not from the sale of properties.
- Location is everything in real estate. Look at the locations of the properties in the trust. You may want to avoid REITs that have invested in overbuilt or depressed locations.

Caveats

- Avoid REITs that are blind pools. These are set up generally by well-known management firms that raise funds to invest in unidentified properties. You want to see the makeup of the real estate assets and liabilities in any project before you invest.
- Do not invest more than 10 percent of your total investment portfolio in real estate.

DUAL FUNDS

A dual fund is a hybrid type of closed-end fund that has two classes of stock. One class receives the interest or dividends from the investments, while the other class receives the capital gains or losses from the sale of the investments in the fund. The latter class is known as the common stockholders. There is generally an expiration date for dual funds whereby the common stockholders vote to determine whether to liquidate the fund or to continue it on an open-end basis. There are not many dual funds traded on the markets.

HOW TO BUY AND SELL CLOSED-END FUNDS

When closed-end funds and unit investment trusts are newly issued, the shares are underwritten by brokerage firms and sold by brokers. Brokerage fees can be as high as 8 percent, which means that the investment is immediately reduced by that amount. For instance, if a fund or trust sells one million shares at $10 per share for $10 million, it will have only $9.2 million to invest after deducting the $800,000 (8 percent) for brokerage commissions. This means that after shareholders have paid $10 per share to invest in the new fund or trust, the shares will drop in value and trade at a discount. This is a quick erosion in capital and is a well-documented phenomenon for closed-end funds and unit investment trusts. This will not be a topic of conversation brought up by the brokers who stand to earn high commissions from the sale of these shares. Many brokers assert that closed-end funds are sold commission-free. This is a play on words, because while the fund may be commission-free, in its place is a hefty underwriting charge that is absorbed by the shareholders. Investors would do better to wait until the funds or trusts are listed on the stock exchanges than to buy them at issue and see the shares drop in price.

Another reason not to buy closed-end funds or unit investment trusts at issue is that the portfolio of assets has not yet been constituted, so investors do not know what they are getting, and they most certainly won't know what the yields will be. Unit investment trust sponsors do not like to see the shares of their trusts fall to discounts, so they often advertise above-market yields to keep the shares from trading at discounts to their net asset values.

The advice from expert Thomas Herzfeld, who follows closed-end funds and unit investment trusts, is to pay attention to the prices of the funds you are interested in and buy them when the discount is 3 percent wider than the normal discount for the fund (Thau).

Two University of North Florida professors studied the different trading strategies of closed-end funds over six five-year periods from January 1967 through December 1996. They found that a strategy that outperformed the S&P 500 Index by 525 percent over that period was to buy closed-end funds at 21 percent discounts to their net asset values and sell them when the gap narrowed to 19 percent discounts. The worst strategy they revealed was to buy at a 3 percent discount and sell when the funds were trading at the net asset values. Their results were not adjusted for capital gains and commissions, which would reduce their overall returns but would not invalidate the findings of their study (Barker, pp. 113–114).

This anomaly for beating the market suggests a higher-risk strategy for typical investors in that it advocates trading stocks as opposed to investing in stocks. On-line investing certainly makes it easier to do this, but there are also the additional risks of on-line trading (see Chapter 4, which outlines some of these risks). This strategy makes more sense for tax-free accounts (retirement accounts), but would investors want to expose their retirement money to greater risk?

Common sense suggests that besides the attractiveness of buying into a fund when its shares are selling below their net asset values, there are other factors to consider:

- The yield, particularly if investors are buying into the fund in order to get the income. Examine the yield, total return, and expense ratios before investing.
- The frequency with which dividends are paid: semiannually, quarterly, or monthly.
- The composition and the credit quality of the assets.
- The average length of time to maturity of the portfolio investments.

Information on closed-end funds can be found in Thomas J. Herzfeld Advisors annual *Encyclopedia of Closed-End Funds*, *Value Line Investment Survey*, *Standard & Poor's Record Sheets*, *Moody's*

Finance Manuals, and Wiesenberger's *Investment Companies* (in most public libraries). There are also several Internet sites that offer free information on closed-end funds:

www.morningstar.net
www.site-by-site.com
www.icefi.com

Share prices of the listed closed-end funds, unit investment trusts, and REITs can be found in the stock exchange sections of the daily newspapers as well as on many Websites on the Internet. For example, the following is a quote of the Argentina Fund listed in the daily newspapers on March 22, 1999:

								52 Weeks			

Hi	Low	Stock	Sym	Div	Yld %	P/E	Vol 100s	High	Low	Last	Chg
$13^5/_{16}$	$6^1/_2$	Argentina Fd	AF	.45e	4.8	—	136	$9^5/_8$	$9^3/_8$	$9^7/_{16}$	$-^3/_{16}$

Reading from left to right:

- The first two columns indicate the year's high of $13.3125 per share and the low of $6.50 per share.
- The name of the stock is the Argentina Fund, with the ticker symbol AF.
- The dividend expected is $0.45 per share.
- The yield percentage is 4.8 percent, which is the dividend divided by the last price of the day (.45 ÷ 9.4375).
- The volume indicates the number of shares traded that day, 13,600 shares.
- The high, low, and last indicate that the high price on the day quoted was $9.625; the low price for that day's trading was $9.375; and the last price was the closing price of $9.4375 per share.
- The change column indicates that the share price closed down 3/16th of a point from the previous day's close.

Barron's, the weekly financial newspaper, has a separate section that includes a comprehensive list of closed-end funds, including unit investment trusts. For example, the information provided below on the Argentina Fund is from *Barron's* World Equity Funds for the week ending March 22, 1999. It provides different information from that offered in the daily financial newspapers:

Fund Name	Stock Exchange	NAV	Market Price	Prem/ Discount	52-Week Market Return
Argentina Fd	N	12.14	$9^7/_{16}$	−22.2	−24.3

- The Argentina Fund trades on the New York Stock Exchange.
- The net asset value as of the week's close was $12.14 per share.
- The closing market price for the week was $9.4375 per share.
- The −22.2 indicates that the market price was trading at a 22.2 percent discount to its net asset value. A + would indicate that the fund or trust is trading at a premium to its net asset value.
- The 52-week return for the Argentina Fund is a negative 24.3 percent.

By combining the information in the daily newspapers with that provided in *Barron's*, investors can better follow the closed-end funds they are interested in buying or selling. Shares listed on the exchanges are sold through brokers.

Before buying closed-end funds or trusts, ask your broker or call the fund sponsor for the annual or quarterly report.

WHAT ARE THE ADVANTAGES OF CLOSED-END FUNDS AND UNIT INVESTMENT TRUSTS?

- Investors can buy into closed-end funds and trusts trading at discounts to their net asset values, which may offer the potential for capital gains and increased yields. The downside of this strategy is that it could result in capital losses if the discount to the net asset value widens.

- The shares of the larger, more actively traded closed-end funds and trusts can easily be bought and sold on the stock exchanges. The less actively traded funds will not be as liquid.
- For income-seeking investors, most unit investment trusts pay dividends on a monthly basis.
- Unit investment trusts have maturities, at which time investors will have all (or most) of their capital returned to them.

WHAT ARE THE DISADVANTAGES OF CLOSED-END FUNDS AND UNIT INVESTMENT TRUSTS?

- Closed-end funds, unit investment trusts, and REITs are subject to interest rate risk. Unit investment trusts have no protection against a rise in interest rates because their portfolios of investments are fixed.
- There is the risk that the share prices of the funds and trusts move independently of the value of the securities held in their portfolios. More investors exiting the fund or trust than buying will have the effect of driving the price down, despite the fact that the assets in the fund are doing well. It often represents a buying opportunity when a fund's shares are trading at a deep discount to its net asset value.
- Brokerage commissions and management fees can be high, which eats into the yields of closed-end funds and unit investment trusts.
- Some of the shares of the smaller, less actively traded funds and trusts may be illiquid.
- Buying into funds and trusts when they are first offered to shareholders means that you are investing in an unknown portfolio of assets. This is of particular significance for unit investment trusts in that investors cannot gauge the level of risk in the composition of the assets and whether the trust will use leverage to try and increase yields.
- Since the portfolios are fixed, unit investment trusts offer little protection against the credit deterioration of their

assets. Only after a significant deterioration in credit quality will the portfolio manager change the assets.

CAVEATS

- Investors should avoid investing in closed-end funds and unit investment trusts when they are first offered to the public because a percentage of their initial funds will go toward paying underwriting fees and selling commissions. For example, if investors pay $10 per share and $0.80 goes toward these expenses, net asset values will fall to $9.20 directly after issuance.
- Compare the long-term performance of closed-end funds, unit investment trusts, and REITs before investing. Some have not performed well and investors may want to avoid those with poor long-term track records.
- Examine the fees charged before buying into closed-end funds and investment trusts. Fees can be quite high.

ARE CLOSED-END FUNDS AND UNIT INVESTMENT TRUSTS SUITABLE FOR YOU?

Under certain conditions, closed-end funds, unit investment trusts, and REITs have provided investors with profitable returns. When they are trading at premium prices, bargains in these types of investments are hard to find. For example, when a fund is trading at a premium of 2.5 percent to its net asset value, an investor would be paying $1.025 for every dollar of assets (not taking into account brokerage fees to buy the shares).

It is far more advantageous for investors to wait until they are trading at discounts to their net asset values to buy into closed-end funds, unit investment trusts, and REITs. In fact, many investment advisors recommend buying closed-end funds and investment trusts when they are trading at large discounts, by historical standards, to their net asset values and selling them when they have small discounts or premiums.

You should also look for closed-end funds that are to be converted to open-end funds. If the shares of these funds are trading at discounts to their net asset values, they will rise to their net asset value price at the date of conversion. This also represents a buying opportunity.

Unit investment trusts need to be examined carefully before buying because of their inherent characteristics. They have maturity dates, which means that investors will have their principal returned to them at a specified time. Whether they will get all of their principal back is questionable. If interest rates continue to go down and the unit investment trust benefits from the use of leverage, shareholders should get close to all, if not all, of their original principal back. However, if interest rates rise and borrowing costs climb, the return of their entire principal may be jeopardized.

With closed-end funds, unit investment trusts, and REITs, share prices will fluctuate due to supply and demand for the shares on the stock market. Thus, if investors cannot find closed-end funds or investment trusts that are trading at discounts and they do not want the added risks of further fluctuations in price over net asset values, they should consider open-end mutual funds.

REFERENCES

Barker, Robert: "Tricks of the Trade for Closed-End Funds," *Business Week*, March 22, 1999, pp. 113–114.
Byrne, Thomas C.: "Beyond Yield," *Individual Investor*, July, 1994, p. 32.
Dunnan, Nancy: *Guide to Your Investments 1990*, Harper & Row, New York, 1990.
Faerber, Esme: *All About Bonds and Bond Mutual Funds*, McGraw-Hill, New York, 2000.
Thau, Annette: *The Bond Book*, McGraw-Hill, New York, 1992.
Zuckerman, Lawrence: "A Look Under the Hood at Realty Stocks," *The New York Times*, July 16, 1994, p. 35.

CHAPTER 11

Portfolio Management*

KEY CONCEPTS

- Investor objectives
- Characteristics of the investor
- Asset allocation
- Selection of individual investments
- Portfolio management

Managing a portfolio can mean different things to different people. For some people, it means buying the most conservative investments and holding them through maturity, or indefinitely. At the other extreme are investors who change their investments on a regular basis as if they were disposable drinking cups.

Managing a portfolio has some analogies to managing your health. A regimen of eating healthy foods and exercising regularly works well for people who are in good health. However, for a person who has a major illness or something chronically wrong, healthy foods and exercise alone won't rectify the overall problem.

Similarly, managing a portfolio of investments means assembling investment securities that will perform together to achieve the investor's overall objectives. When this has been accomplished,

---

*Portions of this chapter have been previously published by Esmé Faerber in *All About Bonds and Bond Mutual Funds* (McGraw-Hill, New York, 2000).

the investor can sit back and eat an apple a day while monitoring
the securities in the portfolio. If, however, the investment assets are
haphazardly chosen and the investor has not set objectives or goals
for the portfolio, there is no way of telling how well or badly the
portfolio is doing. It can be likened to a walk in space. You don't
know where you are drifting to, which means that you will not
have a clue where you will end up.

Knowing what you want to accomplish from your investments
allows you to manage your portfolio effectively. Buying and selling
investments are relatively easy tasks, but knowing what to buy and
sell is more difficult. In essence, the choice of assets to hold is determined by the investor's objectives and personal characteristics.

INVESTOR OBJECTIVES

The investor's objectives will determine the purpose and time period for the investments. For instance, one investor may be saving
for retirement in five years, and another may be saving for retirement in thirty years. Although their objectives may be the same
(saving for retirement), the time period and elements of risk tolerance are very different.

The first step in any plan is to determine long-range, medium-
range, and short-range objectives. For example, a young family
with small children may have the following objectives:

Short-term

- Set up an emergency fund
- Need for additional income
- Save for a vacation

Medium-term

- Save for a down payment on a house
- Buy a new car

Long-term

- Save for children's education
- Save for retirement

Once objectives have been developed, it becomes easier to see
what the investor can expect from the portfolio. Before setting a

strategy to achieve these objectives, investors should examine their personal circumstances, which will serve as a guide in the selection of the portfolio assets. The following list is a good starting place:

Characteristics of the Investor

Marital status:	Single, married, widower
Family:	No children, young children, teenage children, empty nest
Age:	Under 25, 25–39, 40–60, over 60
Education:	High school graduate, college degree, graduate degree
Income:	Stable and level, future growth prospects
Job/Profession:	Skill and expertise, ability to improve level of earnings
Net Worth/ Size of Portfolio:	Level of income, assets, and net worth will determine the size of the portfolio

These variables will determine the types of investments and the level of risk that can be absorbed in the development and management of the portfolio. Foe example, a nonworking widow who depends entirely on income generated from her investments will not be able to tolerate the high risks of investments in junk bonds, small-company growth stocks, or newly issued public offerings of common stocks. This portfolio of assets would need to generate income, but not at the expense of capital preservation.

Likewise, the sole breadwinner of a young family may be risk-averse, but the circumstances may allow more emphasis on growth assets. A prosperous litigation lawyer can withstand more risk aimed at expanding capital (net worth) rather than generating current income.

Depending on the investor's characteristics, there will be a tradeoff between assets generating current income and assets seeking capital appreciation. If investors opt for capital appreciation assets, they will likely sacrifice on current income.

ALLOCATION OF ASSETS

Asset allocation is a plan to invest in different types of securities so that the capital invested is protected against adverse factors in the marketplace. This, in essence, is the opposite of putting all your eggs in one basket. Imagine an investor with $200,000 to invest having invested it all in Toys 'R Us stock in 1998 at $37 per share. With Toys 'R Us trading at $17 per share a year later, the value of the portfolio would have been cut to less than $100,000.

Developing a portfolio is generally based on the idea of holding a variety of investments rather than concentrating on a single investment. This is to reduce the risks of loss and even out the returns of the different investments. The latter point can be illustrated with the following hypothetical example of a portfolio:

Assume the investor buys:	Total investment
1000 shares of XYZ Co. at $50 per share	$50,000
100 convertible bonds of ABC Co. at $1000 per bond	100,000
Total	$150,000
A year later, the portfolio is valued as follows:	
1000 shares of XYZ Co. at $70 per share	$70,000
100 convertible bonds of ABC Co. at $800 per bond	80,000
Total	$150,000

The investor has spread the risks of loss by owning two different types of securities as well as averaging the returns of the two types of investments. Certainly the investor would have done very much better had he invested totally in XYZ shares, but hindsight always produces the highest returns. The fact that we are not clairvoyant underlines the benefits of diversifying across a broad segment of investments. In other words, diversification seeks a balance between risk and return, the tradeoff discussed in Chapter 2.

Diversification is achieved by selecting a portfolio of investments of different types of securities in different industries. For example, investing in the stocks and bonds of General Motors, Ford, and Chrysler hardly achieves any diversification. By carefully selecting at least the stocks of six to ten different companies in different industries or investing in equity mutual funds, some of the risks of loss on any one security (or fund) will be evened out.

Classifying some of the types of investments on the continuum of risk shown in Figure 11-1, you can see that common stocks are considered the most risky (in terms of variability in share price), followed by long-term bonds, with the shorter maturities on the low-risk end. Bear in mind that there are many other types of investments that are riskier than common stocks, such as commodities, futures contracts, and options. Similarly, there is great variation of quality among common stocks. The common stocks of the well-established blue-chip companies are considered less risky than the bonds of highly leveraged companies with suspect balance sheets.

Speculative common stocks are considered the most risky due to the volatility of their stock prices. Blue-chip, large-cap stocks with established dividend records tend to be less volatile and hence less risky than growth stocks and speculative stocks. However, over long periods of time through which the ups and downs of the stock market can be weathered, common stocks as a group have provided higher returns (see Chapter 2). Common stocks provide the growth in a portfolio and should be included among the investments. The percentage allocated to common stocks will depend on the investor's objectives and personal characteristics. As mentioned earlier, a retired widow who is dependent on the income generated from the investments in the portfolio may have a smaller percentage allocated to common stocks. However, if the portfolio generates more than a sufficient level of income for the widow's current needs, a larger portion of the portfolio could be invested in common stocks to provide more growth for later years.

Bonds are sought by investors primarily for their ability to generate a steady stream of income. However, an often-overlooked fact is that long-term bonds (15- to 30-year maturities) can also be quite risky. Although 30-year U.S. Treasury bonds are safe investments in the sense that the U.S. government is not liable to default

FIGURE 1 1 - 1

Continuum of Risk

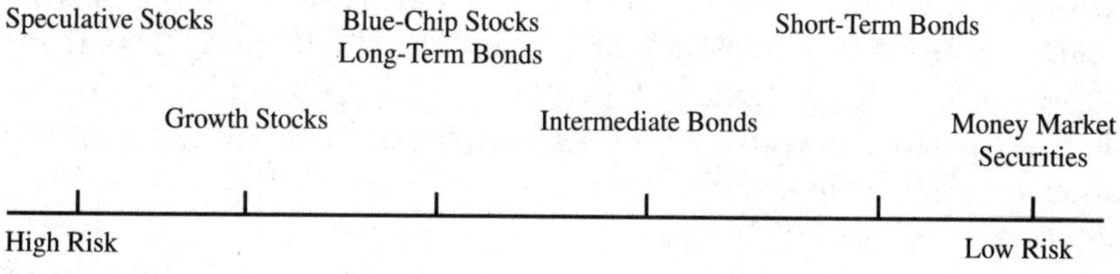

Speculative Stocks	Blue-Chip Stocks		Short-Term Bonds
	Long-Term Bonds		

| | Growth Stocks | | Intermediate Bonds | Money Market Securities |

High Risk   Low Risk on the interest and principal payments, they can be quite volatile in price due to changes in interest rates. Corporate and other types of long-term bonds are more volatile than Treasuries because of their increased risk of default.

Some of the volatility in the price of bonds is reduced by shortening the maturities to the intermediate term.

Low-risk, low-return securities, such as certificates of deposit, Treasury bills, and money market funds, should account for the percentage of the investor's portfolio that will serve liquidity and emergency fund purposes. For a variety of reasons, many investors keep too large a percentage of their portfolios in these low-risk, low-return assets.

Conservative investors who do not feel comfortable keeping only an amount equal to liquidity and emergency needs should increase their percentage. Often, however, the returns from these low-yielding investments over the years do not even keep pace with inflation, not to mention the effects of taxation on the interest.

There isn't a rigid formula for asset allocation. Rather, it is a good idea to think about the concept as a guideline when investing money. The percentage allocated to the different types of assets can always be changed, depending on circumstances. As individual circumstances change, so will the investor's objectives. If the emphasis shifts, for example, from capital growth to greater income generation and preservation of capital, the percentage of the investments in the portfolio can be changed accordingly.

Table 11-1 includes some questions that can help investors determine their asset allocations. Figure 11-2 provides some corresponding asset allocation models. As the figure shows, the most conservative portfolio is not one that consists entirely of bonds and money market securities. This is because the bond and stock markets do not always go up and down in tandem. There are many times when the two markets go in opposite directions. According to Roger Gibson, a Pittsburgh investment advisor, over the past 70 years, a portfolio consisting of 23 percent stocks and 77 percent bonds exhibited the same risk profile as a 100 percent bond portfolio but earned 2 percentage points higher per year. Similarly, at the other end of the risk spectrum is a 100 percent stock portfolio. The stock market cannot always be counted on when you need to withdraw funds, and as was pointed out in Chapter 1, there have been

Table 11-1.

Investor Questionnaire to Determine the Types of Assets in Your Portfolio

---

1. Do you have an emergency fund consisting of at least three months' salary?

   No

   Yes, but less than three months

   Yes

   Investment Planning: These investment funds should be invested in liquid assets (money market securities) to avoid any loss in principal for when the money is needed. The first step is to establish an emergency fund, after which an investment fund can be established.

2. When will you need the investment funds (over and above your emergency fund) that you have invested?

   Within 1 year

   Within 5 years

   Between 5 and 10 years

   Longer than 10 years

   Investment Planning: If you need the money within one year, you need to invest in liquid investments. Money needed within a 5-year time frame should be invested in short-term securities. Investments with a longer than 5-year time frame can be invested more aggressively, depending on your circumstances and your risk tolerance, such as in long-term bonds and stocks.

3. What percentage of your total investment funds is in retirement accounts?

   Below 25%

   Between 25 and 50%

   Between 51 and 75%

   Above 75%

   Investment Planning: The lower the percentage in retirement funds, the more aggressively you can invest.

4. How stable is your income from employment likely to be over the next five years?

   Likely to decrease

   Likely to stay the same

   Likely to keep pace with inflation

   Likely to increase above inflation

   Investment Planning: If there is uncertainty about future earnings, you may have to withdraw funds from your investments, which

Table 11-1. (Continued)

Investor Questionnaire to Determine the Types of Assets
in Your Portfolio

means that a corresponding amount should be invested conservatively. If there is a good chance that employment earnings will increase in the future, you can invest more aggressively.

5. How many dependents do you have?

> None
>
> 1
>
> 2
>
> More than 2

Investment Planning: The greater the number of dependents, the greater the responsibilities. In general, this requires being a little more conservative in your investment approach.

6. What percentage of your earnings goes toward paying off debts, including a motgage?

> Less than 10%
>
> Between 10 and 25%
>
> Between 25 and 50%
>
> Over 50%

Investment Planning: The higher the percentage of your earnings that goes toward paying off debts, the greater the likelihood that you may need to dip into you investment account, which suggests a more conservative approach.

7. With regard to your investment assets, where would you feel comfortable on the scale below:

> I am willing to invest aggressively for the maximum possible growth, even if there is the potential for losses due to market fluctuations.
> I am comfortable with some level of fluctuation in my funds in order to achieve reasonable levels of growth
> I am uncomfortable when my investment funds go down in value due to market fluctuations.

Investment Planning: Your appetitie for risk will determine whether you can invest aggressively, somewhere in the middle, or conservatively.

8. If you could increase your potential returns by taking on more risk, would you feel comfortable?

> Yes
>
> No

Table 11-1. (Continued)

Investor Questionnaire to Determine the Types of Assets in Your Portfolio

Investment Planning: If yes, you can be a little more aggressive in your investments. If no, you should invest in those assets that you feel comfortable with.

9. What rate of return do you expect to earn from your investments?

   Keep ahead of inflation while seeking stablilty of principal.

   Earn returns which are greater than inflation, even if there is some potential for loss in principal.

   Earn high returns regardless of the increased potential for loss in principal.

Investment Planning: Your acceptance of risks of loss in principal will determine whether you should invest aggressively, conservatively, or somewhere in the middle.

10. What do you need from your investment assets?

   Investment income

   Long-term capital growth

Investment Planning: If you need investment income, the investment assets should be allocated more toward bonds. Long-term capital growth can be obtained from diversified investments in common stocks.

FIGURE 11-2

Asset Allocation Models

An evaluation of your answers to the questions in Table 11-1 will assist you in your allocation of investment assets.

A **conservative portfolio** is one in which the investment goals are to preserve capital with some growth. The weighting is geared toward high-quality bonds and some common stocks for growth.

Asset Allocation for a Conservative Portfolio

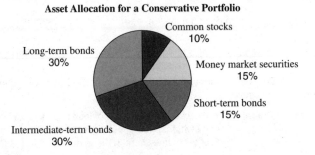

A **balanced portfolio** includes a greater percentage of common stocks, which provides capital growth, and keeps a large percentage of assets in fixed-income securities which provide income.

Asset Allocation for a Balanced Portfolio

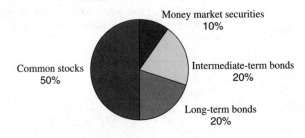

An **aggressive portfolio** is weighted more toward common stocks, which provide capital growth.

Asset Allocation for an Aggressive Portfolio

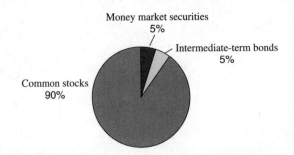

FIGURE 11-3

Portfolio Allocation for a Couple Seeking Long-Term Growth

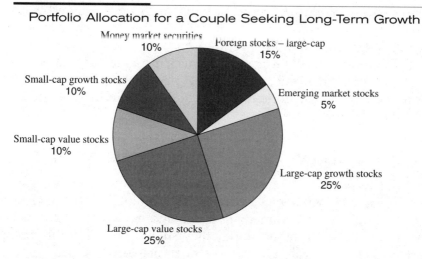

many shorter periods of time when bonds outperformed stocks. Thus, an aggressive portfolio would consist of 90 percent stocks, but still have 10 percent in bonds (Clements, p. C1).

An example of asset allocation for a young, childless couple, both of whom are working professionals, might look like this:

20%	Foreign stocks or international mutual funds
25%	Common stocks with emphasis on growth—large-cap
25%	Common stocks with emphasis on value—large-cap
20%	Common stocks with small- and mid-cap emphasis
10%	Money market securities
100%	

See Figure 11-3 for a further breakdown of the types of stocks in this portfolio.

However, if the wife decides to give up her career to stay home to care for an infant, the allocation of assets might change to provide for greater income generation. The portfolio might be altered to look like this:

15%	Foreign stocks/mutual funds
50%	Common stocks with half invested in blue-chip companies and the rest in growth stocks
10%	Corporate or Treasury bonds
10%	Intermediate-term municipal bonds
15%	Money market securities
100%	

What may work for one couple may not work for another couple. Asset allocation depends very much on the investment objectives, the personal and financial situation of each investor, and the total amount of the portfolio.

The most important aspect of investing is to have an asset allocation plan that reflects the broad mix of assets to strive for. Once these broad categories are determined, the individual assets can be purchased.

SELECTION OF INDIVIDUAL INVESTMENTS

In order to match your objectives with specific investments, you need to identify the characteristics of the different investments and their risks. Funds for immediate needs and emergency purposes should be liquid. In other works, they should be able to be converted easily into cash without loss of principal. These would be money market mutual funds, checking accounts, and savings accounts. These are readily convertible into cash. By increasing the time horizon from immediate needs to short-term needs, investors can marginally increase their rates of return by investing in certificates of deposit, Treasury bills, and commercial paper. However, of these, only Treasury bills are marketable, which means that they can be sold on the secondary market before maturity.

These individual investments (savings accounts, certificates of deposit, money market mutual funds, Treasury bills, and commercial paper) provide some taxable income; are liquid, but not marketable (except for Treasury bills); and do not offer the possibility of capital gains or losses. Although investors will not lose any of their principal by investing in this group of investments, there is a risk that the returns from these investments will not keep pace with inflation.

The financing of intermediate-term objectives, which stretch several years into the future—such as the purchase of a car, house, or appliance, or the funding of a child's education—and the need for funds for emergencies that might crop up in the future will require investments that are relatively safe. These investments need to produce a greater rate of return than a savings account or short-term money market securities. Short-term to intermediate-term bonds offer increased rates of return over money market securities as well as the possibility of capital gains or losses if the investor needs the money before maturity. Although investors will get increased rates of return from intermediate-term securities, they will find that these are not as liquid as short-term securities. Treasury notes and bonds have no credit risk or risk of default. This means that with Treasury notes and bonds, there is no need to diversify. With corporate bonds, it is a good idea for investors to spread the risks of default (and call) by buying the bonds of different issuers. Similarly, it is a good idea to diversify when investing in municipal bonds and some of the smaller agency bonds.

Long-term objectives, such as saving for retirement or an infant's college education 18 years hence, require investments that offer long-term growth prospects as well as greater returns. The level of risk that can be withstood on these investments will depend on the individual investor's circumstances.

A more conservative long-term portfolio would consist of long-term bonds, blue-chip stocks, and conservative growth stocks. The emphasis of this strategy is to invest in good quality bonds and the stocks of established companies that pay dividends and offer the prospect of steady growth over a period of time. Securities offering capital growth are important even in conservative portfolios to provide some cover against any possible erosion in future purchasing power due to inflation.

The growth-oriented part of a portfolio would seek to generate long-term capital gains and growth in the value of the stocks. Investors would look for stocks in growth industries and identify the more dominant stocks in those industries.

A more speculative portfolio, in a case where the investor can absorb greater levels of risk to strive for greater growth and returns, would include growth stocks; stocks of small, emerging companies; convertible bonds; junk bonds; real estate; options; commodities; and futures. Including these last three types of investments does not mean these should play a major role in a portfolio. For a speculative investor who understands the fine points of these investments, such securities should account for no more than 5 percent of the total portfolio. The other assets mentioned offer the investor the opportunity for large gains, but the risks of loss are also greater. Foreign bonds and stocks should also be considered, but investors should do their homework first so that they understand the risks fully. International mutual funds may be more helpful to spread some of the risks, although in the short term, there will always be currency risks when investing in offshore investments. Over the long term, the exchange fluctuations tend to even out and are not a significant factor.

Some investors may not feel comfortable buying individual bonds and stocks; they should stick with mutual funds. Investors willing to make their own investment decisions on individual securities can eliminate the fees and expenses charged by mutual funds.

When considering the different types of securities to choose for a portfolio, investors should weigh the characteristics of the type of investment along with the risks. (See Table 11-2 for a summary of strategies to reduce different types of risks.)

PORTFOLIO MANAGEMENT

Investors need to be continually aware not only that their objectives and individual characteristics change over time but also that their investments need to be monitored due to changing financial

TABLE 11-2

Summary of Strategies to Manage Risk

Investment	Risk	Strategy
Common stock	Market Risk	Invest for a long period of time.
	Financial risk	Diversify; Invest in companies with low leverage.
	Interest rate risk	Active or passive strategy, depending on the investor's time horizon.
	Declining market rates of interest	Increase the percentage of the portfolio allocated to stocks.
	Increasing market rates of interest	Decrease the percentage of the portfolio allocated to stocks.
	Credit risk	Invest in good-quality stocks.
	Purchasing power risk (when inflation increases)	Requires active portfolio management. Invest in stocks that will weather the effects of inflation better, such as gold stocks and oil stocks.

conditions and markets. Companies change, and their securities may no longer meet the criteria for which they were purchased. For example, IBM, which a few years ago posted the largest loss in its history, also recently posted its largest quarterly profit. It is not the same company it was 10 years ago. IBM's securities (stocks and bonds), once considered about as reliable as a fallen angel, are now considered to be a core holding in many portfolios.

Not all investments in the portfolio will realize their projected returns, so investors managing their portfolios will need to sell these and replace them with other investments. This does not mean that all or most of the investments in the portfolio should be continuously turned over. Only those investments that are not likely to achieve the goals specified should be liquidated.

The management of bond portfolios does not generally require as much attention as stock portfolios. In fact, bonds are much more conducive to a passive management style because they pay a fixed stream of income and mature at a specified date. By selecting a convenient maturity date for the issue, the investor can wait until the issue matures to get back the principal. Not only does this strategy minimize transaction costs, it also renders fluctuations in the value of the issue before maturity meaningless. However, if, for any reason, the investor needs the money before maturity, the current market value becomes important.

Many investors follow a more active management style than the buy-and-hold strategy, and they will continue to react to changing economic and financial conditions. Anticipating changes in interest rates could prompt investors to reallocate the types of investments in their portfolios. If higher rates of interest are anticipated, the investor has a number of options. Profits can be taken by selling stocks that have appreciated, or the investor might decide to sell stocks in the interest-sensitive industries, such as financial stocks, cyclical sector stocks in the automotive and home-building industries, and utility stocks. Some investors might buy stocks in the pharmaceutical and food industries, which tend to weather the effects of higher market interest rates better than other sectors of the economy.

Other investors might decide to hold their existing stocks but not invest any new money in the stock market until interest rates start to level off. True market timers might liquidate all their stock positions and wait on the sidelines for more favorable conditions.

Purchasing power risk from inflation hurts all financial investments to some degree or another. However, traditionally, returns on stocks tend to outperform those of bonds and money market securities in low to moderate inflation scenarios. Mining stocks, such as gold and platinum, and aluminum stocks have been good hedges against inflation.

Even a passively managed portfolio should be examined at various intervals with regard to the returns on the different investments as well as to changing economic conditions. Not all investments will achieve their anticipated returns, and if they turn out to be poor performers, they will probably need to be liquidated.

Investors who do not have the knowledge and skills to manage their portfolios may turn to professional advisors. Financial planners and accountants offer advice on the planning and management of portfolios. For investors who do not wish to be involved in the management of their assets, there are professional money managers and trust departments of various institutions. Their fees are often a stated percentage of the total dollar amount of the portfolio, which often requires that the portfolio be substantial in dollar terms.

CONCLUSION

Portfolio management begins with clear objectives. With careful analysis of personal and financial characteristics, an asset allocation plan of the categories of investments for the portfolio is made. The next step is the choice of individual investments and the extent of diversification among these investments. Finally, the management of the portfolio will be guided by the investment objectives. Managing a successful portfolio is more than selecting good investments.

Investors should invest only in those investments they fully understand. If the investor does not follow or fully understand the nuances of investing in individual stocks or bonds, he or she should stick with mutual funds. Besides the investments mentioned in this book, there are many others that were not discussed. This does not mean that they are not important or that they do not have a place in your portfolio. Investing in stocks provides growth to a portfolio, and historically, over long periods of time, stocks have outperformed other financial instruments.

REFERENCES

Clements, Jonathan: "Portfolio for the Conservative and the Bold," *The Wall Street Journal*, November 10, 1998, p. C1.

Faerber, Esme: *All About Bonds and Bond Mutual Funds*, McGraw-Hill, New York, 2000.

INDEX